Those Who Know

For Corrine,

May the Creator
bless you!
In Spirit,

Deanne

20TH
anniversary
edition

THOSE WHO KNOW

Profiles of Alberta's Aboriginal Elders

Dianne Meili

NeWest Press

Copyright © Dianne Meili 2012

LIBRARY AND ARCHIVES CANADA CATALOGUING IN PUBLICATION

Meili, Dianne, 1957–

Those who know : profiles of Alberta's aboriginal elders / by Dianne Meili.
— 20th anniversary ed.

Also issued in electronic format.

ISBN 978-1-927063-13-2

1. Elders (Native peoples) — Alberta — Biography.
2. Elders (Native peoples) — Alberta — Interviews.
I. Title.

E78.A34M44 2012   971.23004'9700922   C2011-906884-2

Editor for the Board: Don Kerr
Cover and interior design: Natalie Olsen, Kisscut Design
Author photo: Claire Beaulieu

 Canada Council   Conseil des Arts   Canadian   Patrimoine
for the Arts   du Canada   Heritage   canadien

 accessCOPYRIGHT   edmonton   **Government**
FOUNDATION   arts council   **of Alberta** ■

NeWest Press acknowledges the financial support of the Alberta Multimedia Development Fund and the Edmonton Arts Council for our publishing program. We further acknowledge the financial support of the Government of Canada through the Canada Book Fund (CBF) for our publishing activities. We acknowledge the support of the Canada Council for the Arts which last year invested $24.3 million in writing and publishing throughout Canada.

#201, 8540–109 Street
Edmonton, Alberta T6G 1E6
780.432.9427
NeWest Press   www.newestpress.com

No bison were harmed in the making of this book.
printed and bound in Canada 1 2 3 4 5 13 12

This book is dedicated to all who do the best that they can
to follow the powerful, old ways of our ancestors.

Contents

Acknowledgements

I want to acknowledge the individuals who helped me in writing the first edition of *Those Who Know,* as well as this new Landmark Edition. To all the elders who agreed to appear in this book, I thank you from the bottom of my heart. I also thank those whose stories were not included but who provided me with excellent information so that I could better understand what I was writing about.

The list of people to be acknowledged for their help is lengthy, and if I have missed anyone, you know who you are. Thanks to my friend Susan Mayse, who originally inspired me to research this book and who first approached NeWest Press with the idea of publishing it.

I thank those who aided me in seeking financial assistance for the original book, including Bert Crowfoot, Paul Saturley, the late Kim McLain, Roy Louis, Strater Crowfoot, Betty Davis, Eva Radford, Merv Kowalchuk, and Leith Campbell. My gratitude also goes out to those who put me up in their homes while I was on the road researching this book, helped identify and set up interviews with elders, translated various Aboriginal languages into English, and corrected some of the completed manuscript. Included among them are: Leona Shandruk, Sharon Strawberry, Alana Boysis, Claire Beaulieu, Rick Lightning, Molly Chisaakay, Vanessa Smalleyes, Maggie Deedza, the late Denys Auger, Elzear Orr, Rachel Simeon, Peter Freeman, Rosemary D'or, Matilda Blackman, Dorothy McDonald, Ella Paul, Steve Andreas, Theresa Grandjambe, Marg Stewart, Rick Tailfeathers, Camille Piché, Sister Lorraine, Muskwa, Father Charlie deHarveng, Martha Campiou, Cookie Simpson, Terry Lusty, and the late Dr. Anne Anderson.

Thank you to the family members who provided updates for the elders who originally appeared in the first edition of Those Who Know: Marcel Desjarlais, Arlene Desjarlais, Chehala Leonard, Francis Tootoosis, Rachelle McDonald, Arnold Steinhauer, David Martel, William Yatchotay, Lorelee Waterchief, Liz Letendre, Mable Giroux, Laura Auger, Beverly Jacobs, Mary Anne Blackman, Lucille Wright, Roy Meneen, Percy Strawberry, Daphne Good Eagle, Kelly Good Eagle, Perry Lightning, Dick Lightning, Elizabeth Yatsallie, Loretta Yakkineah, Reggie Crowshoe, Wayne Roan, Elmer Rattlesnake, Henry Nanooch, Roy Salopree, Darlene Hooka Nooza, Roderick Burnstick, Ambie John, Arnold Mountain Horse, Rod Hyde, Eileen Horseman, Cara Big Plume, Theresa Grandjambe, Ryan Grandjambe, Madeline Habitant, and Theresa Cardinal.

Regarding this Landmark edition, I want to especially thank my husband Rick Moyse and my son Jolon for looking after me, and our household, while I wrote frantically during those last few months before deadline.

Finally, I am grateful to the Alberta Historical Resources Foundation, Culture and Community Services, for providing research funding for this Landmark Edition of Those Who Know.

Preface
by Dr. Emma LaRocque

professor, Department of Native Studies, University of Manitoba

When *Those Who Know* was first published, Aboriginal traditional knowledge and religions were not as well known or appreciated as they are today. Ideas of both "traditional knowledge" (TK) and "Elders" have since gained greater popularity generally, and in the academic world greater research and some debate. This book certainly contributes to this development. However, with such a spurt of interest in Aboriginal cultures and values, there has been a tendency to not only stereotype and universalize such knowledge, but also to limit it to the past, often with the assumption that the only knowledge contemporary Aboriginal peoples can claim is "traditional," and that only "Elders" can have such knowledge. Much more can be said on this discussion.

Perhaps because of these problematic treatments of TK (now IK, or Indigenous Knowledge), I made a point of reading these portraits from a more materialist perspective. But first it must be said that these individuals are indeed imbued with highly developed senses of spirituality. The worldviews expressed here are outside the box of western science. These folks easily move in and out of things unseen. Or seen. Or felt. Or dreamed. But the dreaming is not fanciful, it is in fact practical. Many tell of dreams that showed the searcher or the hunter where or how to locate places or animals. As anthropologist Robin Ridington explains in his article [TK], oral-based Aboriginal hunting societies approach knowledge rather than materials as technology: "They code information about their world differently from those of us whose discourse is conditioned by written documents." Accordingly, there are spirits of the dead. There are unsettling prophecies of the future. There are historical and mythological characters and shape-shifters and spirit travellers that appear in a wide variety of forms and contexts.

To those unfamiliar with these ways of seeing, these stories will astound. But these Native elders most definitely know the difference between *atowkehwin* (in Cree, stories of legendary bent) and *achimoowin* (relaying stories based on factual events). These folks are not confused between faith and fact, or the past and the present, or between what is Christian and what is Native, or between what is seen and what is unseen. They have amazing abilities to integrate the ambiguities, the binaries (to western thought) or even the contradictions and burdens that have come with colonization. This is in fact what draws me to these lives. Their adaptability. And the other is that most of these elders do not flaunt their spirituality. They do not assume guru-ship, or even "eldership" as it has become vogue today. One is struck by their quiet humility and sincere drive to help and to give. For most of these elders, their spirituality is not that of what has been popularized; rather, it is that which is grounded in their languages, lands and skills.

And what skills and resourcefulness they possess. Most of these folks grew up in or learned to live well in land-based cultures. Most of them were born in the early 1900s and grew up with minimal industrial technologies or modern amenities at their disposal. These came later in their lives. There was no central heating, no electricity, no running water. No indoor toilets. No fridges. No stoves. As such, most lived through very harsh conditions. They are not shy to say this. To be sure, they love(d) the land but they have no romanticized notions of what it is like to live with raw nature. These peoples trekked through extreme winters. Gave birth alone or only with the husband (who was usually imposed upon girls who reached puberty). These men and women confronted dangerous animals. Or took care of animals such as horses, cows and dogs. Moved weighty obstacles or built dwellings, invented clay stoves. And of course, tools, transportation vehicles, trapping and hunting techniques and a host of other ingenious technologies suited for their cultures. They worked incessantly and very hard. They had medicines that cured, but they also faced illnesses. Death. Isolation. And many also experienced the punitive hardships, loneliness and cultural confusion in mission schools. These are men and women with intrepid and tenacious spirits. They are to be admired for their incredible strength and determination and for their physical, psychological and cultural survival. As a young and untrained reporter for *The Native People* news magazine (now *Windspeaker*) in the early 1970s I had the privilege of meeting some of these people profiled here.

Individual and cultural portraitures have intrinsic value. And these offer us important glimpses into worlds and eras little known by historians. But they must also be read with care and context. There are some limitations to the methodology, which the author herself alludes to. For example, the author's specific questions to each informant are not revealed, the profiles are restricted to Alberta and except for one Métis couple added to the new edition, to First Nation peoples from reserves. Most importantly, the portraits are only snippets of these people's lives. While snippets are interesting and easy to read, they do lack intellectual coherence. And reading thirty-eight profiles in one sitting can have a mass effect. We need to pay attention to the differences between and among these men and women. There are differences of experience, language, culture, religion, politics, and

opinion. But also because they reflect eras and contexts quite different from our industrialized, urbanized and over-capitalized cultures
today. Not surprisingly, I find some material troubling, especially con-
cerning gender roles and sexuality around which there is a tendency
to essentialize, if not by these individuals themselves, by the modern
readership hungry for identity resolution. One informant even tells
us that we cannot question, we can only enquire. But most of these
men and women would eschew fundamentalism that is at variance
from the ethic of tolerance that marks Aboriginal spirituality. For
those such as myself who grew up very similarly to these men and
women (indicating cultural continuity), I do find remarkable consistency in their appreciation and profound knowledge of the land,
and the spirits of the land, all of which is tempered by their earthy
humour and gracious approaches to life.

Land-based Aboriginal cultures are intricate and nuanced. They
offer hope and direction for environmental renewal and responsible living. Still, we must take care how we translate this knowledge
to our contemporary worlds. What is clear is that these men and
women reflect personalities and cultures that are resilient, dynamic,
un-ideological, relevant and gracious. Ultimately, it is the individual men and women whose knowledge, whose candor, whose tears,
whose laughter, humanize us all. And leave us a rich legacy from
which we can continue building.

Introduction

Henry Laboucan places his black cowboy hat on the table and smoothes his long grey hair. In a restaurant booth on a quiet winter afternoon in Edmonton, we transcend the mundane and slip back through the years when elders like Peter O'Chiese, Eddie Bellerose, and Robert Smallboy were still alive. Henry spent a lot of time with these celebrated men after they chose him to help mediate between themselves and government officials so they could bring cultural programming into jails.

The elders knew that Aboriginal men were starving for spirituality in prison. They were successful in their bid to be able to enter jails and share ceremony and teachings with inmates who were trying to change their lives for the better.

Henry shares a story of how Peter O'Chiese would shoo him away when he tried to help the old man chop wood. "I mean, here's this elder at ninety-nine years of age still swinging an axe," Henry recalls.

"But he didn't want any help. He just said that cutting wood was his life."

Henry opens his ever-present notebook to a clean page and draws a broken circle on it. He moves his pen a quarter of the way around it. "This was my childhood, when I was four or five years old. I remember having a good time. Some of those old people at that time were so powerful. They could levitate," he comments. He points to a space in the circle and tells me it represents the time he spent in residential school, and the magic died for him.

In the middle of the circle he draws a smaller circle and writes the word "wisdom keepers" inside. "We need to gather the strongest of the strong elders we still have and learn from them. If we don't, everything is going to go. We won't have anything of that powerful way of life left," he states.

He's right, and he has summed up why I wanted to develop this Landmark Edition of *Those Who Know*. When I first thought about the prospect, I had some hesitation. All but two of the elders I'd interviewed twenty years ago had passed away and I thought it might be too sad to revisit their stories. I also believed that elders' roles in their communities had lessened and their wisdom was being ignored. With resources being exploited in this province more aggressively than ever, I knew that Aboriginal people's link to the land was becoming more fragile, and the clash of cultures was an even bigger problem than it had been two decades ago.

Ultimately, I decided that there was never a more important time to hear from the elders than now. And so I began, starting out the same way I had twenty years ago, with my notepad and car, driving roads I hadn't travelled down since the early 1990s.

The trip north to Fox Lake was especially enjoyable at the height of summer. The highway north of Red Earth Creek was deserted and the ditches were aflame with fuchsia-coloured fireweed. I stopped along the way to swim in Lesser Slave Lake and arrived at Fox Lake First Nation during the Sixth Annual Leon Jr. Memorial Handgame Tournament which Rachel and Leon Nanooch host every year in honour of their departed son. More than thirty teams had signed up for the tournament and the drumming went on into the wee hours of the morning. Exciting stuff, but I drove away from the crowd a few times that weekend to sit with Henri Nanooch, a quiet, gracious artist who is the son of the late Eve Nanooch, whom I spoke with and profiled long ago. We talked about his mother and how much things had changed in Fox Lake.

A couple of months later, I headed off in the other direction to visit my Blackfoot and Tsuut'ina friends. The towering wind turbines beating against the western horizon of the looming Rocky Mountains assaulted my eyes. Harvesting the southern Alberta wind for electricity near Pincher Creek, they looked alien, but there were familiar sights too: the flat-topped rise of Chief Mountain brought tears to my eyes, as did the sight of the gnarled cottonwoods growing along the banks of the Oldman River, so sacred to the Blackfoot Nation.

Later, as I called on the adult relatives of almost all of the elders who had appeared in the first edition of this book, things got even better. All of them had read with pride their family member's story in the first edition of *Those Who Know* and were eager to fill in the last twenty years. All of the families were as happy to reconnect with me as I was to speak with them. That's when I realized that these elders hadn't left completely; they were living on through their descendents.

The new elders I've added to this book were inspiring to sit with. I know the spirits are still with us through the healing works being performed by many of them, especially Arnold Mountain Horse.

Who is an elder is a debatable question, but I think my friend Cliff Gladue's definition fits as well as any. He says an elder is someone who is in control of his or her emotions and who is a keeper of the culture. The people in this book have transcended jealousy, sadness, anger and hate, and they live fully in the present. They are at peace with themselves and the world around them. They've forgiven those who've hurt them, and, most importantly, they've forgiven themselves for anything they might not be proud of. Loving, sharing, and helping people, they work for the Creator and care about passing their language, spirituality, customs and traditions to young people. They are in touch with the unseen world of spirit and have an intimate relationship with their natural surroundings.

Everyone has their own bliss. For me, it was sitting on Tom Crane Bear's couch until two in the morning, listening to him describe the evening he and a friend retrieved a pipe which had been left to sit by itself for a time in a mountainous place. As they walked toward it, stopping four times, twice a giant eagle flew over them. Paradise was also enjoying a crackling fire under a full moon while the late Albert Lightning shared stories about the May-may-quay-so-wuk — the little people.

William Delver, son-in-law of Chief Blue Quill, the namesake of Blue Quills First Nation College — a former residential school near St. Paul which members of seven bands reclaimed and turned into their own educational institution in 1971 — saw the future of his grandchildren and great-grandchildren when he said they would live during a time when "kipimâcihonâwâw ka-wehcasin; inehiyâw-iwinâwâw wî-âyiman ka-miciminamihk." His words mean "earning a living will be easy; being Cree (Aboriginal) will be hard to hold."

Months before I wrote this introduction, things were happening on many fronts. The sad situation at Attawapiskat was occurring, and many in Canada seemed a step closer to understanding the "Indian" condition in this country. Prime Minister Stephen Harper held a meeting with Aboriginal leaders to discuss their concerns about education, health, governance and land claims, and an incredibly thought-provoking series called 8th Fire, about the relationship between Aboriginal peoples and the settler community, was airing on CBC.

All around Edmonton, Aboriginal language classes were springing up and I continued to hear of new places to go for sweatlodge ceremonies and other cultural activities.

I have full confidence that culture will never die, it just might change a little to blend with the times.

I hope this book and the elders' knowledge in it make it a little harder for William Delver to have been right. I pray that in some small way it will help our children hold onto this powerful way of life well into the future.

DIANNE MEILI
February 8, 2012
Stony Plain, Alberta

1

Tom Crane Bear

Siksika, Siksika First Nation

"Tom's house is the last one on the right before you cross the bridge," Lorelee Waterchief, a guidance counsellor at the Old Sun College on the north end of Siksika First Nation tells me. "He'll be home."

Though I've interviewed more than sixty elders in my time, I'm still shy about showing up on someone's doorstep and asking them questions about their life. Especially Tom Crane Bear; he is a venerated member of "The Spiritual Elders of the World," and an advisor at The Banff Centre. I swallow my fear, say a little prayer, then jump in my car to retrace my journey south to the Bow River to find his house.

I knock tentatively and then Tom opens the door. He smiles when he hears why I've come to speak with him and offers me a place on the couch in his living room. He's ironing his shirts on this Thursday evening and is happy for a little company.

Here we are in Blackfoot country and the first thing we talk about is Cree people.

"My dad was adopted by a kind old Cree man — George Baptiste at Hobbema," Tom recalls. "He raised me too, partially, as my grandfather. He took me as one of his real children. We used to snare a lot of rabbits, the old man and the old lady and me. We'd go out and check our snares in the evening. We'd get three rabbits, sometimes more. I'd carry them home. The old people would skin them and I ate them. With the potatoes we grew — that's what I was raised on. That was back in the early '30s, before Hobbema got rich."

Tom remembers working in the bush with his moosum and kokum Mary making posts. "Moosum would cut down the trees, and me and kokum would cut off all the branches and stack them. At the end of the week we'd take those posts to town and sell them."

Tom muses that he can still see the little house he grew up in with George and Mary and the clearing where they cut wood with a swede saw. "But one day the old man came to me and told me my dad was driving up north to get me. He told me I was old enough to go to school now." When Tom protested, George put his hand on his shoulder and told him if he didn't go to school the police would pick his dad up and send him to jail in Lethbridge.

"The old couple told me they loved me and they would miss me. That was the last time I talked with him for eleven years. I finally went back to Hobbema when I could and that wasn't until the '50s."

Delving into childhood memories, Tom shared with me that he had a grade seven education and left residential school at the age of fourteen. He would return to the books when he was fifty-three to complete his high school education.

"This was in the 1940s, and when you came of age you had to leave the school. The other option was for me to stay and help with the farm, but I would have to pay to live there. I thought to myself no way am I paying to stay here so I left."

Tom returned home to help his family. His father had infantile paralysis, and so Tom had to help him meet mobility challenges, like going outside to the outhouse. He soon realized he'd have to find a job to support his parents, his three sisters, and younger brother.

"I went to work as a post hole digger. I had to do ten holes before noon, and then ten after noon. I was paid two dollars a day." Tom took time off on Thursdays to get rations like meat, flour, and tea, "to keep my family from starving."

Giving thirty-dollar payments to his mother made Tom feel good because she used the money to buy essentials for his siblings.

"But mom knew I also liked hanging around town and playing pool, stuff like that. She knew I worked hard and told me, 'don't get mad for the things you're doing. There's a reason for it. Don't rebel.'"

Tom kept on working, leaving home only to go threshing for non-native farmers in the fall.

"I worked hard, and today I'm still working. My mother told me to never give up and that I would live to be an old man. I decided to keep on going until my legs gave out. And only once have I been on my back since then and that was in 2007. I had a stroke and it took me back a lot. I felt sorry for myself. I was lying in bed one day telling myself that I'd be better off dead. And then, all of a sudden my door opened and my little grandson came in. 'Grandpa,' he said, and those were his first words. It changed me, and from there I got better. I could talk and walk again."

But back in the prime of his life, Tom never laid down for long. He was handsome, vital, and he wasn't afraid of hard work. The good wages he made during the week kept him in the good life — and for him, that was rollicking weekends of drinking and carousing. He fell in love with a woman who liked to party as much as he did, and together they walked the painful road of addiction.

"I was just about as bad a drunk as you'll ever meet," he says. "I'd fight in the street and steal from anybody to get that bottle. One time I even put on dark glasses and I had a white cane. I got an old jam can from the garbage and I stood on a corner. I heard those quarters, those dimes, and those pennies start to drop in and I thought oh boy, I'm gonna get a bottle of wine tonight.

"I even spent time in the nut house. My aunt thought I was kind of crazy and she wanted me assessed. I was sitting in the office and a doctor was asking me all kinds of questions. I was answering like a normal guy, but then all of a sudden, the door opened and a bunch of little horses came in. They were jumping and biting each other in the neck like they do when they're playing. I asked the doctor who let all those little horses in, and that was it. I was committed."

Tom thinks the years of abusing his body as an alcoholic were to blame for the mental health issues he endured. "When I was in treatment, people would come in through the walls and offer me a drink. I'd go through the motions of opening the bottle and taking a drink, and to anybody watching me. . . well, I was just miming. But for me, it was real."

Later, when he was staying in Hobbema, Tom found himself on a dirt road trying to walk off a particularly bad hangover. He came to a yard where a woman sat in the shade. "She motioned to me and I walked toward her. She said, 'My son, what is it you want?' I told her I could use a drink of water and she sent me into the house."

Inside was John Cattleman, who told Tom he'd been waiting for him. The old man spoke for a long time and Tom remembers his speech almost word for word: "When I go to town and we get our groceries every week, I see you. You look good, but there's something wrong with you. You look straight, but I want to see you look like that every day. I'll tell you something. You don't own your body. It's owned by some power way beyond our reach. It's not a human being, it's a spirit. That spirit created you and he meant you to be a messenger. By behaving badly, you are being a messenger, all right, but you should turn around and show people your good side. This spirit chose you to be a messenger. He wants you to be a helper to your people and for those coming into life behind you.

"You know, the Creator loves you, just like He loves all people. But He doesn't live inside you anymore when you have your own will inside of you. Your body is His home. He directs you to all good things in life. When your spirit is outside of you, it protects you but it doesn't guide you. You wouldn't want to live inside a house that's

dirty. Well, that's you right now. You're not clean. You're like a garbage can."

Tom went home and told his wife what the old man said to him.
She shrugged off his words and told Tom the elder obviously didn't
know anything about drinking.

But John Cattleman's words stuck. Tom saw a glimmer of truth in
what he'd said about pushing away the Creator's will when he used
his own will to drink. "I didn't go to treatment, but I decided to start
sitting through some AA meetings. Once you're addicted you will stay
addicted unless you have the will to fight. And I did fight. I worked
hard to stay away from my old friends and stay sober."

As do many people who come out of the other side of drinking or
drugs to find new life, Tom wanted to help others feel as good as he
did. He trained in addictions treatment in 1982 at the Nechi Institute
just outside of Edmonton, and upon discovering how personally re-
warding it was to see real results in the people he worked with, he
added "life skills coach" to his repertoire.

"That really escalated my experience of helping people," he says.
More and more he felt as though he was becoming the person John
Cattleman saw in him. A fateful turn of events at a wellness conference in Albuquerque, New Mexico would propel Tom into the role
the elder foretold he would assume.

"On the first evening, organizers divided all of us in the audience into smaller groups. We were sharing about ourselves. Billy
Rogers, the man in charge, tapped me on the shoulder and told
me he had heard me talking and he wanted me to be the main
speaker the next morning. He told me to open with a prayer and
then tell my story. I went into that gathering and there were about
six hundred people waiting to hear something. The organizer introduced me as a professor and I talked for an hour. I just told the
truth and, boy, I must have said something right because everyone
came forward after to tell me how I had touched them. And that's
how it all began."

Billy was so impressed he contacted his superiors at the Oklahoma

State University in Continuing Education and Health to introduce the idea of hiring Tom to teach the wellness program. They approved, and he spent the next few years teaching in Oklahoma.

"I talked about honesty, kindness, love and trust. You have to have all of these four things if you're going to get well. Some people quit drinking but they're still not living right. When you're not living right you're always afraid. When you're honest with yourself you have to remember where you come from, but you have to walk away from your past when you get well. Forget about your B.S. and realize it's your front and it's a lie. You'll never get anywhere with yourself until you stop conning yourself."

Tom thinks people respond to him so positively because of his honesty. "I am from the university of hard knocks. I learned from the people I used to drink with how to get along in life. A lot of them were intelligent people, professional people like lawyers and Ph.D.s who had hit skid row, like me. They had so much wisdom between them, and as we sat around by the river in the evening sharing rubbing alcohol or a bottle of wine, if I really listened, I learned a lot."

Not long after Tom returned to Canada from Oklahoma, he was unexpectedly given a pipe by his nephew Glen Eagle Speaker, who was withdrawing from the Blackfoot sacred societies he had belonged to.

"He brought it out and said, 'this is for you.' I was actually scared of it. I had a family and I didn't want to devote myself to it. I kept it in my closet for three years and then I decided to give it back to him. I drove to his place. He wasn't home but his mother was there. I told her I was bringing the pipe back to her son and she asked me why. I told her I was scared of it and she laughed her little old lady laugh and said, 'Hmmm. It's not the pipe you're scared of. It's your own conscience you're scared of.' She told me I could go see Eddie Bad Eagle in Brocket to be initiated into the pipe circle and have it transferred to me properly. I thought about it, and then I drove down towards Pincher Creek to see Eddie in Pekuni country."

Tom and his friend Campbell, who also wanted his pipe blessed, showed up on Eddie's doorstep and told him what they wanted. He told them, as part of the transferral, they would have to go through six sweats. "After we went through those sweats I was finally purified enough to touch that pipe. The old man Joe Crowshoe performed the initiation ceremony for us, and then he took the pipes and told us to come back on the next full moon. 'Then you'll be in the pipe circle,' he told us."

The full moon was on a Sunday. Tom and his friend drove south again, stopping on the way at a powwow held at the late Rufus Goodstriker's Cross Bell Ranch. When they got to Brocket, Eddie Bad Eagle told them where the pipes were and offered directions to a place up in the mountains where they could find them. He also gave specific instructions regarding the way the pipes should be approached. They were alive and sacred now.

"He told us we'd have to walk towards them, but we'd have to stop four times before we got there. At our first stop I realized we had no sweetgrass — no sacred incense with us — so Campbell volunteered to go back and get a braid that I had in the car. It was getting dark and I glanced back toward the car watching for him. I could see the lit end of that sweetgrass he held glowing and kind of sparking as he walked toward me. There was tall grass all around us and it was really dry. I was worried he'd start it on fire. So, when he was standing by me again I asked him why he lit it and he answered, 'I never lit it! It started by itself.'

"At the second stop, something almost touched me. I could feel something heavy coming from behind me. I didn't look up at it, but I knew it was powerful. It didn't make any noise, I just heard the wind in his wings. It was a big eagle. I saw it as it passed in front of me. By God, that eagle had to have a wingspan of about twelve feet. I watched it fly ahead for a bit and then it disappeared into the coulee. We came to the third stop and nothing happened. Then, at the final stop, that eagle came again, and once more it disappeared into the coulee.

"Today, I still have my pipe, and if the opportunity comes up, I'll use it. But I don't say, 'we're gonna have a pipe ceremony — let's all get together.' I don't advertise that way. If the time is right, I will use it for people.

"You know, in my drinking days and for a time after that, I didn't believe in God. I thought we came into this earth, we died, and that was that. But now I believe in the Creator so much. I know we can come back as spirits and be right beside our loved ones but they don't know we're there."

In the 1990s, Tom served as an elder advisor to Corrections Canada in Ottawa and to the Siksika Nation's Police Commission and Siksika Land Claims. "We have a huge land claim, and now our chief and council want to become involved in litigation. Next week they want me to come before them and speak from what I know about it from my work with the land claims commission. Sometime between 1905 and 1910, about 190,000 acres of our land was sold by the Indian agent. He wanted funds for our reserve, but only a few million came into our coffers. He must have been a rich man when he died because he skimmed a lot, as I have come to understand. We've been after the government for sixty years for some kind of restitution. The chief and council want some advice as they move toward finally resolving this outstanding issue.

"They're kind of resurrecting the dead to have me come in and give a presentation such a long time after being on the land claims commission," he jokes.

Tom has also participated in watershed meetings and advised on proposals affecting the Bow River that runs through the Siksika nation. "I've dealt with big-business developers who want to add one thousand rooms, plus three more conference areas, to their hotel with a nice view of the river. I asked them how effective their water treatment plant is to deal with the used water and sewage they create, but they said they only have minimal treatment facilities. Most of their sewage goes right into the river. I said wild animals eat the plants along the river and, at one time, before pollution, these plants were medicine and that's why deer and buffalo were healthy and never got diseases. We don't drink that water because it is full of mercury." Calgary has a big impact on the Bow River and "farmers along creeks that flow into it contribute chemicals and animal waste to cause further contamination, either directly or through ground water that affects the water table."

The Banff Centre has been a large part of Tom's life since he became the spiritual advisor for its Aboriginal programs. When I spoke with him in December 2011, he told me he's often called upon to provide guidance to programs other than First Nations ones. The Banff Centre president and Aboriginal program staff nominated him for a National Aboriginal Achievement Award, which he received in the Culture, Heritage and Spirituality category in 2010. When he received it on national television that year, he said he wished he could split the award among the many people who assisted him in his life's journey. He especially acknowledged Hobbema, Kanai, and Siksika elders who helped him triumph over his addiction, and taught him much about First Nations culture, heritage, and spirituality.

Tom took the award to The Banff Centre to share with staff there, and then he left it at the world-class Blackfoot Crossing Historical Park Interpretive Centre in his community. He appreciates the recognition the glass statue stands for, but he's not attached to it. "We don't own anything, really. Material things are gifts for the work we do here on earth — they're just commodities. Money is given by the grace of spirit, and when we die and we go back home, we don't take a thing with us."

Often referred to as a "walking dictionary" on Aboriginal culture, it's interesting to hear Tom speak about Tunnel Mountain, on which The Banff Centre was built. His grandmother told him there was a buffalo up where the sacred springs are. She knew the area had long been a gathering place for many peoples who visited the hot springs for healing purposes and renewal.

"This mountain that the school sits on is a buffalo — inne (in the Blackfoot language) — that's what it's called. Back in time, an old lady once said: 'in a spring make a dance for me. I will give you the powers, the songs, the way you should live.'" He continues, "Before that, we didn't know anything." Tom figures that's how the secret Buffalo Women's Society began. "They used to have Sundances — so I hear — in this valley. They'd gather and celebrate this mountain here — the buffalo. . . the buffalo was the main staple food for the Indians. . . so they praised this mountain with the songs that this mountain gave to these old ladies. Ceremonies are said to have gone on for days and days. Then, after the last one was held, just as quickly as everyone had gathered to praise the sacred mountain, they left." [1]

When I ask Tom about his work as a Spiritual Elder of the World, he informs me he's attended meetings in Asia, New Zealand, Australia and Canada. "Fifteen years ago there were eighty-five elders, but now there are well over a hundred in the group," he says. He's off to New Zealand this spring with his adopted daughter if all goes well.

"That's not bad for a guy who never took a bath and used to eat out of the garbage can," he quips.

Tom had three biological daughters, but his oldest died a few years ago. At The Banff Centre, he met Janice Tanton, an artist and Program Manager for Aboriginal Leadership and Management in Leadership Development. The two got along well. Janice dreamed and designed a tipi to mark the seventy-fifth anniversary of The Banff Centre. The design was ceremonially transferred to her and Brian Calliou, Program Manager for Aboriginal Leadership, by Blackfoot elders Bruce and Anne-Marie Wolfchild. Tom gave Janice the name Iniskimaki (Buffalo Stone Woman). "There has to be a man and a woman who look after that tipi, and so Janice and Brian got together to do that. She asked if I would adopt her and I said 'yes'. Now she represents the daughter that I lost and I treat her just like I treat my other two. I don't leave her out of anything."

We end the evening coming full circle to talk about the Cree and Blackfoot again.

"I was at a banquet and we were discussing the historic battle between the two nations. I talked about the Saskatchewan River and how the Blackfoot stayed on the south side and pushed the Cree to the north side. A man named Louis Rain stood up — he was Cree. He said, 'Mr. Crane Bear, you are absolutely right about this. We used to have fun taking pot shots at you guys trying to cross the river. But if any of you ever made it to the other side, boy, we all ran like hell into the bushes.'"

1   Don Hill, *On Sleeping Buffalo*, Alberta Views Magazine, December 2010.

2

Rose Auger

Osohkahpawiskwew (Woman Who Stands Strong)
Iyinew (Cree), Mithatahkaw Sipiy (Driftpile First Nation)

"It is only in our recent history, with the arrival of those who follow patriarchal ways, that men have taken over. Most feel threatened by women, but they must stop and remember the loving power of their grandmothers and mothers." The late Rose Auger said this some twenty years ago and it would become one of her most often repeated quotes. Until her passing in June 2006, the Iyinew (Cree) woman, whose name was Osohkahpawiskwew ("Woman Who Stands Strong"), was an outspoken advocate of Aboriginal rights, especially those of women.

Rose's third and fourth generation grandmothers' names were in the language of her matrilineal ancestry: Marie Wapastim (White Horse) and Nikimay-eyim (which translates loosely as "Will Sacrifice to Help"). Her patrilineage is much easier to follow, of course, in a patriarchal system. "Her maiden name was Campiou, from the word Campion — originally Champion — before it became misspelled in the records," says Rose's youngest daughter Laura Auger. Her mother was a champion of women, Laura explains, because she understood that her people's history is rooted in the matrilineal society of the Algonquin language speakers that includes the Leni Lenape, or Delaware, Nation. They lived along the North Atlantic coast at the time of contact. Before colonization, Cree children belonged to the mother's clan. Hereditary leadership was passed through the maternal line, and women elders could remove leaders of whom they disapproved.

Cree men dominated society in the wake of the colonial system in the 1970s, '80s, and '90s. Women were victimized and left out of leadership roles. Rose fought for them, and spoke her mind to chiefs and in speeches she gave at conferences. She had connections, too, as a recognized healer, and was adopted into the Bear Clan by friend Tom Porter, a Mohawk elder who helped launch the White Roots of Peace. Committed to the preservation of Aboriginal tradition, this group of adults and youths helped light the flames of activism across North America in the 1970s. She and her peers spoke to audiences across Turtle Island.

Rose witnessed firsthand women's roles in Mohawk matriarchal leadership and was inspired to uplift women in western communities. She saw how colonized her people were and taught them the intelligence of traditional values.

"She'd interrupt a council meeting and ask, 'how come we don't know this?' or, 'why aren't we doing that?' because she wanted leadership to acknowledge ancestral values," Laura explains. She said what was on her mind, and lived by the adage, "when you walk with Creator you have no reason to fear anyone or anything."

According to Beverly Jacobs, president of the Native Women's Association of Canada between 2004 and 2009, "Rose taught me how to not be afraid. She taught me to say what needs to be said and to know what to say." The two met at the wake of the late Harold Cardinal and became instant friends. As Beverly established initiatives like Sisters in Spirit, raising awareness about Canada's missing and murdered Aboriginal women, Rose was a trusted advisor. "She gave me strength to do my job and she still does. Her son, Fred, sits on some of the same advisory committees that I do and we talk about Rose all the time."

Rose worked with Aboriginal offenders for more than thirty years and Beverly witnessed the strong relationships she had with female offenders in the prisons they visited together. Rose was a leading proponent of allowing Aboriginal ceremony and teaching into correctional facilities, and she established The Buffalo Robe Medicine Society in Alberta back in 1980 to help juvenile offenders experience culture-based healing. From 1977 to 1995, she was an elder with the United States Youth and Elders Council and was a healer with the Regional Psychiatric Centre in Saskatoon. She received a Culture, Heritage and Spirituality Award from the National Aboriginal Achievement Foundation in 1996.

As the oldest of sixteen children, Rose helped parent her siblings. "A constant theme in her life was 'you have to fend for yourself,' because her father was deemed too successful an entrepreneur by the Indian Agent and he was kicked off the reserve," says Laura. Rose grew up in a very hard-working family despite being disenfranchised and isolated by the government of the day.

As a child, Rose said she could take away people's pain by rubbing her hands over them, but then she would carry the pain and she would cry. Her elder relatives went into ceremony to ask the spirits to hold off with Rose's gifts until she was older. She knew one of her grandfathers could heal tuberculosis, but she also knew he wasn't allowed to practise his kind of healing in the open. Her own mother was raised Catholic in the convent and spoke her language, but remembered little of the old ways. Rose's grandmothers told her stories of relatives who could do many supernatural things.

"My mom hung on to those stories, even if everyone else seemed brainwashed by the Church. She was Indian when it was hard to be Indian," Laura explains. "She began with bringing back traditional dancing and was instrumental in reviving our ceremonies. She was determined to, and ultimately did, find her place in the world as the daughter of powerful people."

Rose's spiritual search took her far from northern Alberta as she struggled to recover what had been lost. Sometimes she doubted her ability to stay on her spiritual path. "In my early years I made a lot of mistakes. I kept worrying, 'I can't do this, I'm not holy enough, I won't be able to do this. I've just done too many things that are not good,'" she said in an interview with a Carleton University student. "And the holy man who passed the sweatlodge to me kept saying, 'It's not your choice, the spirits chose you, you have to do it. You have no choice.'"

THE SPRING OF 1989

Rose Auger scoops up a handful of black dirt and surveys the freshly tilled garden plot behind the Faust community hall. Closing her eyes, she imagines green plants poking through the soil. Her ancestors didn't grow food, but Rose sees her garden as a necessary "tradition" for the coming years.

"It's not hard to figure out we have to create another way of sustaining ourselves. Indians especially have to keep our earth intact. If we have no more land, we cannot carry out our religion, our traditional ways. We cannot even pick medicine plants."

The Cree medicine woman's moccasins leave tiny imprints in the soft garden dirt as we head back to her two-storey log house, passing by a sweatlodge and woodpile in her yard. Inside her large kitchen, Rose sets coffee cups steaming with strawberry-mint tea on the table and sits down. Her dark eyes are piercing and her expression intense as she continues talking about self-reliance in the future.

"Many Indian people live on reservations. They have all kinds of land. They can sustain themselves by raising domestic animals and growing food. We have to find our own natural way of surviving and go back to our ceremonies. Now we have TV, bingo halls, and things like that. It's all out there, and it deals with trying to be economically stable. Well, it's a fantasy, a dream, and it's destroying our children and our homes. We have to get back to our traditional life, because then you become whole, you're happy, you're at peace. You can put in a garden, you can pick your own medicines, your own natural foods. There is so much you can do for yourself that keeps you healthy. You are outside doing these things. In the other world, you sit and you lay and you eat and eat and become very unhealthy."

With an unhealthy body, things just get worse, says Rose, suggesting the sweatlodge is a good place to become healthy again, a place where "your body, mind, and spirit are all brought back into balance. It's a purifier of your self, and it takes toxins out of your body. It cleans your soul, your spirit." Rose laughs and refers to the sweatlodge as her people's "treatment centre" because it was used to "put everything in place." She insists, "What we had was far superior to anything in this new world to keep us healthy and happy and give us a clear vision of what life should be. In the sweatlodge, when you feel a spirit, you can't deny it. If you have prepared yourself, and the pipe-holder leading the sweat is strong, you can't deny spiritual power. It might come in the form of emotions, but you feel something."

People today have forgotten how to live, Rose insists, and she knows many Native people who are not willing to sacrifice living the strict and powerful way according to the Creator's laws. She believes this unwillingness will eventually bring destruction.

"There is a prophecy. We know the time is coming. It's a time of purification. There will be floods, eruptions. . . many things. The earth is starting to rebel against what is going on — it's so unbalanced. The purification is going to happen, and when it does we are going to have to start over. We are near to that time."

The medicine people and prophets Rose travels to meet with in southern Alberta, Saskatchewan, and the United States have said for many years the people need to prepare themselves for the purification. "The time may come when we can't find water, so we should learn to find water. If we can't find medicines. . . we have to revive our powers to communicate and be guided as to how we are going to find what we need. For instance, you may be guided to the mountains to a place where you can survive."

Medicine bundles, sacred songs, and ancient ceremonies used by First Nations on this continent to survive long ago are needed. These sacred things kept the spirits of the people open to the Creator's guidance and love and kept them firmly connected to Manito, the Great Spirit.

The word "disconnected" comes up often when Rose discusses the way most people live today. She suggests the first Europeans who landed in North America became disconnected from their homelands and were no longer "at one" with their Creator when they left ancestral roots behind. They lost the most important part of themselves, their spirit connection, she says.

"The emphasis was put on economic development instead of human development. Human development is the finding of your identity by looking at your history, your roots. It's a way of life that guides you and helps you to know the right thing to do." Without this kind of human development, people disconnect from the guidance of the Creator and look only to themselves for direction, Rose explains. With the spirit connection gone, the mind and body take over, and they "get stuck on themselves and nothing else matters." The mind and body are self-centred. They seek to be satisfied with the least effort and become attached to material things. When people come to Rose to regain their lost spiritual connection, she helps them to realize the world does not revolve around them.

"We have to relate to what's around us — be it a tree, a blade of grass, or clear spring water," she says, stressing each person must understand he or she is no more important than the Creator's other miracles. This realization does not come easily to most people who have learned to over-individualize and worry mostly about their own comfort, rendering life much more complicated than it was meant to be. They have grown up using their minds and not nurturing their spirits, Rose explains. A person must be totally sincere in wanting to know the truth about life and be willing to break down old, deeply ingrained ideas.

Most people, especially young people, want knowledge right away, but it doesn't happen like that, says Rose. People's beliefs are layered around them, and the layers are hard to peel off because they are so tough from years of reinforcement. Just like an onion, the layers must be gently peeled away until the soft heart at the centre is exposed. This can take years, but as long as that person continues to move around the medicine circle toward the Creator, that is okay, she adds.

Rose's house is often a home to young people — sometimes offenders in trouble with the law and foster kids deemed "the worst of the worst" — who want to find their identity and re-establish their connection to the Creator. They pray in the sweatlodge, work in the garden, and, Rose hopes, begin to become more aware of the beauty of the land around them. Spiritual training begins with a give-away, an offering to show sincerity to the teacher. "When you work with an elder, the elder is gifted in a certain way and he uses the gift to help you. So for me, you must bring four colours [of cloth], three packs of tobacco, and a gift. It should be something that makes you feel good to give away or something that hurts you to give away."

Once the offering is made, the giver receives his or her Indian name in a ceremony. This is an important rite because it gives the seeker an identity; it reflects their true nature. It is who they are. "You have a helper in the spirit world who is with you all the time. It's like your double in the spirit world. That's who you are. That's your Indian name, your real name. You begin to understand yourself, why you are the way you are, because your name teaches you that."

The name-giving ceremony symbolizes the beginning of the journey along the "red road" for those who want to follow it back to their Creator. The road is long, and the way of it is neither easy nor comfortable for the mind and body. It means upholding a "strict and powerful" way of living, but in the end, as Rose puts it, "It's all there is."

THE SPRING OF 1991

The journey from Edmonton back home to Peace River seems longer than usual. Just north of Whitecourt, I drive past the Highway 32 turn-off, brake, execute a quick U-turn and head north toward Kinuso. The decision rewards me with glimpses of deer and a honey-gold sunset over the Swan Hills. "Now, will Rose be home?" I wonder.

My car fills with symphonic music blended with loon calls, seagull cries, timber wolf howls, and an environmental message. At the end of side two, a man reads from a diary dated 2040, saying, "My regrets are wasted as I sit indoors like all the others on this planet. The view from the window is always shocking and repugnant. It offers a vision of destructive ignorance, a vision of lust, a vision of wilderness lost.

Mankind has brutally devastated the ecosystems of this world with all his varied waste. Yet, I am fortunate, being a man of age and experience. I can still see the brilliant colours of seasons past. . . the true pungent smell of a pine on a crisp and cold morning. Those things that nature once offered so freely and in such abundance, I remember. And I can dream." [1]

Tears well up as I feel, more than see, the beauty surrounding me, imagining it gone in a few decades. How appropriate it is to have these emotions before coming to see Rose, because she made me understand how important spirituality is to saving our planet. Listening to her words about the Creator's intentions for us, my doubt about the spirit world melted and I was able to believe in it. All things do have a spirit, and we must show respect, for we all influence each other and we are all connected, she said.

The light is on as I pull into her driveway. Rose is in the living room on the telephone, and the house is chaotic as several young people pack to leave on a trip somewhere. When she finally sits down with me, I tell her about my tears. She nods and her eyes nail mine as she describes an international conference she attended last summer in Quito, Ecuador, to discuss preparations for consciousness-raising activities in 1992. She hopes her people will unite to make others aware of the five hundred years of oppression and environmental destruction First Nations have endured since Europeans arrived on the island in 1492.

"Indian people must wake up! They are asleep! They know honesty and respect, but many just exist by stealing. That has never been our way. We are born of a people who walked softly on this earth, moving with the seasons and eating birds and fish while letting young animals grow. We were in touch, but now we are not!" she almost shouts.

"We don't need all this materialism. Once you're on the red road, you just flow with your life," Rose was quoted as saying in an interview with a Carleton University student. "And the part that most people find difficult is the part to give. To give of their time, of themselves, to give without expectations. When you give, you give from your heart. And you know the Creator's going to give you what you need. And a lot of the time you don't even know what that is. But you just know that you do this and it will be given to you.

"Someone who is always giving away things, he just walks free. He doesn't accumulate a bunch of stuff that weighs him down. He's just free. He's so free in life. That's how our people were. They roamed this world because they never got weighed down in the material- istic world. They just had survival. They just had their spirituality. 'Wunskaw.' This means wake up. Part of this waking up means re- placing women to their rightful place in society. It's been less than one hundred years that men lost touch with reality. There's no power or medicine that has all force unless it's balanced. The woman must be there also, but she has been left out! When we still had our cul- ture, we had the balance. The woman made ceremonies, and she was recognized as being united with the moon, the earth, and all the forces on it. Men have taken over. Most feel threatened by holy women. They must stop and remember, remember the loving power of their grandmothers and mothers!"

I mention the teachings of Eddie Bellerose, an elder living in Ed- monton, who so eloquently described the insight he gained into female energy as he watched his young son trying to button his own shirt one morning. Eddie noted the boy's struggling, rough-handed fingers fumbling with the buttons. "Boys are born clumsy, knowing nothing of love. Girls are more gentle and proper. Mothers breast-feed and hold babies close, teaching about love and bonding," Eddie had said. If a woman is really in tune with her inside being, she knows the name of her baby (reflecting the child's nature) at the moment of conception. Women are like Mother Earth — giving and giving, always trying to give more, he said.

"Women are understanding their own truth. When they come alive, then their homes and their families will come alive," Rose agreed. "The woman's way is a life of giving. There's no glory, and it's a humble place. But women enjoy life, and they help others to do the same. Women know the importance of togetherness. They know it's more important than punching a clock. The Blackfoot people have the woman in her rightful place. The women's societies are strong."

Rose's words comply with those of a poem written by Saskatchewan's SkyBlue Mary Morin, called "Ahow, Holy Woman." In many circles the virgin, who symbolizes Mother Earth ready to bring forth creation, is forgotten at the Sundance. Women who sang the mourning song to bring down the sacred tree of life for the centre Sundance pole, and rode the wagon that carried the pole, now walk behind in the shadows of the men who ride inside.[2]

"Men need to do research into their family trees and find out where women fitted in, traditionally," Rose concludes. "If they truly have power, they will be given guidance to discover the strength of women and work with her again. And, women will work with men, in balance."

1   Dan Gibson, *Harmony, Exploring Nature with Music* (Toronto, Ontario: Dan Gibson Productions Limited), n.d.
2   Jeanne Perreault and Sylvia Vance, *Writing the Circle: Native Women of Western Canada, An Anthology* (Edmonton, Alberta: NeWest Publishers Limited, 1990), p. 219.

3

Tibeyimisuw

(Jimmy Meneen) Cree, Tall Cree First Nation

Roy Meneen, Tibeyimisuw's grandson, is proud to say he's a fifth generation ancestor of Tall Cree, the leader of his people who signed Treaty Eight. "I'm glad to be a part of this family, and I feel so fortunate to have been raised by my grandparents," he states. "With them, there was never anxiety. There was no worrying. They just took everything in stride. Nothing was dictated to me. I was told in story-form how to behave. My grandfather might say something like, 'This is not right. You will see for yourself in time,' and I always did — and still am — coming to see what he meant."

Roy says, first and foremost, Tibeyimisuw inspired him to live his life to the fullest and to take the high road, no matter what. "Whether it's good or bad, you have to take the positive in everything," he told me. Tibeyimisuw also taught Roy to be an environmentalist and to never forget that all life comes from the land. Without exposing the sacred, Roy shared that his grandfather knew how to work with the spirits of plants and animals.

During the last week of his life, Tibeyimisuw visited the house in his North

Tall Cree community where his grandmother had passed away. Roy said Tibeyimisuw heard a drum beating and knew his time to leave this earth was coming.
To his last breath, he was still singing with his drum. "When the doctor wanted
to transport him to Edmonton, he told him 'no, my time is up.'" It was hard
for the doctor to let the old man go, too, because he was one of those rare pro-
fessionals who wanted to know how Aboriginal people survived. Tibeyimisuw
had taken the doctor out in the spring to tap birch trees for sap and shared information about the natural world with him. The doctor thought a lot of the
elder and promised to look after the people in isolated northern communities
like Fox Lake and Garden River because he knew they had hardship.

"All through my upbringing my grandfather gave me everything. He never
held anything back. I want to be a good elder and give back accordingly," Roy
says, especially now that he has his own grandchildren. He had the chance to
take an elder's role this summer at a youth camp east of Fort Vermillion and
admits he was disheartened at first to see kids walking back and forth with
their cell phones the first day.

"But by the following day they were getting more focused on the gathering," he observed, suggesting future camps should focus more on culture and
language and less on fashion models, rappers and hockey players who are often
brought in to speak to youth at conferences. He was gratified to meet a Dene
elder who had known Tibeyimisuw at Steen River, north of High Level, in the
late 1920s. "He sang a song my grandfather had taught him and we went down
that memory road together. It was good to reminisce and hear things about my
grandfather from a different perspective."

Tibeyimisuw (Tuh-bay-i-mi-soo) passed away on November 17, 1990,
taking with him more than a century's worth of memories. His Cree
name means "One Who is His Own Boss," and as he spoke of his
life it was obvious he had lived up to the powerful title. I was lucky
enough to spend time with him in February and August before his
death. Both times, he responded energetically to questions about
early life in northern Alberta and motioned with gnarled fingers to
explain things like how to load and shoot a long-barrelled musket.
He retained his wit well into his one-hundredth year, laughing about

how he once walked a distance of about ninety-five kilometres in one day, to prove to himself he could do it, and now could barely cross the road from his house to his grandson's. He recognized life as a circle and "now I'm going back to being a child. I guess I used to be pretty strong, just the same. We shot a bear once, and I packed it home on my back." His parents Joseph and Victoria died when he was young, so he learned to help himself as a child.

He remembers being left behind in the bush by his uncle and older brother to set a lynx snare and was so little he became frustrated and cried because he couldn't tie it in place because his fingers were too numb from the cold.

"It took a while, but I finally got it. After that I began to know how to snare lynx. Then I was sent out to hunt mostly. The children were told to get out of bed before daylight. I was taught to respect the day and night. Not like today. When we as elders are getting up today the kids are just going to sleep."

When he killed his first moose, he had to tie a rope around its legs and the other end around a tree to turn the body belly-up so he could gut it. He remembers the land between Wabasca Lakes and his North Tall Cree Reserve when it "used to look like a prairie — there were no trees. This land was occupied by the Beaver until the Cree moved in."

In his long life, Tibeyimisuw remembers living in stick lean-tos and travelling great distances. "We camped any place. Wherever we shovelled snow away, that's where we camped. Some people did not even have a tipi, they camped in lean-tos, that's how poor people were. We ate whatever we could kill; there was no store-bought food. No flour or lard, just tea and ammunition. We made shredded dry meat and moose grease for ourselves and the store managers." [1]

Clever with his hands, Tibeyimisuw built "anything a man could use — dog sleds, canoes, snowshoes." He made canoes from birch and spruce, noting that vessels made of the latter material had to be left in the water or they dried out. He had even built dugout boats in his life. When he needed special nails to construct the last canoe he worked on, he special-ordered them but soon realized he couldn't see to pound them into the wood.

"That's when I knew it was time to stop building canoes," he jokes.

He didn't hesitate a moment to answer, "Killing a moose," when asked to name the best experience of his long life. "If I killed a moose, then that was everything. It meant food. Being free in the bush and providing — everyone valued that."

The last time I saw him, after sharing some highlights of his life and several truths he had come to learn, Tibeyimisuw mentioned he wouldn't live much longer and sent me off with these cautioning words, "If you are given something from an elder, it's not finished there. What really matters, above all, is what you do with it."

As translated by his grandson Roy, the elder tells his life story:

"I was born at Trout Lake. There were four of us children in my family baptized in 1896 and I think I was about six years old then, so I believe I turned one hundred last year [January 1990]. Our last name is not really Meneen. It's Letendre, and our family comes from around Loon Lake. When my parents died my grandfather came to bring us to my great-grandfather Tall Cree's land. We were children; my brother was three years old. I can't say how old I was.

"I remember a time when there was only the bow and arrow. I remember the first two types of guns that came into this part of the country. Muskets, I guess, were the first, and they sure took a long time to go off. It went 'sssssssss' after you loaded it, and by the time it went off your moose would already be gone. But those guns were something new to us. Really powerful. Times were hard, and we could hardly believe our eyes when we saw the first guns.

"We ate off the land, and we ate anything except mink and fox. The merchants at the trading posts depended on Indian hunters for their food. About sixty-three years ago, I went to trap and hunt with the Dene people. I spent nine years with the Slavey Indians. People all over the north had hardship.

"In my childhood days, I can remember my people would be walking and crying from moving from shelter to shelter. We had no socks, rubbers, or rubber boots. To keep from freezing, we had rabbit skin wrapped around us. When the men would see a good camping place, with lots of good wood, they'd hang their packsacks on a tree and then the women would catch up and make camp.

"One time, my great-grandmother's mother-in-law was going to have a baby. They plowed the snow for her, and she had it. They rested for one hour, and then everybody started walking again.

"We used to use spruce boughs for our tipis; we didn't use hides for our shelter until later. When my grandfather's mother caught on to making a tipi from hides, she made it from the skins of nine moose. It had to be carried in two sections, and it was very heavy.

"I remember moving from the south Tall Cree Reserve to Fort Vermilion. We had one horse and on it were all our belongings. On top of all that were three children riding. On that old trail we used, there was only room for one horse, it was so narrow. It took them one year to build it wide enough for wagons. I always travelled that road, and wherever there was a soft spot it used to take us about four hours to pull the wagon out.

"Travelling north from Trout Lake, when we got to Jackpine Creek [about sixty kilometres east of the Peace River, on the same latitude as Manning] we could hear the steamboat blowing its horn. It took a crew of eight to keep feeding the stoves of the *D.A. Thomas*. Along with that, there were four teams of horses that were used to carry things from one boat to the other. One boat came from Peace River and the other from Fort Vermilion, and they met in the middle.

"One time, for the challenge of it, I left Fort Vermilion at sunrise and walked to the South Tall Cree Reserve by night. That's about sixty miles on a very crooked road.

"Not until I was twenty years old did I see the first building built here on the North Tall Cree Reserve. I remember there used to be a big lake right here. This was Beaver territory, and there were trails that went all around the lake.

"We always had dog teams, but the horse didn't come around here for quite a while. Then, one person brought a stud and mare to Trout

Lake. My grandmother couldn't believe this animal. It was so big! When it snorted, she got scared and ran away.

"I remember we all used to get together every year to have a lodge and give offerings to the Creator. A lot of people were specially gifted, but the church destroyed that. Still, a lot of these powers are coming back. Roy here, my grandson, is about thirty-six, and I've been teaching him some of what there is to know. But he's a mere child compared to all there is to know. The powers were never meant to be used for bad purposes but now they are. A long time ago, medicine men fought with each other. It's best to keep quiet about your power.

"Chiefs were spiritual men with powers. One time, there was a war between the Woodland Cree and the Plains Cree. They met as the Plains Cree moved farther north and the Woods Cree moved farther south. The Woods Cree captured two women from the Plains Cree, and then two or three years later the Plains Cree came back to get them. This Woods' chief invited everyone in the camp to come together so they could see what the Plains Cree were doing, then he left to check on them spiritually and he had a string of small bells on his wrist. He saw that there were eight of them sitting in a circle. They heard the bells and fell back, but one had a mirror on his chest and he could see something had come to check up on them.

"So now, the Woods Cree made plans to shoot the enemy. They did shoot one and they wounded him, and then the next time they went to fight the Plains Cree they found the grave of this enemy who had died from his injury. A lot of people wonder how the Slave River got its name, and it was named for this dead 'slave' man.

"I had a good life, and today I'm grateful that I'm alive and still have my memory. Today, you see how old I am, but one thing I've never experienced is standing in a court of the law. But you never know, that could change and I might go to court tomorrow.

"My beliefs are that we are created by one Creator and we all pray to one God. We are all related in some way to each other. Some people say we're not related, but they're wrong. One Creator made us all. He gives us signs. Some people can be out in the bush, and maybe a dead tree will stand up like a young one. The elders would say God was telling them they will live a long life.

"I think the old way is the good way, but why it got wiped out puzzles me. It really depends on the way you're brought up. You have to follow one way — you can't follow the middle road on this one. When I remember the old days and the people I grew up with, it's hard for me to come back into today. . . it's hard to come back into the present.

"All these things I tell you — they're all gone. The people I grew up with are all gone."

1   Excerpted from an interview conducted by the Office of Specific Claims and
     Research, 1978, Alberta.

4

Wallace Mountain Horse SR.

Kainai (Blood), Blood First Nation

Sipisttooki'si, as Wallace was named in his Blackfoot language, was born on February 27, 1927. He distinguished himself as a spiritual leader of the sacred Horn Society and came from a family deeply committed to Blood culture. On a windy night in the autumn of 2011, I sat late into the night with his son Arnold, listening to his stories and realising his life is a fitting tribute to his father's. Arnold travels the country treating people with his medicine and I share his story in the next chapter.

"My dad kept doing his spiritual work until about 1993," Arnold tells me. "Then he developed cataracts and his eyesight failed." A couple of years later he had operations to remove the growths and had some good years until he passed away on November 26, 1997 at the age of seventy.

As the evening dew collects on slender sagebrush leaves, releasing their pungent odour into the cool air, a young man wrapped in a colourful blanket approaches Wallace Mountain Horse's tipi. Soon to be inducted into the Horn Society, the senior spiritual order of the Blackfoot, the young man is concerned about the responsibilities he must carry when he holds a sacred bundle. The vows commit him to travel the powerful path of his ancestors' religion, avoiding behaviour that goes against the Creator.

Teacher and student walk toward the centre of the tipi circle to sit cross-legged in the grass. Their seated forms are visible in the light of the full, prairie moon hanging low, its glow answered on the Belly Buttes, just east of Stand Off, by campfires inside canvas-walled tipis. Throughout the several days of ritual before the bundle transfer occurs, sincere initiates repeatedly call upon good-natured Wallace for counselling. After the transfer, he will be kept busy conducting sweatlodge ceremonies to purify society members.

"When I'm called upon in these sweats to pass a message to the Creator by members of this society, I have to put myself on the line," Wallace confides. "I have to sacrifice and confess how I'm going about my life properly so He will hear my prayers. I dare not pretend I'm something I'm not in the face of the Creator. I can't commit myself in a way that would make God avoid accepting what I'm seeking for these people."

Wallace, sixty-four, is proud of the new breed of traditionalists. "These fellows and their wives who are taking the initiative to belong to societies, they're the ones who are really trying to go about life in the best way they can. They're still thinking about their relatives and the best way they can help them out. They really care about their families and others.

"Other bands have lost their bundles, sold them to museums or collectors. Others have gone to the religion the white people brought with them, but it's not that perfect for us because we're making mistakes with it."

Wallace is quick to point out he was raised in a mission school and respects Christian doctrine. His wife was a devout Catholic, and he combines non-Native and Native religious concepts to better understand "how things were provided for us in the beginning and how I should live as a human being. But some people here are using what was provided for us by the Creator. There is still life in our religion. . . in the ceremonies and the bundles."

Affirmation to believe in what the Creator taught so long ago comes in many ways, Wallace says. A society member told him that in a dream she encountered four people — an old man and woman and two young boys. The man said he came to prevent society members from losing confidence in themselves. Refreshing her in religious ways, he entreated her to remain faithful and confirmed her prayers were being heard. He introduced himself as the Sun, his wife as the Moon, and his two sons as Mars and Jupiter — four powerful entities.

To explain the dream's significance, Wallace tells me the people in the dream are characters from the legend of Scarface, who introduced the sweatlodge on earth. Wallace describes Scarface as a disfigured, sad young man, horrible to behold. His only desire was to marry a beautiful woman, but she repeatedly put him off. Disgusted, and believing his face would never be whole, she finally vowed to marry him if he could rid himself of his scar.

"He was seeking to everyone. . . he even made a raft and went out on the lake to ask the spirits if they could help him. They said, 'Nothing on earth can remove your scar.' Well, the Creator finally stepped in — in the form of a man — and told him the only one who could help him was the Sun. Scarface thought about that and wondered how he could get up in the sky to see him. Finally, he decided to walk east in the direction of the Sun's lodge, and, mystically, he was taken upward."

Wallace explains that Scarface walked for days and finally came upon a camp, asking the man who lived there if he could remove his scar. The man was powerless to grant such a request but encouraged the young man to keep walking. He came upon two more camps and was repeatedly told to keep walking. Discouraged, Scarface almost gave up, but suddenly he spied another camp. There, a man told him he would get to his destination if he walked a little farther to a big lake.

"When you get there, dig yourself a hole and cover yourself real good. The Sun has a son, Mars, and he always hangs around that lake because he has nothing else to do. When he comes near you, take hold of him and ask him to pity you."

Scarface did as he was told and succeeded in making friends with the Sun's son. He was taken to Sun's lodge, but when Sun came home that night, his wife, the Moon, had to light incense to purify the place before he could come in. When Scarface told the Sun his reason for coming to see him, the Sun ordered four sweatlodges to be erected. After each sweat, the scar became fainter and fainter, until mother Moon could scarcely tell the two boys apart.

Before Scarface returned to earth, Sun gave him a bone whistle to attract the woman he desired to be his wife. When he blew it, the woman came to his lodge and, seeing his scar had disappeared, agreed to marry him. After a time, Scarface honoured a promise he had made to Mars and took his wife to a hill and blew his whistle. His wife vanished, but Sun rewarded Scarface by giving him the sweatlodge to take back to his people.

"'It's a communication place for you to seek anything you want or assist anybody that needs help through religion and me,' the Sun told Scarface. 'I'll hear all your requests. This is your tool to help a person, providing you're doing it for a good purpose,'" concludes Wallace.

"So, we've been given these things by the Creator, and we receive encouragement that we're going about things the right way," Wallace says, adding that society members take vows to follow a moral lifestyle according to the Creator's laws and are revered by others who ask them to pray for them.

Wallace, as spiritual director of societies on the Blood Reserve, is heavily depended upon to instruct initiates in the "things they are still holding at this stage in time." He was a member of the Horn Society for twenty-three years and began learning songs and rituals at a young age from elders who spoke only Blackfoot.

"I guess it's a good thing I speak two languages because some of the new members have a hard time with Blackfoot and I have to explain things to them in English. Still, it's not that good, because there are some Blackfoot words that have no English equivalent.

"When I was a society member, we had no help from cultural grants or band assistance to keep the religion going. Jobs were pretty scarce, and we had to dig into our own pockets to keep the religion going. Sometimes, I wondered why we had to sacrifice so much to the Creator, but now I know. My reward is being able to help these new society members along."

Anticipating a return to Blackfoot religion by young people, Wallace claims the pendulum of progress is swinging from "outward living" to "inward searching." He says critical issues — a dying Mother Earth and declining moral values — are pushing kids to reject the empty ways of mainstream society and return to the religion they thought was "crazy and something to get rid of.

"Take these four planets — Earth, Moon, Jupiter, and Mars. Well, to the white man, they are just planets. But to us, they're spirits. Our way of life tells us that when the Creator made the world he put life in everything. Without life in these things, they would rot. Where there is life, there's spirit. So, when He made the earth, He put life in it, a spiritual life. That's why it can renew itself. Everything in nature has life and a spirit. It was shown to us by the Creator to live amongst all His other Creations. That's what makes life so pleasant, to have all these relations."

Humans must understand respect for these spirits and how they are inter-related. Wallace contends the first inkling most people have of spiritual awareness is realizing that all they see is not everything and that there is much more going on below the surface. They realize that they are perfect creations of God but they are not outstanding in the vast sea of beings. The spiritual path they tread is a stripping away of self-important ideas, burning out the fire of ego until the real, humble self remains in the ashes and surrenders to the Creator's will. Finally, the seeker realizes he or she functions within a single field of shared consciousness — plants, minerals, other humans, and vegetation — that are all projections of a single God. Through spiritual practices such as praying, serving the Creator, and sacrificing, the humbled seeker becomes sensitized to subtle energy and can benefit from more advanced communication with other spirits, finally earning the right to request their help.

Seekers must demonstrate their sincerity in making the request and "really come out with their faith" in the form of personal sacrifice to convince the Creator "to accept you as a person who is living his life on the right track," Wallace stresses.

"It's like when you have a child and that kid wants something real bad. He'll cry for it. Then it gets down to the point where you give in to that kid and you give him what he's crying for. Well, that's how God works. If you want Him to respond to whatever it is you're seeking, you're going to have to show Him you desperately need it and you'll stand behind your intentions. If you want a power from an animal or a rock or a bird, you have to prove how much you're willing to put yourself through to receive it."

Wallace often talks about his friend, Buster Yellow Kidney, a medicine man who fasted and underwent hardship to gain the help of several spirits he works with to heal people.

"When he has a lodge, he calls for the spirits of an old man and an old woman, a rock and a bear, and he's got some others. I think the bear is the most powerful. But, when the rock comes, I guess it's just like something really heavy hits the floor and shakes the whole place. And those spirits know if someone doesn't believe in them. They'll do something embarrassing to someone if they're just there for curiosity."

Wallace's son-in-law Andrew, plagued with severe coughing spells that caused him to black out, went to Browning, Montana, in the summer of 1990, to fast and pray for healing under Buster's guidance.

"The spirits told Buster that Andrew has a gland that gets blocked when he coughs. When it closes up, he loses his breath and collapses. Andrew felt hands, really cold, stroking his throat in the sweatlodge. Buster keeps a lot of herbs in tin cans and the spirits told him which ones to give Andrew for a medicine to drink. After that, he didn't have any more blackouts. But Andrew smokes so much. He still has trouble with his throat. He's going back to see Buster again this year.

"In the lodge, it has to be kept dark in preparation for the spirits to come. My wife Eileen went to Buster, and she said she could feel the spirits' hands all over her body. She thought the spirits were small people from the way their hands felt."

Satan and other unwholesome forces are called upon to produce evil, and even if a seeker seems to have escaped paying the consequences in this world for bad medicine they create, he or she will suffer in the next, Wallace warns. "And we are always being tested as we prepare for the next world. The Creator put us here with so much for our use and gives us a route to go by, but our own self-will is strong," Wallace says, reiterating a Bible story to illustrate his point.

"The Creator made man, knowing that no matter how strong He made him, his will could be broken. Adam and Eve disregarded the Creator's will and mankind was put on earth. So we made a mistake and must bear out our multiplication on earth. But God explains to us how to live, and if we do it he forgives the original sin and has a good place provided for us for the second stage of our lives."

The experiences of his late wife Eileen, who suffered from tuberculosis in her younger days, convinced Wallace to accept the concept of a promised paradise in exchange for a life well lived. Before meeting Wallace in 1954, Eileen underwent an operation to remove several of her ribs, and she told Wallace years later that the mysteries revealed to her in the recovery room were unforgettable.

"She was out cold for four days. She remembers having dreams, but they were more than dreams. While she was lying in bed, she began thinking how nice it would be to see her folks back home. 'I'll go down and see how they're doing right now,' she thought, and she went out the window of the Charles Camsell Hospital in Edmonton. She says she looked back and saw her body lying on the white bed. Within no time, she was down here where her parents lived, but she couldn't get near the place because the dogs were barking at her. That barking was so powerful it was just like a wind, she said. The vibration hit her and kept her away.

"Finally, since she couldn't get any closer to the house, she thought she'd better go back, but before she left she went and stood on the roof of St. Mary's School and thought, 'This is where I was before I got sick.' Then, she was back at the hospital, and she couldn't get in the door. We always laughed about this. She said the nurses must have been changing shifts, and the door kept swinging open and shut before she could get through. Then, she remembered how she got out of the building, and she went up to the window. She looked in to see her body lying there and just went back into it.

"As Eileen lay there, still unconscious, she began to see a cloud of smoke above her, forming into the image of Saint Theresa holding roses. The saint dropped the flowers, and as they fell they turned to water," Wallace says.

"It took her breath away and she started coming to in the shock. She asked for a drink of water, and then the nurses came running."

Eileen also shared her vision of the after world, a place unparalleled by beauty on this earth, a paradise filled with flowers, birds, and animals. "She said she didn't have any words to make me understand how wonderful it really was to her. And after she looked at it for a while, she said she heard a voice that sounded like her father's. He told her, 'Daughter, try to come to this place when your time comes. Try hard to go about life the way you were shown, in a religious way.' She saw a bright light quite a distance away, and she knew it was the Creator. She'd seen the place provided for people who are going about life honestly."

The night Eileen went into the hospital for the last time, Wallace prayed to the Creator. Her life had been filled with pain, and he requested that she pass gently into the next world without suffering when her time was at hand. If the Creator granted the favour, he vowed to devote his life to spiritual purpose. "And that's what happened. My daughter told me she was sitting with her one night, and she asked her to turn out the light because she was tired. My daughter thought she'd fallen asleep until she noticed how still she was."

Eileen passed away in the spring of 1990. Since then, Wallace believes she has attempted to convey a healing message to the family.

"When my wife was alive, she never really liked the Blackfoot religion. She was such a strong Catholic, she just didn't believe in it. But my daughter had a dream about her a while ago. My wife told her she understands now that Indian religion is not bad. Her Catholic way is not the only way of God. She said she was happy where she was and that she's busy all the time helping others."

Wallace has upheld the vow he made before Eileen's death. Though he is sought out by the Blood Band to advise on such worldly matters as policing and agriculture — acting as an outspoken counsellor between 1970 and 1974, spiritual matters remain closest to his heart. He tries his best to teach young people who come to him, as his own elders advised him long ago.

"I guess I was in my twenties when I came into the Blackfoot religion. The elders knew I was trying to be reliable, and they told me to work hard and never spend my money foolishly. If I saw an elder, I'd give him a dollar or two and he'd go buy something he hadn't had for a long time, maybe some meat. He'd buy a pound of hamburger for fifty cents and maybe two pounds of sausage for twenty-five cents. After that, there was still lots of money left over for tobacco and papers and matches, then the money was shot. The elders would approach me and say, 'Even though I'm old, I want to show you how you can live successfully.' They could see ahead to things that I might fall into, and they warned me about these things. They would always give me examples from their own lives. They told me I'd live long if I took their advice seriously. And you know, all those people I knew who participated in the religion lived to be eighty, ninety, and one hundred. That's because they lived God's life."

Wallace started powwow dancing when he was five years old, "for pleasure, not competition." The only time he joined a contest was when *Circle of the Sun* was being filmed in his community and he performed the chicken dance and hoop dance. He was beaten by Jeffrey Bull Shields, a man twenty years younger than him.

In 1967, along with Dan Weasel Moccasin, Allan Spear Chief, Pete Standing Alone, Charlie Bull Shields, and the late Jim Bottle and Jim Prairie Chicken, Wallace organized a well-received Kainai Indian Days. The idea was to promote goodwill between band members and visiting tribes through feasts, visiting and parades within a tipi camp.

In 1975, the Kainai Indian Days Committee handed over the responsibility of organizing the event to a younger group. The event is held every July to this day, and is a way of teaching Blood youth about the old ways.

Wallace says today's young generation badly need their elders' advice and respond quickly to love and respect shown them by adults. He relates the story of how he kept a runaway foster child close to home by offering him trust and unlimited freedom. "A Lethbridge social worker called me up years ago to see if I could look after this kid. I said I'd try, and they brought him over. He was about eight or nine. I could see he was a kid who couldn't be told what to do. I didn't say too much to him at first and just accepted him. He ran away and my son caught up with him before he got to the highway."

Wallace told the boy he understood what it must be like to be mistreated by parents and to feel uncared for. He made it clear he accepted the foster child as one of his own children, and he could do whatever he liked within household rules.

"All I asked him to do was let me know where he was if he was going to be late or was visiting a friend. I made sure he knew I considered him one of my people and that I cared about him. I told him the house had four doors, and they'd be left open. I wouldn't lock him in, and he was free to come and go and eat whenever he wanted, but he had to make a choice to stay with us or go back to wherever he came from.

"He sat there and finally said, 'I'll stay.' Well, I shook his hand and we were friends. Maybe it was the first time he'd been treated like a human, because he turned out to be a really good kid. He stayed with us for four years."

The unselfish, protective love most parents have for their children is the kind of feeling people should have for each other, Wallace says.

"When I was young, parents loved their children so much they could hardly stand to let them go out into the world on their own. So, they picked out their daughter or son's mate, someone who lived a good life and would continue to be a good influence. That was the intention behind arranged marriages."

Wallace says harmonious, healthy societies find it natural to help each other, because its members have peace of mind knowing they are a single expression of the Creator. "So we have to get back to caring for each other instead of competing, because we are all one. It's not that hard to live a good life if you always remember what you're preparing for. You just have to realize your body will die, but your spirit, the thing that makes you think, goes on to the next life. Everything you do in this life prepares you for the next."

5

Arnold Mountain Horse

Kainai (Blood), Blood First Nation

"We were all so excited when the weekend would come along. One by one they started coming. Four or five elders would come and spend the whole weekend with us and we knew there would be lots of storytelling."

Arnold Mountain Horse, son of the late Wallace Mountain Horse, is telling me about a special time in his childhood when his father would invite his friends to come and share stories and songs in the living room of his Moses Lake home just outside of Cardston in southern Alberta. We're sitting in that same house — it's actually a converted community hall — on a windy night in October, twenty years after I first interviewed Wallace.

"Someone would give us a dollar and tell us kids to go to town and buy whatever we wanted to eat. 'But don't stay there too long. Come back and listen to the stories we will be telling later on,' the old men would say, and so we'd hurry to get our candy or whatever," Arnold says.

Old Blackfoot elders like Willie Whitefeathers and Mark Old Shoe, and Jim Bottle and Earl Willows and their wives would settle on chairs around the room. Arnold and his brothers and sisters, and sometimes a few of their friends, would sit on blankets and pillows spread out on the floor.

"First they'd be telling us what was right behaviour and what was wrong, but as it got later they'd start to tell old stories. They'd talk about people going out on vision quests and seeking their powers. Animals would approach them and give them some of their power. The stories would be so unbelievable, but you knew coming from these old people they were real."

A popular story that was often told in Arnold's parents' living room, and is even included in Beverly Hungry Wolf's book *The Ways of My Grandmothers*, involved a Blood man whose beloved wife was captured during a Cree raid on his camp. When Yellow-Painted Lodge heard she was still alive, he gathered horses and gifts to give the Cree in exchange for his wife. When he arrived at the enemy's camp he found his wife and she told him to be careful because her captor was a very powerful medicine man.

When the Cree returned from hunting, he saw the horses outside his lodge and knew why Yellow-Painted Lodge was waiting for him. A wager was quickly established: if the Blood could prove his medicine was stronger than the Cree's, then Yellow-Painted Lodge could take his wife back and the Cree would accept the horses in trade.

The Cree took a small, red-painted wooden figure of a man from a pouch and started to sing and drum. Suddenly animated, the figure advanced toward Yellow-Painted Lodge and his wife became alarmed. "Don't let that thing touch you or you will be dead!" she shouted. Her husband stayed calm and merely removed a small pouch tied to one of his braids. From the pouch he removed a piece of rawhide cut into the shape of a spider and this he placed on a patch of dried grass. He sang his own power song and covered the spider with his hand for a moment and blew on it between his fingers. When he lifted his hand, the spider had become real and was walking around on the grass.

Yellow-Painted Lodge placed the spider on the ground in the path of the little red man. The spider jumped on the figure and, in a flash, bound it tightly with his thread, dragging it along behind him as he climbed up one of the lodge poles.

The Cree warrior realized he was defeated. He begged Yellow-Painted Lodge to spare his life and told him to take back his wife and keep his horses. Yellow-Painted Lodge sang another song and the spider dropped his burden and hurried back to the bunch of dried grass. After Yellow-Painted Lodge covered the spider again with his hand and blew on it, it again looked like a spider-shaped piece of rawhide. He put it back in its little bag and tied it back onto his braid. The little red figure of a man lay crumpled up where the spider had dropped it.

Yellow-Painted Lodge saw a chance to soothe relations between his people and the Cree, so he told the man to keep the horses and give him and his wife a meal before they returned home. He invited the Cree to visit him any time at his camp and to be his brother. The Cree was happy to oblige because he knew that no further trouble would come once Yellow-Painted Lodge had accepted food in his tipi.

A short time later, Yellow-Painted Lodge was visiting the lodge of his friend Little Bear, who had a very sick baby. Little Bear asked his visitor to hold the baby and pray for his son to live. Yellow-Painted Lodge told Little Bear to make a sweet pine smudge and then he took out his rawhide spider and placed it on a bunch of dried grass. He said: "If my power comes alive, I will give its name to this baby and he will grow up to be a strong man." He repeated his ceremony to make the spider come alive and soon it began to move. It ran across the floor to Little Bear. They saw it. Then it went back to Yellow-Painted Lodge, who put it away. He said: "Since my power has come alive for your child, I will give him the name Spider." [1]

Arnold says many people of the Buffalo Days knew the man named Spider, who was an outstanding dancer in his beautifully beaded regalia. He, indeed, grew to be an old man.

Another favourite story the old ones told was about a hunter who followed a herd of sheep to a mountain summit where he discovered a deep pit belching smoke and gas. After passing out from breathing the dense, suffocating clouds surrounding him, he found himself in the lodge of the Thunder Maker, in the form of a huge bird, with his wife and many children around him. The Thunder Maker smoked his pipe and told the man his name was Many Drums. He instructed him to make a pipe like the one he smoked and to add it to his bundle. Ever after, he should smoke the pipe after hearing the first thunder rolling in the springtime. If he were ever to find himself in a heavy thunderstorm, all he would have to do is pray to Thunder-maker and ask him to pity him and no harm would come to him.

According to Arnold, after an elder had told a powerful story about medicine power, he often backed it up by "reaching for his hand drum and singing the song that was sung when the event happened," such a long time ago. "There were stories about how the milky way was formed and how a woman might fall in love with a star and go into the heavens to live with him. I never wanted to fall asleep when they were telling these stories, but I always did. Sometimes I'd wake up in the morning and they'd still be telling them."

When Arnold was about seven, a healer named Scraping White visited his family and began preparing the young boy for the future.

"It would be very early in the morning and my mom would stoke the fire in the stove. She'd put the kettle on and when the water was boiling inside it would shake. I'd hear that and I'd jump up to get a basin of water for Old Man Scraping White. He would always sleep on the floor. He'd wash up while my mom was cooking and I'd help him get ready. He had a gunnysack full of clothes and I'd find the shirt he was going to wear that day. My mom would iron it for him and then he'd get dressed.

"You know, he let me take out his medicine bag. Most people were afraid to touch someone's medicine bag, but not me. The old man always wore a red scarf and I'd spread it out on the floor. I'd take out his paint and put it out where he could see it because his eyes weren't very good. I'd get a charcoal and he'd make a smudge with that bit of fire and then he'd get a mirror. He'd paint his face and then he'd paint mine. While he was doing this, the kids would be very calm, not jumping around like they usually did."

During one visit, after Old Man Scraping White had eaten and was ready to leave, he pulled Wallace aside and told him: "Your son here, in the future he's going to be doing what I'm doing. I've seen his path in his lifetime and he's going to help the people."

"About five years before my dad passed away, he asked me if I remembered what Old Man Scraping White had predicted so long ago," says Arnold. "I told him I did, and I think more than ever what the old man said is coming into play.

"In my early twenties I had the opportunity to be in the centre of the tipis at the Sun Dance with all of the elders, running the ceremonies. Many times we sat up late, my dad and the old men, and we'd go through the songs in the Horn Society. I was so fortunate to visualize our spiritual ways through them. It makes me think how I was able to keep all that information that the elders gave me back then."

It also amazes Arnold to think about how "dead right" the elders were with their predictions.

"They said things would change big time with our ceremonies. It's been over fifteen years since I stepped into the Sun Dance encampment and it was very emotional for me this past summer. Things have changed so much — not only with the Horn Society, but the Buffalo Women's Society as well. They were surprised to see me on those grounds. We stood there for a good hour and I saw how our sacred circle is not the same anymore. It was once a sacred place not only for our Blackfoot tribe but for others who are seeking as well. I told a ceremonial leader that our circle is starting to look like an RV park and he looked around and finally said I was right."

Arnold would like to see things go back to "the humbleness that has always been behind our sacred ways. The younger generation need to have the respect that our elders of twenty to thirty years ago had. Long time ago, we had elders who watched out for every child in our community. If they were sitting in front of one of the stores in town and they saw a child doing something bad, they'd go out of their way to settle that child. The parents would understand — he's disciplining that child because he loves him. He wants to help that child make a good way in life. An elder disciplined me and I went crying to my dad about it. He said, 'Well, what did you do?' and I told him. He told me that old man was right to do what he did and that the elder would put a needle through my ears the next time I was bad."

Arnold thinks one of the reasons he was given so much knowledge from the old ones at such a young age was to make things right with ceremony that involves handling bundles.

"Everything in that bundle has a life. In order to wake up the bundle a song has to be sung for each part. It's very emotional seeing all that goes on at a ceremony. We are losing a lot of our spiritual ways and it's just as the elders said. They talked about how they had pity for our generation twenty-five years into the future. Some of the same songs are being sung for the same bundles, and some of the songs that belong to a certain bundle aren't being used. I'm pretty sure I have enough information to make things right again. I'm just sorting out what I was taught and getting things straight in my mind. I feel like I want to step up and share the truth of our spiritual ways. A lot of people aren't going to like it."

Arnold observes that an emphasis on money has replaced the old, humble ways of caring for sacred items passed down from owners to receivers, in good faith that "the new holder would carry it humbly. Owning a bundle was not based on how much a person could afford to pay for it." Arnold has heard people give as much as $45,000 for a bundle these days.

"The old people said it over and over: 'Never put a price on something that you're going to do for a person if it involves our Creator.' It's not for money. It's between you and that guy up there, the one who gave us life. You're only taking up that spot (as a healer) to extend the help the Creator gives us."

People from all over the world visit Arnold for help with medical problems, including a woman from Japan who contacted him some time after she had returned home.

"She called and the family was crying. The girl's mother had a stroke in her garden and was paralyzed and still in a coma. I asked her if she still had some of the medicine I gave her when she was in Canada and she said she did. I told her to try and get it into her mom's intravenous bag, and that I would pray for her at the same time. They managed to get the medicine into her drip bag and I prayed for her. If you mean it from your heart, and not your head, your prayers will travel a long way. A couple of weeks later the girl phoned to say they had brought the old lady home and she was already back working in her garden."

Last spring, Arnold was invited as a healer to work with people in Fort Simpson in the Northwest Territories. He worked with numerous community members and was then taken to visit patients in the elders lodge.

"There were people there who were pretty sick. I sat and talked with them through my interpreter and I asked what their requests were. The last old lady I spoke with broke my heart. She was blind and she spoke not a word of English. I went into her room and I held her hand. After a while she looked up, though she couldn't see me, and cried. She told me she felt like she had a leash on her neck. She was led around like an animal and fed like a baby, then put back in her room."

She confided in Arnold that no one should have to live like she did. She had been blind since her early thirties and now she was somewhere close to eighty. She was so visually impaired that she couldn't see whether it was day or night; she vowed she would give anything to be able to see her brothers and sisters again, and to lay eyes on her grandchildren for the first time.

"I held her hand and told her, 'I'm going to beg my grandfathers so they can meet your request.' Then I went into the sweatlodge and the grandfathers told me what to make for her. I had some of that medicine in my bag and I made up the solution. I told her to put two drops of it a day in her eyes until it was all gone.

"That was about the third week of April. Around the first week of June, I got a phone call. That morning the old lady said she woke up and saw a person at the foot of her bed. At first she thought she was dreaming, but then she jumped up and became fully awake. It was a nurse at the foot of her bed and she asked the old lady if she could see. The lady replied she could a little but everything was in shadow. They sat her up and got her ready for the day. By the afternoon she started to see clearer. By the end of that week her family came and picked her up.

"The old woman told me, 'something amazing happened here. This is a miracle that has happened since you talked to me. My whole family has gotten together and we have a gift of $8,000 for you.' I told her I didn't want that money. All I wanted was a picture of her smiling. I told her to take that money and gather the elders in her community together and make a feast. If everyone would pray together, that would make me happy.

"I cannot account for what the Creator has done. What the Creator can do. . . I still don't believe it sometimes. I always remember the teachings my dad and the elders gave me and maybe that's why my prayers are answered. Maybe that's why things happen in a good way.

"There was a big meeting in Hamburg, Germany with people from Poland, Czechoslovakia, England and Germany. The delegates wanted me to come and show them medicine. I wish I could give information out, but I was told not to expose myself in any form. I can only help those who come to me. If you come to me then maybe I can help you. It was given to me from the Creator to help people. It wasn't given to me to make money.

"There was a doctor at the Tom Baker Cancer Centre in Calgary who said to me, "I have millions of dollars of equipment here but what you have to help people is way beyond anything I have."

1   Beverly Hungry Wolf, *The Ways of My Grandmothers* (New York, William Morrow and Company, Inc., 1980) pp. 73, 74.

6

Alexis Seniantha

Dene Tha', Chateh (Dene Tha' First Nation)

Years after I spent time with Alexis in the early 1990s, I heard he'd moved from his home community in Chateh, one of three Dene Tha' communities in northern Alberta, to a retirement home and palliative care centre in Peace River, six hundred kilometres to the south. I hoped he had his drum with him and could still sing because these things were so much a part of him. Several of his relatives assured me he was still talking about spiritual knowledge, like his visions, spirit travel, communicating with animals and receiving their help, and the importance of dreaming, while he lived at the centre. He gave his drum to David Providence, a younger man (whose profile is included in this book) who would carry on his leadership role. Alexis passed away on December 1, 1998.

Maggie Eht-Chillay lies on a couch, breath rattling from her heaving chest. Her son Henry is worried her lungs won't hold out this time and she will die from emphysema. She has taken no food in days and hasn't the strength to talk.

Bending over her, the prophet from Chateh holds her emaciated hand and speaks softly. He has travelled 170 kilometres north of his home community to Meander River to bring comfort and pray for the ninety-year-old woman. Taking his drum from a white cloth bag, Alexis Seniantha beats it slowly. He sings about wanting to be "where my Father's land is," and that "we are pitiful" on this earth.

"If something happens to us, our souls fly to heaven like a [prairie] chicken," Alexis assures Maggie. He sings another song, a more light-hearted one, then speaks again. "You don't have anything to say about your future. There is a God and it's true. I saw my Father with my eyes."

Alexis's last song for Maggie is about Mother Earth and how God created the world for people. He explains his own mother once sang it for him, telling him to remember it in times of sickness. As the last drumbeat fades, Alexis sets down his drum. Suddenly, Maggie struggles to sit up and begins talking. The strength in her voice astonishes Henry.

"Before, she couldn't even talk clearly!" he exclaims. Easily exhausted, Maggie thanks the prophet and lies back.

Henry tells Alexis that as a shy young man years ago he felt threatened by Alexis when the older man urged him to drum and sing for the people. "But now I see you're just an old man," he says. Henry is not being disrespectful. He is expressing his realization that Alexis is not to be feared. He is grateful to the kind elder who pushed him into becoming a shin Dene (song man). Although Henry is helping to keep the Dene tradition of praying with the drum and song alive, there are some who fear that when Alexis dies, there will be no one to take his place as a spiritual leader.

To the Dene Tha' (Common Peoples), Alexis is Ndátin — A Dreamer. He has developed a strong mind and lived a clean life. He can direct his dreams and receives messages from God. He is devoted to helping his people and for years has been the head prophet amongst the Dene Tha', named the spiritual leader by Nógha (which means wolverine, pronounced No-ah), before he died in the 1930s. Dene Tha' in their seventies remember Nógha riding his horse throughout northern Alberta, conducting Tea Dances wherever he went, urging them to honour the Creator. Nógha received his power from wolverine, an animal portrayed in many Dene legends as being able to see things that are hidden. He looked into the future, and the old people who heard him forecast the changes to be brought by white newcomers say his words were true.

Alexis's granddaughter Molly Chisaakay says her grandfather was made a drumkeeper and was expected to follow a rigid code of ethics at a very young age.

"He felt he wasn't worthy. He had such a big responsibility. In spiritual leadership, it's not about how much you gain or lose, it's responsibility. When you take the drum, you have to be in tune with what it stands for. You have to live what you say about living a good and humble way by accepting the teachings of the drum. My grandfather could have drank alcohol when everyone else was, but he couldn't go against the teachings of the drum. But that's not to say he judges those who do."

As a child, Alexis listened carefully to his uncle Nógha's prophecies and to the advice of other elders. He heard over and over again stories about animal people and powerful ancestors who had performed heroic deeds. His senses were trained to detect information from the spirit world that went unnoticed by others. His elders told him it would be good for him to sleep beside a tree that had been split by lightning and touched by the Thunderbird if he wanted to seek his vision.[1] Some children who became prophets had the ability to journey to heaven, and Alexis, now eighty-three, often speaks about travelling in spirit above the earth. He uses his hands expressively, grabbing his shoulders and shaking them when describing how he was thrown out of heaven.

"I was sick and just about died. If I put an offering in the fire for myself, I knew I might live. I wanted to know what's happening so I placed an offering in the fire. I started to sleep. I don't know what happened. I must have gone to my Father's land. He saw me. 'What do you want over here?' He asked me.

"I said, 'I'm very tired and ill but I wanted to go to You.' He was smiling, looking at me.

"'Way down, people are pitiful. Work for them,' He said. I was grabbed and pushed out. There was nothing but blue sky. That's where I was set free. He's holding my arm. I went back to the earth. I was so thankful when I saw the world. My feet were together, on the ground again."

Before the dream ended, angels told Alexis where to find a moose on earth so he could hunt it.

"'Look over here,' I was told. I saw a cow moose. 'Hurry up to get that moose,' they told me. 'The moose won't go any farther, so just turn back [to get it],' they told me." Alexis describes how he woke up and felt better. His wife paddled him in a canoe to hunt the moose he had been shown.

"So all day, we went back. I could breathe good by then," he recalls. "So many difficulties and such a hard way of living. But when you've got to live, then you've got to live. It's not that difficult," Alexis says, referring to the help God provides to people who live straight lives.

"It is true there is a God, a Creator. He made the world for us. The clouds are high. That's where my Father's world is. It's very nice. But because I am here on earth, I'm going to help others."

Since Alexis has been to heaven in his dream, he has earned the right to direct Tea Dance (Dahot s'ethe) ceremonies for his people. Tea Dances are spiritual community celebrations for petitioning the Creator, thanksgiving and socializing. The reason to have a Tea Dance is revealed to the spiritual leaders of the community through their dreams. A Tea Dance might be held to ask for a successful hunting season or good weather. It might also be held to commemorate a meeting with another neighbouring community or as a burial ceremony for someone who has recently died.

Drummers, facing east, stand before a central fire within a fenced circle with openings to the north and south. Dancers move between the singers and the fire in a clockwise direction, the way the sun moves across the sky. In the Tea Dance you are making your trail to heaven as you dance, the Dene Tha' elders say. The ceremony is a meaningful blending of Christian and Dene tradition, and the elders make no delineation between the two. For example, as men, women, and children place their tobacco offering on the fire, they kneel and solemnly touch their forehead, chest, and shoulders, making the sign of the cross on their bodies as Catholics do.

"There's a spiritual meaning behind everything at the Tea Dance," explains Molly. "The drum represents the circle of life. It's made of an animal skin and wood, the Creator's gifts to us, and you have to heat it up near fire for it to sound good. There's a real power behind it. The drum brings people together and awakens something. When you hear it and dance, it's a way of expressing yourself, rejoicing. You realize you have this powerful connection between yourself, the Creator, and everyone else. If you're at a Tea Dance, you just don't want to sit down."

The Dene Tha' talk to the Creator with the drum which holds symbolic meaning, Molly says, and singing is an ancient practice. There are songs soliciting the Creator's blessing, honour songs for elders, women, and children, and some for different dances. "A feeling can just well up from inside and you let it out, like you're crying for the people," Molly explains.

At Tea Dances, Alexis invites the people to pray, dance, share, and live clean lives. He wants them to look closer at life and concentrate on positives so they will fly straight to their Father's land when they die. "It looks really nice there. There is no dirt in that land. There is tall grass, but it's not the same as here. The ends are sharp. It looks different. Like cattails. I saw it with my eyes. I thought it looked very beautiful."

Before the dancing begins, Alexis and other elders place tobacco and food offerings on the fire, then they may talk to the people about what they see coming ahead. Information about the availability of animals for hunting or the severity of the coming winter are just two examples of what they might share.

"I know my own journey and I am becoming more aware," Alexis tells his people. "Before I go to sleep, I pray to the Creator. I see the pain in my people and feel it with my family. In my dream, I look ahead. What is going to happen? When I do look, I'm wondering if I'm going to be around to see what is going to happen. The angels tell me, 'You are going to stay as long as you can through tough times.'"

The ability to direct dreams and look ahead is a spiritual gift prophets have long used to help their people survive. Falling asleep, a person who has dreaming abilities can travel, in spirit, to locate animals in the bush. When the dreamer awakens, he or she describes the locations of the animals encountered in the dream, and the hunters go to those spots and make the kill. In the same way God showed Alexis where to find the moose, the dreamer helps his or her people to find what they need spiritually, by relating God's messages to them and reminding them that an all-knowing creative force watches over them.

"At the Tea Dance, we pray. The people want me to talk. Even if I say something to them, they don't believe it. They'll see. Heeeeee! They'll wonder why they didn't change. I am taught everything. I know. This drinking business. The people think nobody sees them do bad things to each other. But if they die, they will see. They'll wish they had obeyed the pitiful old man. I know it's very hard."

Alexis prays constantly for his people. "When I go to bed, I pray, then sleep. In the morning, I get up and pray again. After that I drink tea. I don't eat, I just drink tea. I look at what is happening. Why do people drink? I pray they won't do that. It should be quiet. They should just pray. Myself, I don't bother with liquor. Never once has liquor touched my mouth."

Alexis knows alcohol is the symptom of a larger problem. He realizes how complex the world has become with the impact of the dominant society. He mentions a simpler time when he was young and living off the land.

"We lived at Tu Lonh [Zama Lake, located north of Chateh]. I lived in a tent, but it's nice. We were heading farther and farther out with our traps. Out there, I killed three moose. Three cow moose.

It's wonderful to be able to feed everyone, I thought. We went for furs. My traps were still set. We set camp for the night. At the next camp, I killed three moose — one fat cow and two young, quite big. Next morning, we started on our journey. We headed back for Zama Lake. I had good dogs, and our blankets, all our belongings were packed on the sled. We returned to our tent and I cut some of the wood and made a fire and went back out to work. When it got warm, I went inside."

Molly recalls the fascinating story her grandfather told her when she asked how he and her grandmother, Betsy Metchooyeah, became husband and wife.

"My grandmother was an orphan. She was a good trapper. She knew how to take care of herself. I think she was about twelve years old when my grandfather picked her. He brought her a whole load of gifts, and she was trying on the dresses and shoes, putting ribbons in her hair, putting on make-up, eating candy, just having fun. But when reality set in, she stopped to think, 'You're going to be married.' She stayed away for two days to think about it. When she came back, she brought food. She said to my grandfather, 'This is my answer. We will have some nourishment and so our marriage will bear fruit.'

"My grandmother was small, but she stood her ground. She never said anything without good reason. She was a trapper and she told my grandfather she had her own ways and they must not go on each other's trapline or they might have accidents or arguments. She told him not to bring anything into it [the marriage] or there would be problems. . . just to bring himself and they would start their lives new, together."

Molly marvels at the maturity of her grandparents at such a young age. She says they lived together for two years without sexual relations until her grandmother began menstruating and underwent a period of isolation and ritual between "the earth and herself." After that, she had her first child.

"My grandfather told me they had a good life together. I think his parents taught him well. His mother told him, 'If you strike a woman, you have destroyed something.'"

Life in the early 1900s was simple but hard, Alexis admits. Death was always close by, and he recalls the sorrow he felt when his brother Billy died. He had been well respected by the people and once killed a grizzly bear that had been terrorizing the camp.

"One day, my brother went outside his house. As he walked back by the pile of sawdust, he just fell like that. When I got to where he was, I was shocked. I cried with all my heart. He had told me before not to cry, but I couldn't help it." Later, Alexis says he was confronted by his brother's spirit. "I looked inside his house. I saw him crawling in his house. He crawled a bit farther and then got up. He said, 'Just like I told you before, I would fly like a grouse to heaven. Why are you holding me back?'" Alexis confirms the grief of the living can hold dead relatives and friends back from starting their journey to heaven, but when someone does make it safely to the other side they send a song back to earthly friends or relatives. The Dene say when this happens a person will receive a song in their sleep and, upon awakening, find it impossible to forget.

According to Nógha's prophecies, if the Dene people really listen to the messages and songs sent from heaven and pray with all their strength, they and the world will not be destroyed. The people must not let go of the traditions like placing tobacco on the fire and praying at Tea Dances. Alexis continues passing along these teachings and is one of only four recognized elders in Chateh who speak about spiritual matters at gatherings.

As Molly notes, Alexis has a distinct personal way of teaching, too. "Elders tell stories in a general, simple, symbolic way. You have to translate them to your life situation. My grandfather has always told me to listen. When I would talk and talk about my problems, he would tell me to take time to be quiet and listen. I remember being outside and while I talked my grandfather chopped wood. . . never said anything. Then, he finally said something like, 'You can learn a lot from wood.' I think he was telling me to be quiet, like a piece of wood, or to concentrate on chopping it or something like that. Maybe I'd get an answer from inside myself, from my spirit, if I'd let it come. He never told me what to do.

"Some people think our elders are wishy-washy and should be more aggressive about stopping today's problems. But they cannot go against tradition and they never force things. They are trusting and almost innocent in that way. They are so spiritual, and some people have gone so far away from that, they can't understand anymore." Molly says her grandparents raised her in a way that developed her awareness and respect toward other living things, which also have a spiritual life.

"We were out walking one day and I stepped on a flower. I said, 'I'm going to pick it,' but my grandmother told me to leave it.

"She said, 'Nature is strong. As we pass, it's going to open up again, so leave it alone. We're not here to destroy nature. The Creator cares about that flower.' At night, by the fire, she'd say, 'Look at the stars, then look at our fire. It's small and you can only see its sparks from a little ways away. But the stars, you can see their light forever. That's our Creator. That's how powerful He is.' When we left camp, we always made sure everything was left clean behind us."

Alexis speaks about God and tradition so people can make the choice to live fulfilling lives. He reminds them of Nógha's faultless vision and how he foresaw bad times, making it all the more important that they pray and stay true to their traditions.

Nógha spoke of "yellow papers" that would fool the people. Alexis believes these to be the government welfare cheques that impaired the work ethic once so critical to Dene survival. He predicted the land will be criss-crossed with lines, and the cut-lines slashed by oil companies that moved into the Chateh area not long ago have proved his words true. The prophet also foresaw strong winds and speculated about "something terrible coming." He said the earth will not move because it is "tremendous," but things would move on the surface of the earth. Another of Nógha's prophecies states that, "if you all forget to pray, then there will be no sun for a month. In the morning, the sun will rise, followed by the moon, and as they climb higher they will eclipse each other at noon. The sun will stop there, midway in its path, for one hour. Together, the sun and moon will set and there will be darkness." [2]

Alexis grew up with the prophecies and knows the healing power of prayer. Many credit him with inspiring Dene in his own community and in places like Fort Rae and Fort Edzo in the Northwest Territories to revive their traditional Tea-Dance religion.

"In fact," says Father Camille Piché, the Catholic priest at Assumption, "a little while ago, when Alexis was sick in the hospital in Edmonton, the people up north saw blood-red northern lights and they worried they were a sign that Alexis wasn't going to live much longer. Everyone thinks so much of the prophet."

Though Alexis may talk about apocalyptic times to come, he believes people will be safe if they pray for guidance on life's journey and treat the earth and each other with love and respect. He knows there are immense spiritual forces to help those who ask for assistance and stop hurting themselves and others. That is why he calls Tea Dances and finds the energy to attend meetings and gatherings, gently reminding the people to pray.

And as long as he is alive, they will.

1   Pat Moore, Angela Wheelock, and the Dene Wodih Society, *Wolverine Myths and Visions — Dene Traditions from Northern Alberta* (Edmonton, Alberta: The University of Alberta Press, 1990), p. 75.

2   Ibid., p. 79.

7

Beverly Hungry Wolf

Kanai (Blood), Kanai First Nation

Beverly Hungry Wolf is dancing on Banff's main street to live music from a band hired to play during Alberta Arts Days. She is on a break from the Aboriginal Emerging Writers Course she helps teach and is a spiritual advisor for, and she and a student are clearly enjoying themselves, gyrating "old school" to the music as crowds walk by. The dance is a testament to the sixty-one-year-old's self-confidence and free spirit.

Beverly is "elder certified" when it comes to making a contribution to her community. She preserved invaluable stories of the "Buffalo Days" of her Blackfoot people, especially women, in *The Ways of My Grandmothers*, published in 1980, and *Daughters of the Buffalo Women*, released in 1996. She is also a language keeper and teaches Blackfoot* in a community Headstart program.

---

* The Blackfoot language is spoken by the Kanai, Blackfeet, Siksika, and Piikani Nations in the Blackfoot Confederacy.

"In residential school I was told our people were evil and stupid and dirty, and we were so brainwashed," Beverly says. When she got older, in her twenties, she wanted to learn about where she came from. She decided she would go sit with people older than her own parents and find out if they were so bad. "I sat with the old ones and asked lots of questions and my books are the result of that time," she explains. It was also the '60s and suddenly, during the hippie movement, it was "cool" to be Indian.

Blood families were traditionally tight-knit and Beverly was raised with love and generosity. "I wasn't even expected to work. My father told me I was a child and my only job was to be a child. If I did help out, oh, I was praised to high heaven. One time my mom tried to force me to do the dishes, and because I didn't want to I got a little bit of a whipping. My grandmother jumped on her and took my side right away."

Beverly's father believed in "letting me get out of working as a child because he trusted I saw how neat and orderly my parents kept things, even though I didn't help keep it that way, and so I would automatically follow suit when I owned my own home."

When Beverly first approached her grandmothers, "it took me a while to understand that these old women had the information I wanted, but that they took it for granted that I should know what they knew. They didn't understand I was raised differently in the mission school.

"For example, when I asked my grandmother, 'How do you make drymeat?' she answered, 'Oh, you just take the meat and you cut it open.' I said, 'Really?' and my grandfather was sitting there and he said, 'No, old lady, ask her how she would do it.' So she asked me and I told her how I would do it. She said, 'Oh, no. You don't do it that way. You take the muscles and you cut all the muscle packages apart, and when you're done, you just have the bone. There's a real knack for taking those muscles apart, otherwise you have a lot of skin and stuff in between and you want to just have the meat."

That first query led to more questions about women's work and traditional ways, and as she delved deeper into the sacred ways of her ancestors, Beverly eventually became a medicine pipe holder. She was taught how to take care of the pipe and at the same time, "learned how to treat my family, my community, and my tribe. I had a big responsibility in sharing the knowledge that I was given, so that when I passed on my medicine pipe I would do it correctly. I would do it in the same way my grandmother passed hers to me."

Beverly was taught traditional skills, like tanning hides, picking plants, roasting intestinal meats, making berry soup, and caring for two hundred or more ceremony guests.

"All through my real education, I saw how gentle and beautiful my grandmothers were. I thought to myself, 'How could they be bad? They've never done anything unkind to anyone — they don't even drink alcohol. They pray hard morning and night, and they pray before they're going to travel somewhere.'"

The idea for writing a book about the ways of her Blood grandmothers came from Beverly's mother, Ruth Little Bear. Ruth kept a handwritten manuscript from her own father about Blood history and she thought she would like to write something similar about the life of women. When Beverly married her German husband, Adolph (who was given the Blackfoot name Hungry Wolf), Ruth was delighted to learn he was a writer. Here was a son-in-law who could not only start a family with her daughter and support them, he could direct the project she herself never got around to. When Adolph and Beverly discussed the project, he was adamant that she should work on the project herself, and so she began.

Beverly first recorded stories from her mother, and then reached out to other older women, who by custom were her grandmothers, for their recollections. The old ones told her stories from their own grandmothers — about how they kept their camps, cooked and prepared food, and processed the hides from animals their husbands killed. They shared legends of how the sacred Natoas headdress, worn by holy women at Sundance ceremonies, first came to the people from an elk, and myths about women who married dogs or regenerated the buffalo population when it was almost extinct.

"I became the hands and feet of those old ladies. I would go and visit my grandmothers and I would clean their houses or take them for drives. They would be sharing their knowledge as we went. At first, I don't think they knew what to make of me, but they understood the importance of sharing what they knew and were generous. I think, for them it was special and unique to have someone who was very young pay attention and want to learn the old ways instead of modern education."

Beverly was fortified by stories of strong women. A much-loved legend she recounts in *The Ways of My Grandmothers* involves Running Eagle, who became the most famous woman in Blackfoot history. As a young girl, she practiced hunting buffalo with her father and saved his life when they were suddenly attacked by an enemy war party while out on the plains. When her father had his horse shot out from beneath him, she rode back to rescue him against a volley of arrows — a brave deed her people praised for days.

She settled down to women's work when her mother became ill and she had to look after her brothers and sisters. However, when Crow warriors killed her father on the war trail, she enlisted the help of a widow woman to look after her siblings while she avenged him. Despite the misgivings of the Blackfoot war party leader who wanted to leave her behind, Running Eagle joined in and distinguished her prowess by killing a Crow warrior who was attempting to steal her people's horses.

Dismissing men who felt she should stay in camp tanning hides and cooking, Running Eagle fasted for spiritual power and became so successful in raids and in battle that she began leading war parties. Still, men tried to halt her masculine career by attempting to marry her until she finally explained she belonged to the Sun, who came to her in a vision, and that she would die if she broke her vows to him.

No one is sure how many Blackfoot enemies Running Eagle killed, nor how many horses she captured, but it is known that she died as she lived — on the war trail. In a long, drawn-out battle involving clubs and knives, she was fatally struck in the back of the head by a Flathead warrior.

Some of Beverly's grandmothers admitted that their lives were humdrum compared to the war and hunting exploits of their male counterparts. In later years, when intertribal wars and buffalo hunts ended, they were still busy scrubbing floors and cooking for their families while their husbands worked in the fields and with live-stock, or spent time visiting with friends to relive their glory days.

The wife of a spiritual husband was kept doubly busy during an-nual ceremonies like the Sundance because she had to feed and entertain her husband's visitors, all the while keeping up with her own religious work.

Beverly's mother retained incredibly detailed memories of watch-ing her own grandmother set up her tipi and proceed to use only a couple of kettles and a frying pan over an open fire to feed ten visitors or more during the Sundance. Ruth was Beverly's best friend when she was alive and was open in sharing women's knowledge with her daughter about issues like childbirth, preventing pregnancy, early courtship and craftwork.

For example, in *The Ways of My Grandmothers*, Beverly's grand-mother, AnadaAki, shares her experience of giving birth: "Right after my baby was born and taken care of, my mother started to clean me. After I was cleaned, she started massaging my bones back into place. I was given some broth to drink and then she laid me down to rest." The baby and the mother were dressed in old rags that had been cleaned. They would continue to dress like this for the first thirty days after the birth. The new mother usually stayed with her own mother during this time, away from her husband. No sick per-son could stay around the home where she was taken care of and she didn't do any heavy work during this period.

Every four days the new mother was bathed and given a cleansing ceremony. Her mother would wash her and then cover her up with a blanket. She sat by the altar, where incense was lit. The incense went up under her blanket and purified her body. To bring the mother's body back into shape, in addition to the massages, she was made to wear a "belt" or girdle of rawhide. This was wide enough to cover her abdomen, and tied firmly. She did not use pins on any of the rag clothing but rather tied her baby's rag bundle together with buckskin cords. This was a trial period, to make sure everybody would survive the new birth. In those days children often died in their first days, and it was not unusual for mothers to die from childbirth.

At the end of thirty days, mother and child would move camp and, after being cleansed once more, they would get dressed in their new clothes. Usually the child got a new cradleboard, and around this time, the father came to take his newborn to a noted elder whose prayers were known to be strong. This holy man would paint the child's face with sacred earth mixed with grease while he was praying and then announce the name he had chosen for the child.

When Beverly had her first child, Wolf, with her husband Adolph, her father took him to raise in his own home. Though she was angry at the time, she realized he was keeping with Blackfoot tradition.

"Often grandparents take one of their grandchildren to raise and keep them company. In the Blackfoot way, these children are called "old people children." Some of these children grew to be very wise, especially in tribal lore, while others grew up to be lazy and spoiled. My father took my son Wolf and he told me later, 'your boy has kept me and your mother young.'"

In 1973, when her second son, Okan, was a month old, Beverly and Adolph moved to a secluded area in B.C. For the next thirty years, the family lived without electricity and running water. The couple home-schooled their children and Adolph ran a publishing business out of their house. Beverly lived many of her grandmothers' teachings: sewing moccasins and cooking wild meat, and sometimes living in a tipi. She also kept a garden, baked her own bread, made jam from berries, kept a root cellar, and raised chickens.

To say the couple had returned to the land and were living a healthy lifestyle is an understatement, but it was not to last. By 1998, after Beverly's parents died, the marriage began to falter.

"I knew I had to let Adolph go because I wasn't happy. And when you're dealing with things like sacred bundles, you can't pretend to be happy in front of spiritual things. You can't be carrying sadness when you are asking for love and kindness in your prayers."

With the break-up, Beverly had to support herself and she began teaching Blackfoot at a community college in Montana. During that time, an Aboriginal producer who had read her books suggested she start writing scripts so she could bring her grandmothers' stories to life in film. When he suggested she attend an eight-week writers' boot camp, she jumped at the chance, and later attended Aboriginal Film and Video Studies at Vancouver's Capilano College.

These days she's up by five in the morning to work on the many projects she has on the go. Her writing themes are still focused on women, and her latest is called *Sweetgrass Burners*, about women who live in two worlds as they combine modern, successful lifestyles with traditional ceremony and prayer.

Beverly's life continues to be informed by the teachings her grandmothers shared with her, but she's especially thankful to her grandfathers who taught her about a woman's status in Blood society. "They told me, 'we hold a woman highly because she is a giver of life.' They made me realize how honoured women were and that made me feel like a special person. In traditional meetings, women talked first and then the men. If it was a war issue, the men got together to discuss strategy, but in a general meeting the women were always given the first chance because they kept the family; they're the ones who kept the lodge. They knew what the tribe needed to survive. If the community was low on meat, they'd tell the men to go on a hunt; if they were down in berry supplies, they'd say, 'we need to go to the berry patches,' and if tipi poles were needed, they'd tell the men to cut more."

Beverly's grandfathers told her women were never forbidden to do holy work, and that if a dream person came to them and told them,

'This is your power,' then it was the woman's duty to use the gift given to her, just as it would be a man's.

"Of all the Aboriginal societies I've looked at, it seems our ways are the most balanced. You can't do anything without a man, and you can't do anything without a woman. Bundle keepers are usually a man and wife, or maybe a sister and brother if they aren't married. In our ways, all the holy things were given to the woman; we shared with the men by teaching them the ceremonies. Unlike a lot of other nations, we don't take sweat baths because women don't need that purification; we cleanse ourselves each month during menstruation."

That's not to say other nations don't have ceremonies that honour women, Beverly points out. "I was in Hobbema at this wonderful coming-of-age ceremony for a girl who was becoming a woman. It made the girl feel important about getting her period instead of like it was an ugly, dirty punishment. The church has a way of taking sacred things and making them evil. You can look at menstruation like it is a hindrance and it is ugly, or you can celebrate it because it means you enter into the mystery of being able to bring new life into existence.

"Snakes are another thing the church has put down. To traditional people they are sacred because they move so close to Mother Earth, but certain religions portray them as wicked."

Paradoxically, Beverly's father was a deacon in the church even though his grandfather Eagle Plume had been an important holy man, and another of his grandfathers was documented as having lived four lifetimes as a reincarnated being. At each of his deaths, a relative such as his great-grandmother would sing his power songs and bring him back to life as a baby. During each lifetime, he didn't live to be very old, but he would talk in-depth and give great detail about his other lives.

"Finally, after his fourth life, the old people said, 'He's lived enough lives,' and they let him go," Beverly explains.

When she informed her father she was returning to Blackfoot religion, he remained supportive of her, telling her to, "find the religion you want to be a part of, and when you find it just be sure to follow it well."

"I think I brought my father back to our Indian ways because I shared so much about them with him; he could appreciate the wisdom and beauty in the old time religion. He continued to practice his Catholic ways but he was a weather dancer for the Sundance and he was a drummer for the medicine pipe. Both my parents helped my grandparents with the Sundance; my mom would bake bread and take it up to my grandmother and if they were having a big gathering she'd prepare big meals and take them up to the camp. Both of my parents took big support roles in our ceremonies."

The hierarchy of spiritual societies is intact within the Blackfoot Nation, Beverly says, though she doesn't belong to one herself right now. She was once part of the Crazy Dogs Society, the members of which are servants for the Sundance people.

"I'm not active at the moment because I passed on all the holy things I had. The person who passed them to me is my 'holy parent' and now I'm a 'holy parent' to my daughter because I gave her the Beaver bundle and medicine pipe bundle in a transfer ceremony. She wanted to keep those because she wanted to do the Sundance. She's not doing that any more but she's continuing her holy work with the medicine pipe."

Young people are keeping the societies alive although only three still exist: the Horn Society, Crazy Dogs and the Pigeon Society for males. "And we also have the Ladies Buffalo Society," Beverly explains. "In the old days, the Pigeons protected the inside of the camp. They were the youngest society but they were the ones who reprimanded the older people if they were acting out of line. The Crazy Dogs were our first response in war. They protected the outside of the camp — beyond our tipi circle. Finally, the Horn Society was made up of the war leaders. We used to have a Bull Society made up of really old men, but they gave their head dresses to the Ladies Buffalo Society and the Horn Society. And we used to have the youngest society — the Flies."

Beverly stresses the commitment to carry a bundle is serious. "The community expects you not to drink or drug; you have to be a role model. Today, a lot of young people are getting involved with holy work — some do it well, and some fall off the wagon. Still, they always manage to sober up for the main part of the bundle opening or transfer.

"And you should see our Sundance Circles; when I first started going up to the Belly Buttes, where they are held, there were maybe six or seven tipis and maybe thirty tents. Now we have a full circle of tipis and there are hardly any modern tents."

This past summer, Beverly was heartened to visit the Sundance circle and see two little girls dancing, "and there was a little boy, too, who was one of my students at a place I worked at before. He was dancing the way the old Horns dance — in a jumping kind of movement. Seeing that was good for me. I thought to myself, 'Okay, our culture is not going to die. We have those little kids; it's become a good thing for our young people to become involved.'"

Beverly was proud to see the Crazy Dogs Society in action, too, as they escorted a policeman off the Sundance grounds.

"He was a member of our own police force, but the Crazy Dogs told him, 'No, up here we have our own police force. You can come back when you're dressed normally but don't come up here in your uniform.'"

The Blood people have been holding their ceremonies on the Belly Buttes for "hundreds and hundreds and hundreds" of years, Beverly says. "We've made our offerings in the same place and there's never been a break. Up there, it's sacred. It's like coming home. Sometimes I get sad because my grandparents aren't there, but I will always go up. This year I had a death in the family but I still went up there. I'd have to be pretty much dead before I stopped going."

When I mention to Beverly I once had my face painted by Joe Crowshoe in the springtime, she tells me I must have been at a medicine pipe ceremony.

"The medicine pipes are opened in the spring. The Beaver bundles you open every month but you don't once the water has frozen. When it gets cold enough to freeze water you don't work with them any more. In the spring, when the water starts flowing, then we open them again.

"The different societies and bundles have different face-painting designs. The Beaver Bundle just has four dots on the face and then the arms get painted, too. The painting is a blessing. You're coming to be blessed by the articles in the bundle. Lots of people who have cancer go to these holy ceremonies and they come out of it. There is power in those bundles and I've seen people get healed from heart problems and liver problems. Even people who are going to jail will ask for help and then pull out of their bad situations."

When Beverly visits the Sundance on the Belly Buttes each year, she finds spiritual renewal. When she helps out with the opening of a sacred bundle, she is empowered.

"When you're living these ways, you know you have the ancestors behind you, pushing you along. You never think 'I'm alone here' because you feel the old ones helping you along."

8

James Grandjambe

Cree, Fort McKay First Nation

At a handgame tournament at the 2011 Fort McKay Treaty Days, I spy James watching the action. I approach him and tell him I'm the one who put him in a book twenty years ago. He smiles and nods at me, and then I ask the young woman standing with him about Onion, James's grandson who was a little boy back in 1992. She tells me there are two Onions — Big Onion and Little Onion because now James's grandson has a son of his own. Later, up at the culture camp, amidst racks of drying fish and meat, we have a little reunion as I snap pictures of James, who is now almost ninety-two, holding his great-grandson Little Onion while Ryan Grandjambe, Big Onion, kneels proudly beside them.

"Moosum still likes going hunting," Ryan confirms. "We go to a few areas around here but industry is really taking its toll. You can't go anywhere now. We quad, we take the truck or we boat up and down the Athabasca. We go fishing sometimes, but what we're always after is moose."

Companies like Canadian Natural Resources and Total E&P Canada, are "really developing," so he and James go further and further away from Fort McKay to hunt.

"I go up to Moose Lake," Ryan says, and I recognize it as a place James talked a lot about when I first spoke with him back in 1991. He said it was once a paradise where there were lots of animals to hunt and berries to pick.

James's daughter Theresa, the third of his eight daughters and whom he treated like a son since he had none, remembers walking with her family for three days to get to Moose Lake from Fort McKay.

"That's if we didn't kill a moose. If we killed a moose we'd stop for a while to smoke the meat," Theresa recalls. Along the way, James would show her how to dig the roots of medicinal plants and how to set snares for rabbits and squirrels. At night, the family slept in lean-tos on hand-sewn mattresses Theresa's mother Mary stuffed with feathers.

"My dad would make us girls dolls out of wood to play with, and I remember pulling frozen squirrels on a little sleigh for fun," Theresa says. When she got older and stronger, she easily carried a hindquarter of meat on her shoulders down to the boat when her family was returning from Moose Lake.

"We didn't have toys so we made our own. We didn't have store-bought things like candy or cookies, but we drank the sap from the poplar tree in the springtime and it tasted like watermelon. We loved that. The same with cattails — if you eat the roots of them they taste a bit sweet like watermelon, too."

She recalls how many people would come to see her father for medicine from the land but James says plants are not the same now as they were when he was young. "You have to make an offering to the spirit of that plant in a place that hasn't been disturbed. Now, everything is so contaminated up here the plants aren't the same," says Theresa.

Oilsands activity is taking its toll.

"The spirits look after you when you keep the promises you make to them." James Grandjambe offers this spiritual philosophy as he balances his adopted grandson, Onion, on his knee. Patiently, he plays with him and urges him to get his drum from his bedroom to show the visitors. Onion emerges from his bedroom, proudly banging a star-painted drum and then scoots off to play with some Tonka toys. James says he has been teaching Cree songs to his grandson, but Onion is just a little too shy to sing for strangers.

James resumes telling us when he was Onion's age he was taught to believe in a world many have lost touch with, that of the spirit beings. Life seems hard to some people because help from good spirits is withheld when humans break their covenant with the Creator by disobeying Him.

"If you have a dream that someone's put a curse on you, or they're bothering you, go out and buy food. Make a feast. Then the drum will be used there. The pipe will be used there. And that's your way out of the bad thing you dreamed about. It will not come true, and that's how you get out of that curse. Ask for help from the spirits," James explains, indicating prayer and good deeds overpower evil.

He speaks of a young woman in the community who suffered several miscarriages and became pregnant again. He learned through a vision that if she would make a Tea Dance and feast, her next pregnancy would come to full term. The woman agreed and the feast was made. James had another vision several months later. "It was really bright, and there was a big feast going on. I saw her dancing with a little girl. They were both laughing and happy."

Two more months passed and the woman learned from her doctor she was pregnant with a boy, but James began preparing a Tea Dance "for the little girl that's coming." James then asked the woman's husband to go hunting for meat for the feast, and, a little later, the man's daughter was born.

"So now, all her life that little girl should be making Tea Dance, every year around her birthday, and the spirits will look after her," James says. He didn't tell the girl's mother about his dream "because people don't believe," and he realizes adults and teenagers are often embarrassed by the old beliefs and have lost faith in the spirits.

"If someone would really just show the younger generation how we used to pray and celebrate a long time ago, I'm sure all the kids would really enjoy seeing it. Like the Round Dance, everyone used to look forward to it. It was just like Christmas. When we'd come back from the bush with a whole bunch of dried meat, pounded meat, and everything, we'd have a feast for three days and everybody would dance. Let's say I was holding a scarf, and you were holding the other end. . . we'd dance one round in the circle, and after we finished the scarf would be yours. People gave away horses, blankets, guns, or anything that was valuable."

Today's powwow dancing is "jumping around and the songs don't make sense. It's just screaming," says James. "It's nothing to us because it doesn't mean anything. The kids are not really interested. They just go home after the dance. We were raised on ordinary Tea Dance.

"Before, when there was an elder who was too old to go out and hunt for the feast, but he knows how to smoke the pipe and he knows the prayers, then the younger people would go and get moose meat and get the food ready. Then they'd go to his house and ask him if he would make the ceremony, and the elder used to do that."

From grandfather to father, James's family upheld the tradition of making Tea Dances for years. James's daughter Theresa remembers the huge celebrations, often lasting for days. "They'd make a big fire and a big fence around it. You'd take your own dishes for the feast and whatever you were going to give away. Everybody would dance around the fire. The old people used to shoot up to the spirits with their guns to ask for help so the Tea Dance would be a success. . . just lots of fun, no trouble."

James says, as a feast-maker, "As soon as we were finished cooking the last thing, I'd shoot my gun into the air four times and people would come to me."

When we beg James for a story like he would have heard at a Tea Dance long ago, he stops to think for a moment and then a broad grin lights up his face. He launches into a tale about that traditional hero/trickster of Cree legends who loses more battles than he wins, Wesakychak.

"Wesakychak had a wife and two children, and he started feeling something for his daughter. I guess a long time ago they only lived in families and there were no other people around. He had a crush on her, but he couldn't go to her because his wife would see. So, one day, he pretended to be sick and he told his wife, 'Well, my old lady, I'm going to die soon. Won't you promise me when I die you'll just leave me up in a tree and then keep on going and try to survive without me.' His wife said, 'Sure, I'll do that.' Sure enough, Wesakychak died, and his wife put him up in a tree and then she and the kids left their camping area. They travelled in the bush and then found a good spot. There were a lot of rabbits there and everything, so they set up their tipi.

"Now, before Wesakychak had died, he told his wife that a nice-looking young man would come along some day and he would ask to marry their daughter. 'Make sure you let him marry her,' Wesakychak ordered as his last, dying wish. 'Sure, I'll do that,' his wife answered. So, after they were living in their new place for some time, this one guy came and told Wesakychak's wife, 'I like your daughter. I want to marry her.' So, the mother said, 'Well, daughter, it was your dad's last wish. This is the promise you have to keep. You have to marry this guy.' Wesakychak's daughter married this guy, and they began staying together.

"One night, Wesakychak's son woke his mother up. 'Mom, mom, look at that new man's bum. It looks like my dad's bum. It has a big scar on it, just like dad's.' 'Ah, my son, don't say that. That's not your dad,' his mother said. But, the little boy kept bugging her, so she finally went and looked, and sure enough, it was her husband's bum. She recognized it. So, she went and got a big stick and hit him. Wesakychak jumped up and said, 'Ah, what am I trying to do, being another man? I used my powers to make myself different, but I forgot about that scar I got when I sat on a hot rock. I'm still the same man, after all,' he said."

We all laugh and shake our heads for poor Wesakychak. James mentions Wesakychak stories aren't told too often around Fort McKay these days, and the traditional way of making Tea Dances and ceremonial feasts stopped about twenty years ago after the death of his grandfather on his mother's side. Since then, James tried to make a traditional dance but it turned into a fiddle jamboree. He mourns the knowledge and tradition that died with his elders and doesn't know many people living today who have the spiritual strength they had.

"Long, long time ago there was no sickness in this land. There was only the wetigo. This thing ate people. He could eat up this whole world. There was no way a person could kill him, but my great-grandfather did. My great-grandfather could walk on top of the water."

To illustrate how his ancestors used spiritual power instead of technology, James talks about dreams. "Long time ago, if you wanted to go to Moose Lake, it took three nights of walking from here. If you left your family in Fort McKay and you thought something might be wrong, you could go to an elder and give him tobacco or a print [cloth] and tell him you'd like to find out what's going on back home. He'd go to sleep, and it's just like he's watching TV. He can see what's happening, and he'll tell you from his dream.

"When I was young, I was sick out on the trapline. I was dying, and my breath was almost gone. My grandfather didn't know what to do. He was just sitting there like he was in a trance, and all of a sudden he got up and started writing a letter. Then he went out to his dogs — he had six — and put the letter around one of them's neck and said, 'Here, take this to Fort McKay and take it to the people. Tell them to come here right away, my son is dying.' Well, then that dog started fooling around and peeing on the trees and stuff like that. So, my grandfather told that dog, 'Listen here, I want you to go right now. This is important.' And it was just like he hit him, eh? That dog took off and that same night people came to help.

"My grandfather must have dreamed of a dog, that he would help him, and through his own power he was able to make the dog understand. If you dream of an animal and that animal is helping you, then that's your power. If you're stuck, that animal will help you."

When the topic changes to prophecy, James tells us about an old woman, half Cree and half Chipewyan, who used to live at Moose

Lake (or Namur Lake), about sixty-five kilometres northwest of Fort McKay.

"This is the truth. She had a breakdown and went crazy, but she wasn't violent. She was always talking to herself and telling everybody that white people were going to come and break the land around Moose Lake and put roads all around it. And this was when everything was just bush. It was nice and calm all over. There wasn't even electricity around here yet." The woman tried to describe in Cree the oil-production plants that would be built near Fort McKay and that eventually things would end in war, James says.

"She said white men are going to shoot at us. She never went to school and she never read a book, but she said she saw it all happening. She was the only person to ever talk about the future that I know of."

James still returns to his band's traditional land at Moose Lake. "I was there last summer. I'm happy to see it, even though it's different. Years ago, mostly everyone went to Moose Lake by dog team or packhorse for food. It was paradise over there. There were all kinds of fish, like trout, and ducks, duck eggs, and moose. In the morning, you'd get up and step outside your tipi and you'd see a moose standing on the shore of the lake just outside your door. And you could see fish jumping and ducks swimming around. There were blueberries and cranberries. You didn't have to walk or struggle to get what you wanted to eat."

Though animals and berries are becoming scarce, James wishes young people would learn how to survive in the bush. It scares him to see how dependent on the white-man's ways they have become.

"I always tell my grandchildren, 'Learn how to survive without money. You should get an education but learn the traditional ways, too. You don't know when your steady job will end, when you'll be out of work. That's when your Indian ways will come in handy. You can go out and get food. But if you don't know those ways, how are you going to survive?'"

9

Katie Bull Shield-Wells

Kainai (Blood), Blood First Nation

The sound of sleigh bells ringing out across the field captured the children's attention and they slid down from the woodpile to watch the horse and wagon approaching. Just like every year, it was Dick and Katie Wells coming to deliver Christmas candy to the kids who lived around them. The couple loved children and enjoyed making them happy with the bags of treats they delivered. They weren't rich, but they did own a car and had nice things in their home, like the little clock that marked each hour with the sound of music while a little carved Bavarian couple slid out of one tiny doorway and then disappeared into another. The ornament was an unusual thing to see on the Blood Reserve in the early 1950s.[1]

I read this little snippet about Katie and her husband, Dick, in Beverly Hungry Wolf's 1996 book Daughters of the Buffalo Women. When I spoke with Katie twenty years ago, she focused on frugality and ecology, but I found out a lot more about her just recently in Beverly's book. Katie was progressive in her thinking and was one of the first housewives in her community to work outside her home. *The income she brought in was necessary when the government or-dered non-Aboriginal ranchers to work the land of several Blood farmers because the tribe was in debt. After three years, the debt was paid off and the govern-ment paid the couple $2,200 for their crops. Katie wanted to save the money, but her husband bought a nice car with it instead. She was especially angry with him because he didn't have a license and hardly knew how to drive, but he managed to pass his test eventually and drove his new vehicle everywhere.*

Katie was born on January 2, 1913 and passed away on January 7, 2008.

If everyone treated the earth like elders do, we might find answers to our difficulties, says Katie Bull Shield-Wells. "In my day, we saved ev-erything. Even a pail of water, I'd try to use it again. Today, you know I still have that habit, and here I've got so much water all I have to do is turn a tap."

Socks with holes were repaired and recycled, instead of tossed out. The root houses her husband dug to keep vegetables and perishables like milk and butter cold "were better than refrigerators" and didn't need to be plugged in.

On her drying racks, Katie still makes "lean cuisine" — strips of dry meat without fat, much healthier and better for the teeth than fatty steaks and hamburgers that have to be cooked. Dried foods need only the sun to be processed and they don't need to be stored in refrigerators.

If you want to talk macrobiotics, Katie is a master at using food sources growing near her. Polluting transport vehicles that deliver ex-otic fruits to our supermarkets and destructive agricultural practices that kill our rain forests would no longer be a threat if we depended more on local fruits and wild vegetables like berries and bulrush roots and others that could be grown in small gardens.

Wild mint will keep rodents and bugs away from food and cloth-ing, so why couldn't it be used instead of toxic bug sprays and poisons? There's always a gentler way to treat nature and the crea-tures within it, Katie says.

Beyond the clever hints and tips to change wasteful habits, there is a much more pressing transformation that has to take place first — attitudes. The fact that Indigenous people are close to nature has become stereotypical and legendary now; younger generations are as guilty as anyone of throwing away pop cans and paper products. Cultural indoctrination of man as the dominator of nature has been unconsciously internalized, and we treat the world as something to be used and manipulated.

But when Katie steps on her doorstep to listen to the meadowlarks sing or the frogs croak, she is revelling in the joy the natural world gives her. She speaks of the power of God and how significant humans are within the circle of creation, yet she knows that humans were meant to use respect in their domination.

"Now, the rivers are spoiled. We used to enjoy the water and the pines and woods. Now, even the air is bad, and that's the thing that makes us feel sad. For us, when we talk about the way it was all given to us by the Creator — water to drink and berries to eat — we cry because we don't even know if it's safe anymore. Even the sun affects our skin sometimes. When I sit out now, sometimes I get a rash. I never used to.

"In the morning, I get up early to hear the birds singing and watch them flying around. But you don't see as many as you used to, especially the meadowlarks and magpies. One time, I was driving past a farm and I saw a bunch of partridges. I was so surprised. Where in the world have all our poor birds gone? I suppose they're all poisoned with these chemicals they put on everything."

Katie lives on the Kainai First Nation, which is the largest in Canada. Comprised of 352,600 acres, the land has changed greatly since her nomadic ancestors roamed it.

"They say there was an old lady long ago. She was sitting out there on the prairie in her tipi and she said, 'The next people after us won't hardly see the green grass. All this land is going to be turned over, and it will be black.' She meant the earth was going to be cultivated, and, you know, all there is around here is farming and ranching."

As the black topsoil blows away in drought years and dirt becomes too hard to work from overuse, one has to wonder about the unnat-ural agricultural society foisted upon the Bloods when they were forced onto the reserve after signing Treaty Seven in 1877. Respect for others is fast eroding as newscasts report gang violence, reli-gious wars, and white supremacist groups on the rise. Before she even went to school, Katie's parents taught her to respect them and her elders and to be polite. "If we saw a child who was very rude, my parents would tell me to keep away and 'Don't be led by them, they'll get you into trouble.'

"Today, my grandchildren aren't mean to me, but they don't re-spect me in that way. They get into my things and maybe if they get a chance they just take them, like my blankets. But after I find out they've taken it, I hate to get after them. But I tell them I never dug into my grandparents' things. I never dared do that. I had to ask if I wanted something. I never helped myself."

Futurists predict people will become more religious as they expect the return of Christ or the catastrophic end of the world as we know it. Authors John Naisbitt and Patricia Aburdene write that people will embrace either fundamentalist views of God as an all-powerful source outside themselves or the new age opinion that God is every-where and within us also.[2]

Katie transcends duality and embraces both views, getting spir-itual nourishment from each. Born in 1913, during the mission school era, she was at St. Paul's Anglican School and believes in the word of God as written in the Bible. But she was also "Motoki," a member of the Motokiks old woman's society, and a bundle-keeper. The Motokiks put up a special lodge inside the camp circle at a Sun Dance. For four days they have their meetings and sacred cer-emonies, especially the public dances, when four men with rattles sing the dance songs. The members wear ancient headdresses that they keep inside their medicine bundles throughout most of the year. These, and the Natoas used in the Sun Dance, are the only medicine bundles that belong specifically to women, and they are highly regarded by all the tribe.

She holds fast to her Indian religion based on the belief that God is in every living thing and that when we die we don't go to heaven. We become spirits and merge with all of creation. We shed our bodies and just live in spirit. "Our spirit is the one that goes around — happy, nothing to worry about. We never know, there might be a spirit standing beside us right now," Katie says.

Katie believes a return to simplicity is necessary in the future. She observes that the world is suffering from people trying to make money to buy things to ease their lives and satisfy every little desire. She wonders why some people need a new car every year and begin to let material things run their lives. "We used to work hard for whatever we had, and we didn't expect much. We had to haul water, chop wood, things like that."

Katie thinks education is the way of the future but recalls the simplicity of her mother, who never set foot in a school. "She had a lot of patience. I used to enjoy watching her with the chickens. She had about four hens, and when they laid eggs she used to carefully turn each one and the chicken would brood on them and the eggs kept evenly warmed."

Katie's father, on the other hand, sneaked away from his parents to attend Calgary's Dunbow Industrial School. Though they didn't want him to go, he knew he would need to learn to speak English "because the white society is here." Years later, when Katie turned seven, her parents put her in school even though her grandparents strongly objected. "They told my father he was just throwing his child away, but my dad knew what Indian people were facing with the domination of white society and the federal government, and he knew things would get harder. He said we would have to fight for our rights. I would have to help so I'd better learn how to speak to white people."

In school, she loved studying the past, even if her people were depicted in her "little brown history book" as always declaring war on white people. "The book told us about Christopher Columbus landing here, and about the way we also used to fight with the Cree. The Indians used to fight the white people in wars in the east, but we

[Kainai] didn't because we'd already made treaty when they [Europeans] came up here. We were civilized."

Though Katie wanted to attend secondary school after finishing at St. Paul's when she was sixteen, even if it meant going to a non-Native school, she wasn't given the chance. "I was hoping to keep on with my schooling, but I don't know what happened," Katie says, suspecting the government wouldn't pay for it.

Years later though, she was given a chance to learn more about her tribe's history while exploring the north end of the reserve with an archaeologist who was researching the early whiskey-trading posts like Fort Whoop-Up. Among other findings, she and a group of young people identified numerous tipi rings — rocks used to weight the bottoms of tipis to the ground. "There used to be so many of them, but now there's just the ones on the river bottom. The white farmers lease our land, and they just plow them under. It's such a shame. They don't know how valuable they are."

While exploring the area where the present Head-Smashed-In Buffalo Jump centre now stands, northwest of Fort Macleod, Katie observed groupings of rocks in the hills and drew her group's attention to them.

"I told them, 'You see these rocks? Well, they don't belong here. The old people hauled them up these hills to cook with. They put them in the fire until they were red hot and then put them in the pot to heat whatever was inside.'"

Katie's respect for the old people who came before her and lived so gently on the land is evident in the way she speaks about Holy Running Sun, her mother's father. He went through many ceremonial transfers and owned medicine pipe bundles.

"He used to be a great hero. He never really talked about it, but I know he went on the warpath many times. He must have been over one hundred years old when he died back in the 1930s. And he was still riding horseback. . . he had this old pony. . . when he talked to it, that horse seemed to understand. The old man couldn't see very good, but he just got on that horse and it took him everywhere."

1   Beverly Hungry Wolf, *Daughters of the Buffalo Women-Maintaining the Tribal Faith* (Canadian Caboose Press, 1996).
2   John Naisbitt and Patricia Aburdene, *Megatrends 2000* (New York, New York: William Morrow, 1990).

10

George Kehewin

Cree, Kehewin First Nation

A testament to the fact that George Kehewin, who passed away in 1996, devoted his life to those in trouble with the law is the designation of a gymnasium on the second level of Building 2 at Edmonton's Stan Daniels Healing Centre. Used for social and spiritual purposes, the correctional facility's George Kehewin Ceremonial Room pays homage to the man who long served as the centre's Elder.

"In his later years, he pretty much lived at the centre," says George's youngest daughter Ambie John when I speak with her at a 2011 Blue Quills First Nation College Art Camp. "He was family to a lot of those inmates and so many of them would say he helped them change their lives. He could probably say he's a grandfather to a thousand boys. They weren't outcasts of society to him."

George put up fasts and countless sweatlodge ceremonies for his "warriors," and brought them to his Kehewin home when he could.

Vicky Whalen, an elder who worked for the Edmonton Institution for Women, and for Native Counselling Services, said George helped many inmates go through their pain. "He was kind, soft, gentle. . . like a light bulb — glowing, shining," she said. She looked upon George as a psychologist, even though he didn't have a degree. He would offer encouragement and always said to never forget the basic teachings, such as praying to the Creator and burning sweetgrass, she said.

"Yes, his teachings were simple," Ambie agrees. "He was really down to earth. His spirit name was 'Sweetgrass Elder.'

"When he got sick, we thought he was going to go right away," she recalls. "But he stayed around for two more months until my oldest son, Chance, was born. After that, he passed away. It seemed to us like he felt he could let go then."

"It's not good to hear, 'Don't go to so-and-so's sweatlodge or listen to such-and-such.' Okay, it doesn't happen much, but when it comes from our spiritual leaders, what are we supposed to think?" a young man asks his elders.

His hard-hitting question spawns constructive dialogue between teachers and students at this elders' gathering near Bonnyville in the spring. For four days, spiritual advisors from Alberta, Saskatchewan, and the United States have fielded questions about religious and social issues, and in the evening, groups of people sit at picnic tables or before a fire to discuss what they've heard.

There are no prepared speeches here. Elders speak from the heart — of prophecy, religion, and life experiences — to listeners seated in a circle around them. When a breeze blows, a speaker stops to ask people to "feel the wind. It is like the Great Spirit — you can't see it but you know it's there." Another points to a poplar and spruce tree standing side by side, noting the tolerance amongst nature's species. Messages about the Creator's provision and the interrelatedness of all things are amplified in this natural setting, beside Moose Lake.

A sacred fire is kept burning throughout the assembly in a tipi where morning pipe ceremonies are held. The elders pray especially for a group of young people in drug and alcohol rehabilitation who visit the camp. During the day, individuals pull elders aside to talk one-on-one, and after dark everyone round dances to Dave Jock's small but powerfully loud water drum and his Mohawk songs. One of the more soft-spoken elders at the gathering is sixty-two-year-old George Kehewin, a pipe-holder from nearby Kehewin First Nation. Tall, quiet, and almost seeming to hide behind his sunglasses on the elders' podium, George is as personable as he is knowledgeable — his teachings born of experience.

Fending for himself at an early age, he says he awakened early each morning to make his lunch and walk the miles to the Kehewin school. At thirteen, he was placed in a convent in Onion Lake, Saskatchewan, and was on his own by fifteen. He worked for farmers and eventually married and had children of his own.

"My father was an alcoholic, so I started drinking at an early age. I couldn't stop. Eventually, it got to the point I knew I had to quit somehow, but there weren't any rehabilitation programs in those days. A couple of elders had told me, 'That's not the way we were given to live,' but I didn't listen."

George hit the proverbial rock bottom many alcoholics experience before changing their behaviour. Finding himself without his family and scrounging on Edmonton's skid row, his life had become a monotonous cycle of conning, stealing, and lying to obtain liquor.

"You name it, I'd do anything to get a bottle. All I could think about was satisfying myself," George says, until one day he met his wife on the drag and found she too had succumbed to liquor and was no longer caring for their children.

Eventually, she quit drinking and encouraged George to do the same, or face abandonment. He quit for three months and finally gave in grudgingly to friends pressuring him to attend Alcoholics Anonymous meetings, but it wasn't until his third one that he began to notice what was going on.

"I saw some of my drinking buddies were there, but they'd quit and were working the Alcoholics Anonymous twelve steps. I realized I wanted to have what they had. They were happy, they laughed during those meetings, and they talked about themselves. But what made me mad was, when they told their stories, I thought they were talking about my life."

Despite his misgivings, George continued with AA, and after six months he and his family reunited, "and we started to live together again like normal human beings." He and his wife Julia began to hold AA meetings and, slowly, more and more people started to attend regularly.

He confirms the most difficult thing about sobriety is overcoming peer pressure to drink. Friends laughed at him and called him a "priest trying to be holy." Another assured him he couldn't make it one month without drinking, let alone three.

"I told him he was right, but as long as I was sober today, I felt okay with myself. 'Tomorrow's not here yet, and yesterday has passed,' I told him. He didn't say a word."

Bible stories about persecution gave George answers to put off those who wanted to pull him down, but it was an introduction to a sweatlodge in Edmonton that helped him begin living the principles his elders had spoken of so long ago.

"After twenty-seven years of drinking I didn't know a thing about my culture. I went to that first sweat just because I wanted to know what the hell was going on in there," George admits. But soon after the lodge door closed and water was splashed on the hot rocks, he regretted his curiosity. "I saw the women come in, and I started to think about them. . . I was still young then, you know. I came into that sweat without a purpose — with a negative one, anyway — and I burned."

After four rounds, the pipe-holder leading the ceremony informed George sweatlodges were for praying and nothing else. As long as he continued to come in for other reasons, he would burn. "The next time, I prepared myself mentally, physically, and spiritually, and I made it through. I started to learn more about spirituality and then I made up my mind to fast with my teacher, an elder from Wyoming."

That first, solitary vigil changed him. Time stopped as he reflected on his life and relationships to a depth never before reached. Through the hunger and isolation, George came to realize the Creator had assigned him the ordeal to propel him toward repaying a debt long overdue.

"I could so easily be six feet under the ground. I had lots of close calls when I was drinking," he says. He now understands a higher power spared him from death to help others kick alcohol and assist in easing family problems. Fasting helped him gain humility and the wisdom to give counsel, and, eventually, he convinced his teacher he had enough integrity and knowledge to be given a pipe and become a spiritual leader.

"I fasted for a sweatlodge. . . and my teacher gave me a pipe so I could hold sweats," George says, explaining his life had changed from greedy self-interest to generous concern for others. He began entering jails to counsel inmates and found them starving for cultural information and needful of prayer. He describes 98 percent of the inmates he meets as "good, smart people" who have awakened from alcoholic binges to find they have pulled a knife on someone or broken another law. Unfortunately, most first-time offenders can't afford the legal fees required to appeal sentences.

"When you go to church or to a sweatlodge, please pray for these inmates. We have to encourage them to carry along with their lives. Many are locked up, I would say, for nothing."

George conducts sweats for parolees "to help their minds so they can improve their attitudes toward parole and, someday, be free." He is a psychologist and a mediator between humans and the Creator, who reminds people they possess an inner light, as it was once described to him.

"An old man told me this after I gave him tobacco and asked him what alcohol does to people. He pointed to an electric bulb and said that's what my spirit was like inside me — glowing, shining, happy, brightness. When I'm sober and in touch with myself, I can do anything and my spirit will stay with me. Once I take my first drink, things are okay and my spirit is still happy, but when I take a second drink, now it's starting to be confused. By the time I'm on my third drink, I'm starting to make trouble and maybe trying to start a fight.

That's because my spirit is above me, outside me and looking down, crying for me. That's when I'm committing a crime, hurting other people or scaring little kids, stuff like that.

"The old man said, 'My child, don't ever try to chase your good spirit out of your body. A bad spirit comes to be inside you then. If you chase your good spirit away, someday it might leave you.' That old man got me thinking, but I didn't listen. Anyway, it came back to me later. . . that I had this good thing inside me."

The pipe George carries is as symbolic to Aboriginal spirituality as the cross or bible is to Christianity, and, with it he leads those who come to him toward the Creator. When he lights tobacco in it, he sends prayers skyward with the smoke.

"A pipe bowl is made of rock, solid and strong. When Saint Peter went to Rome he stood on a rock and said, 'Upon this rock I shall build my church.' We hold a pipe and say, 'Upon this rock I will build my church.' After our Creator fashioned all other spirits — Mother Earth, the moon, the stars — he told his angels he needed one more helper. A rock stood up and said, 'I will be the one to always be with the Indian people until the end of the world. When they do something wrong, I will correct their prayers.' Be careful of what you say and do, rocks are always near."

The wooden pipe-stem is a tree, sacred in all it offers: warmth, shelter, shade, medicine, and tools. Straight and strong, it is the centre pole — the focal point — of fasters in a Sundance lodge as they send their prayers up it, skyward. George says the tree can be likened to the cross Christ died upon and the men who dance are like angels blowing trumpets in Jericho.

"When we make a commitment to make a Sundance, we don't do it for ourselves. This year, I'm making it for my daughter. She was sick over a year ago, and I brought her to every sweat or every spiritual doctor I could. She kept going down, down. She couldn't even care for her kids. I told my wife I was going to make a Sundance for her to be cured, and inside a week she was as normal as you and I. So, I'm thankful. That's why I'm paying for my commitment. I have to suffer. Other people are going to participate, and I'm praying for them, too."

After the first day of the Sundance, George allows dancers the option of partaking in a small feast. Then the pledgers fast and dance for three more exhausting days in a large, circular lodge made of heavy poles and greenery. As one elder from Prince Albert put it, "After you take that last drink of water, you are a spirit."

George further explains, "You're there with the spirits and they will cleanse you. You've got to prepare yourself and have faith to make it through."

On the final day, dancers present gifts to the elders whom they want to pray for them. Whether it is a blanket, cloth, gun, horse, or a little tobacco, "that elder will never refuse it and he'll pray for you the best way he knows how."

Most respected elders have evolved spiritually in part because they have come to terms with the material world and their emotions. They trade the striving and struggling for worldly things for nurturing within themselves the spark of divinity the Creator placed there. They purposefully go without creature comforts their egos would like to have, like nice cars and expensive clothes, to earn the help of many spirits. By performing a required ceremony or singing a certain song, these spirits come quickly to give assistance and do things that seem beyond the human realm of ability.

As George learned the way of becoming a pipe-holder, he was tested many times regarding his attachment to earthly possessions. "I had a gun scope and I loved that thing, but I gave it away," he recalls, adding it made him feel good to do it. Spiritual fulfillment doesn't come from owning many things. When elders see someone sincerely offering a treasured object, they appreciate the act of giving — not the object — because it lets them know the individual is overcoming his own selfishness and ego.

"When you give away, in turn down the line you get what you really need, unexpectedly, because the elders up there [in the spirit world] are praying for you." Detachment from earthly things is a small price to pay for a compassionate and peaceful mind, he contends. But to those who come to him dissatisfied with themselves and not receiving what they think they need, George recommends they ask a lot of questions about spirituality and try to understand.

"Someone here told me she was only halfway toward that full light where she wanted to be but she didn't know how to get there. We talked about nature, and I told her to learn all she could about our spiritual ways. You know, the good thing about it is our Bible is nature and it's all around us. We can read it day by day and never get tired of it because we see it, feel it — we feel the wind, and it's a spirit. We breathe the wind, and without it we couldn't live. Everything is a gift from the Creator. I told her about what I went through, and, now, if I get lonely, I phone somebody to talk to, or, if I can't find another person, I talk to little children. They are the most powerful little things, you know, and they make you happy! They can make your life come back to normal. If you still can't find anyone, take a walk. Or talk to a tree. You don't have to move your lips, talk from your mind. Try to communicate with creation. You'll get something out of it. It'll make you think and something will come."

I ask George if he has words for girls just learning about ceremony who might feel shunned when they are not allowed to attend ceremonies while menstruating. "Women are far, far ahead of men. It's quite hard to understand, but when you start living the Native culture, you will. You are like Mother Earth, who once a year in the spring, washes herself down the river to the ocean. Everything. . . all debris is washed away. Same thing with a woman, except it's every month. It's the power you have. You don't need to be in ceremony. You cannot enter a lodge or a spiritual gathering because you will overpower all the prayers and offerings in there. You are more powerful than all of it, and if you come in you can't fool the spirits. At Sundances, if a woman in her time comes near the lodge, the singers and dancers know. I have to tell the older women to tell the younger ones not to stay around if they are like that. It's not because we don't like them, it's the power they have. They're way ahead of me," George repeats.

Addressing the question of elder rivalry, George points out there are good things and bad things about every society and religion and elders are only human. Everyone is at a different stage in spiritual evolution, and jealousy and misunderstandings can arise because "some people don't like the way others do things." Since sweatlodges and Sundances are places where people pray to the Creator, George turns a deaf ear to what others might say about avoiding another person's ceremonies.

"In my own mind, I go in there to pray. I'm not going in there for the person leading it, I'm going there for God. These are my beliefs in the Creator, so I'm not afraid to enter any lodge."

As I write this, I want to ask him if he knows how similar to the sacred pipe he is. His faith makes him strong, and he is as constant as a rock in his ministering to others. Like a pipe-stem, he is straight and true, yet his experiences have tempered him so that he has softened, like the wood it is carved from.

11

David Providence

Dene Tha', Chateh (Dene Tha' First Nation)

David Providence is passing the hottest hours of this July afternoon
in his house on Third Prairie in Chateh. He's been working in his garden but has come in for a rest on his couch. He stands up to greet my
friend Molly Chisaakay and I when we knock on his door.

As David puts on his glasses, I am struck by how distinguished
he looks. His handsome features are framed by greying hair, and he
is tall and slightly built. I imagine he must have turned girls' heads
across northern Alberta when he was younger. Today he's wearing
jeans and a white T-shirt with a silk-screened image of the late Willie Denechoan on the front, an elder who likely taught David many
songs and transferred many teachings to him.

At eighty-three, David is recognized as the spiritual leader of the
Dene Tha' First Nation because he was given the drum belonging
to the late Alexis Seniantha who was the leading prophet before he
passed away in 1998. I can see why David was chosen to take over the

leadership role because he's charismatic yet humble, is dedicated to the drum and Dene Tha' spirituality, and leads by example rather than persuasion.

To impose yourself on someone and be bold in asking for what you want is not the Dene way, so I didn't want to barge into David's house, interrupt his quiet afternoon, and start firing questions at him. Instead, Molly shows David a copy of the first publication of this book and he smiles as he sees a picture of Alexis Seniantha on the first page. She explains in Dene Tha' why we are visiting and he indicates that he's willing to share a bit about his life.

Molly reads a passage about an even earlier prophet called Nogha (which means "wolverine" in Dene Tha') who was active in the 1920s, when David was still young. As she reads to him, he closes his eyes and nods his head slightly every now and then. The subject matter takes him into a reverie from another time.

"I saw Nogha with my own eyes at a Tea Dance when I was three or four. People were gathered there from all different areas. Nogha was preparing to leave this earth. He was going into the Spirit World. He was asking everyone to come and shake his hand. I played around but I was watching everyone walk up to him."

As a young man, David was always interested in what the older people in his community were doing. "I learned early on that the best way to live my life was to be a drummer and to sing at Tea Dances. As far as I can remember, I was always interested in becoming a drummer."

The Tea Dance David refers to is *Ndahotsethe*, which translates to mean "people dance" in his language. It is a long-standing practice that involves socializing, eating, dancing, praying, and the revealing of prophecy. Other First Nations have Sundances, sweatlodges, shake tent ceremonies and other rituals, but we have the Tea Dance, David explains.

The ceremony is usually performed outdoors, around a central fire, inside a fenced corral. The corral has openings at the north and south entrances and exits, and another two on the east and west sides of the circle. The dreamer or prophet holding the Tea Dance flies his flags on two poles on either side of each opening. Some of these flags have designs on them, received when the dreamer's soul travelled to *echuhdigeh*, "the other land," or *yake*, "heaven." Participants place offerings of tobacco in a washbasin as they pray for the well-being of loved ones, a successful hunt, the safe return of travelling or working loved ones who are out of the community, protection on a long journey, or the health of elders and loved ones. After the tobacco, along with a skillet of melted moose fat (or store-bought lard that stands in for animal grease), is burned in the fire, the people eat a feast usually consisting of meat, potatoes, biscuits and tea. Finally, the prophets tell the people what they have dreamed about. They have "looked ahead" for the community and might address future weather or hunting conditions, possible accidents, or general advice to live by. Speeches are interspersed with songs played by the dreamers and other drummers. Whenever they sing, the participants dance around the fire in a clockwise direction.[1]

David has inherited three flags from the Tea Dance. I notice a white one flying from a pole beside his house today. Molly tells me it either means he has dreamed the night before of someone who has passed on and has messages for the people, or it signifies his status as a dreamer.

In a chance meeting with two Dene Tha' elders, David Martel and William Yatchotay, who travelled to Edmonton for a rally supporting treaty rights a few months after my interview with David, I ask them what being a dreamer means. They tell me a dreamer can leave his or her body and journey to the other land, the spirit world. There, they can speak with relatives who have passed away, or to Christian figures like Jesus or Mary.

"The mind lives in the body while the person is alive on this earth, but it also lives forever in the spirit or soul," William explains. "When you dream, your soul takes a trip away from your body and maybe you are exploring the land — looking for animals, or fighting with someone in a medicine fight, or visiting with people who have passed on. If you're sick, your soul has been away from your body for a while, and then a dreamer can go to the other land and get it back for you."

I had heard David "had a strong mind," and understood he likely had power from animals, though, of course, he never spoke about it. If a recipient speaks about those gifts he is apt to lose them. I ask William and David to explain how medicine power works.

"When you see a plant or animal in the bush, it has a replica in the spirit world. When you are on a vision quest, you don't eat and you drift into that place where the spirit part of that plant or animal can talk to you. Animals are powerful and will often give you some of their leftover powers," David says. "Powers that they give you can override this physical world and that's how come miracle healings can take place on this earth."

George Blondin, a Sahtu Dene from (Deline) Fort Franklin in the Northwest Territories, tells a story in his book *Yamoria the Lawmaker: Stories of the Dene* of how his father, Paul, healed himself with his moose medicine. The doctor said his sick father's lungs were so full of mucus it sounded like boiling porridge "popping" inside them when he used a stethoscope to listen to Paul's chest. The doctor prepared George for the worst and left the hospital in Tulit'a (Fort Norman), fully expecting Paul to die before he returned. But through the night, Paul spoke to the moose power he owned in a strange language and sang his power song. When the doctor came the next morning to examine Paul, he was mystified to find his lungs were "clear as a bell," and he discharged Paul that day.

Born in 1928 to parents who were both from the Northwest Territories, David grew up north of Meander River, seventy kilometres north of High Level. His traditional parents left him alone in the bush at puberty to attract medicine power, and it's likely this power helped him to be successful. He didn't attend school but rather lived a traditional lifestyle, learning to hunt and trap from his father. In his younger days, he raised horses and cows — his cattle were healthy and he rode a horse that was the envy of the community.

"My horse was fast. Spirited. It fought with other horses so I had to be on my guard whenever I rode him," David says. "I had very powerful sled dogs, too."

Molly can vouch for that. She says many years ago her husband wanted to give their small daughter a sled ride and so he took David's dogs for a run.

"Those dogs took off and my husband slipped and got dragged for a while until he fell off," Molly says, laughing at the memory now although it wasn't funny at the time. "The dogs just kept on going and my daughter was sitting in there without a care in the world. We had to drive for miles to catch up with David's sled dogs."

In earlier times, each Dene family in the community was good at making certain things they became known for, and David's father distinguished himself as a snowshoe-maker, while his mother was known for her beadwork. In the winter, David always wore fancy mukluks, beaded to the knees, and a fine moose-hide jacket. He married Mary when he was thirty-four years old, late in life for a Dene Tha' man, and he was a good provider.

"You take up the drum and it's a way of life. I knew if I looked after the drum it would look after me. I'm successful and I'm alive today because I listened to the old prophets talk and I noticed they were successful hunters and trappers. They shared their food with everyone. I remember an elder holding some meat. He said to me: 'See this meat in my hand. You would like to cook it and eat it right now. But next door, people are hungry. Give it to them. Every person who comes along, feed them. Then you will be okay and you will be looked after. You must always share what you have.'

"I tried to do what the elders said. I worked hard to be a drummer and earn my place in the Tea Dance with my community. It was my role to put up the flags when there was going to be a Tea Dance and I rode my horse to let the elders and everyone know that it was going on."

David recalls he was only eleven when he took up the drum. Out of five brothers, he was the only one to learn all of the songs the elders could teach him.

"I started out by learning to sing in Cree first, because there were Cree people at the Tea Dances I went to. It is good that I have drummed since I was young. I never was afraid to take leadership and join in with the drummers at Tea Dances."

All good things are in the drum, David believes. "It helps you to have a strong mind. You have strong mind when the values in your heart come out in the way you live," he says. "I have no schooling but yet I can speak to people in a good way. The drum gives me messages and it is like reading a book. I am given words in dreams, a few words are written, and then I see what I have to speak on. It is through my thoughts, I have those visions in my mind and I share them with the people. I can talk about things that challenge our lives and about changes in our environment.

"I am given messages yearly during the spring and fall. Not much is said, but those few words in my dreams give me strength. I pray to ward off negativity and what people fear the most — sickness. I pray because it helps me and I know it helps others."

Prayer has helped David deal with the death of his wife early in their marriage and to weather the loss of his second oldest daughter in the early 1960s.

"I'm happy to say my children have given me lots of grandchildren and I live for them today. I try to help all our young people to have a good life."

David observes the drummers in the community are getting older and he wants to teach the younger members of the community to take their place. "All we need is a place where they can come together and practice," he insists. He doesn't want to draw attention to himself or boast, but he says he knows most or all Dene drum songs and is willing to pass them on to the youth.

"We must teach and support our little ones to pray. We have to make them understand that when they pray, they are never alone."

Even though David is ready and willing to teach the songs to young drummers, sadly, the will to learn is not always present in the new generation. "It's hard to see the kids gather to hear a rapper, and then hardly anyone shows up when there's a Tea Dance," says Mable Giroux, Dene Tha' Director of Social Development. "I feel sorry for our elders."

But even if every pair of ears in the community isn't listening to him, David maintains prayer and faith are the most important things to keep. "It's really important to have faith in Ndawotá, 'God.' If you do, you're going to get help, and you're going to get food and your grandchildren are going to be healthy. If you pray morning and night, when you ask for something it will be given to you."

David slaps his knees and mentions he beat cancer with his prayer. "For two years I couldn't do much. I couldn't even walk. They helped me at the Grande Prairie hospital but I was also helped in the spirit world. They operated on me, then, in a dream, I saw myself walking between two moose. I was told I would be leaving the hospital in two days, and when I got home I should eat nothing but wild meat that would be given to me. I did what I was told and I am still sitting here today."

When the interview is over, David takes us for a visit to his garden. The plants, mostly potatoes, are healthy and he shows us how high Sousa Creek is running this year, due to heavy rainfall. The stream flows just a few feet from his garden.

We sit in the shade of some tall willows as David shares a few last thoughts.

"Often people wait for me to start the Tea Dance ceremony. I encourage our Dene drummers to take the lead, to pick up their drums and work together as one. I believe in praying together, in celebrating together and in sharing our traditional ways to work together. If we pray, anything can happen. Even the animals that people need, like the grouse, moose and rabbits that seem to have gone away, they will come back.

"My grandfather told us not to lose what has been passed on to us, like our Tea Dance ceremony and Dene songs. Don't wait to begin working together. Just pick up and support each other. We all have to do our share in the community."

1   Jean-Guy A. Goulet, *Ways of Knowing — Experience, Knowledge, and Power Among the Dene Tha'* (Vancouver, British Columbia: UBC Press, 1998, p. 224.

12

Nancy Potts

Stoney, Alexis First Nation

Nancy left this world on January 31, 2006 at the age of seventy-five. Her daughter Liz Letendre told me she died exactly four months and four days after her beloved husband Paul passed away on January 27, 2002. Nancy's work as an honourary elder for the RCMP, with the Alexis First Nation heritage department as a Nakoda language source, and on child welfare committees, kept her engaged and busy, "but over and above everything I think she died of loneliness. She missed my dad. The two were very close," says Liz. Nancy contributed words and stories to the Stony 15, 25 and 30 high school language courses, and provided guidance to young offenders, both one-on-one and in her work with her community's restorative justice program. "Before she left us, she and a bunch of elders got together to share and document what they knew about raising children," Liz explains. Nancy also had a hand in devising a drug and alcohol prevention program for grades three to nine, and contributed content used in Alexis to teach things people need to do to live a good life — Wakan Washtay.

"*Because she helped her parents raise so many of their nieces and nephews and had so many children herself, she knew how children should be raised. My mother fought for child welfare policies that supported struggling families to keep their children instead of giving them up to be fostered,*" Liz says.

THE SUMMER OF 1926

Benjamin shifted his weight on to one stirrup and swung his leg over the horse's back, sliding off. Bending his knees slightly to loosen stiff joints, he led his horse to the creek.

"Grandfather, let me water him," his granddaughter Nancy shouted as she entered into the clearing from a poplar grove. Behind her, Benjamin noticed a thin trail of smoke rising above the trees, some distance into the bush.

Handing her the reins, Benjamin smiled at his little Mukshim. The name means Old Grandmother in Stoney, and he had given it to her after noticing how she performed tasks with the skill of someone who had been doing it all their life, though she was only twelve. The child would watch her aunt pluck and singe a duck, and the next day there she would be on her knees by the fire, plucking and singeing like an old granny hard at work.

"Mukshim, what did you do today?" he asked her after she had returned from the creek and tied the horse to a tree.

"I cooked some bannock, and I made Elizabeth's little girl a rag doll with that old shirt and those old blankets you had in the tent. Do you want to see it?" Nancy replied, disappearing behind the doorflap before her grandfather could answer. When she came out, she held a soft doll with button eyes and wisps of yarn for hair.

"See? It's just like the one I had when we used to go to Tender Lake. Remember? Only this one's better because now I can sew good. The only thing I need is some more stuffing for it."

Yes, she can sew, Benjamin thought to himself, remembering the brightly coloured ribbon shirt she had given him last summer after school let out. He wasn't entirely sure he agreed with everything she learned from the convent nuns in St. Albert, but he had to give them credit for what they had taught his granddaughter about sewing.

"Grandpa, while I get some pussy willows to put inside this dolly, why don't you have your steam bath? The rocks are ready, I think. When I get back, we can eat."

Benjamin watched her go, then entered the tent to undress and wrap a blanket around himself. Walking barefoot back out toward the bush, he paused to break off and tie a few leafy branches together for sprinkling water on the rocks inside the bent-willow lodge. With a pitchfork, he carried glowing stones from the fire to the hut, then lifted the pail Nancy had filled with water and disappeared inside.

Later, refreshed and satisfied after a meal of rabbit stew, Benjamin asked Nancy if she wanted to come with him to see a beaver lodge he had noticed earlier. He knew she loved watching beaver, especially when they walked upright, carrying chunks of wood they couldn't drag into the river. A few times, they had gotten close enough to the animals' work site to hear the beavers' heavy tails dragging behind them as they waddled to the water, holding wood against their chests.

When they got to the riverbank, they sat beside a willow in silence, eyes glued to the hump of the beaver lodge. Soon, a dark head broke the surface and a V-shaped wake signalled the beaver's course downriver toward his dam. The two watched for a long time, until Benjamin turned to his granddaughter.

"Granddaughter, why do you make me sweatbaths?" he asked, almost whispering so as not to disturb the beaver. Pausing a moment, Nancy replied, "Well, you like steam baths. When you get tired from riding horses, it makes you feel better."

Benjamin looked across the river and smiled, pleased with her answer. He chose his next words carefully.

"On this trip, we've stopped four times and every time you've made me a steam bath. You always think of others. You want to make them happy, not just yourself. Now, I would like to know if there's anything you want to know about medicine? I will give you four — one for each of the sweatlodges you built for me."

Benjamin appreciated the fact that his granddaughter expected nothing in return for her labours, and so he did not send her away empty-handed. She had always treated him well and had earned his respect, convincing him that she had sensitivity and awareness and would neither abuse healing power nor underestimate it.

THE SUMMER OF 1991

The subject of her grandfather's gift arises as Stoney elder Nancy Potts explains to me how "the best things in life must be earned." It is an easy thing to say, but it is obvious she has lived it, as the name her grandfather called her reflects.

"My parents told me I was always working like a little old granny, and I caught on to things fast. They only had to show me once," Nancy says. Her natural urge to serve others is evident in the way she cared for her paralyzed sister and, at eighteen, calmly reached inside another sister's labouring, pregnant body to help remove the baby.

"My mother's hands were too big, so I did it. I told my sister, 'This is going to hurt, but you've got to help me.' I wasn't scared. All I could think about was saving her life."

Love begets love, and it is something Nancy was given a lot of while growing up, especially from her grandfather. When she grew up and left her family to get a job, her efforts were fuelled by devotion to her relatives and the belief she had to use "what God granted me to make a living," and to "move my muscles and feel strong about what I could earn."

She got her first job at eighteen, cooking in a camp for two hundred and fifty men. "They used to whistle at me and call me 'squaw,' but I didn't care. I wasn't there for them. I was earning money to help my parents and my brother still at home. Sometimes, I got so frustrated, but I knew I was a person, too. I kept myself clean, and I stayed close to the kitchen area. I could stand on my own two feet."

That stability and self-assurance came, in part, from listening to her grandfather's stories. When he told her about her ancestors, not only was he entertaining but he was intertwining the fibres of her character like the strands of a rope to anchor her and give her a strong identity. He told her about a baby boy — the only survivor of a battle between two Stoney mountain clans — whose name sounds like Kash-Tay-Ohgwa-Dtabin, which roughly translates to mean The One That Survived. In the sixteenth or seventeenth century in the Kootenay Mountains, the Stoney people were fighting each other, and, after one group had surrounded the other, the victors killed their defeated brothers, except for this small baby.

According to Nancy, "One of the people said, 'I lost my little boy a few weeks back, and I want to have this one to represent my son.' So, he just grabbed that little boy and took him for his son and from then on he grew up to be big. He had his own family, and I'm a descendant of him. My husband Paul's people came from the east."

Related to the powerful Sioux nation in the United States, Nancy's break-away people's name, Assiniboine, comes from the term Assini-pwat, or Stone People. The old man who signed Treaty Six was called Assini-pwat, but his name was recorded as Potts, as the last syllable of his Stoney name must have sounded to the ears of non-Native government officials.

"They used his nickname Potts as his last name. It has no power in it," Nancy says derisively, then pronounces her Stoney name, which sounds like A-run-a-nah-jay. "It means Standing on the Earth, and it's strong. You know, I've thought about changing my name, but no one could pronounce it," she laughs.

Her grandfather also told her how she is related to Stoneys in the Paul Band, near Duffield, explaining that in the eighteenth century, two brothers struck out to look for a certain lake but split up when they got to the Stony Plain area. One went north to find Lac Ste. Anne, the other headed straight west to discover the Looking Glass — Wabamun Lake.

"When they saw each other again, they both wanted to stay in the places they found. That's why we're here at Lac Ste. Anne and the others are farther south."

Spiritual ceremonies also served to reinforce Nancy's identity, and between Stoney customs and those of historic allies the Cree, she has noticed differences she sees no harm in discussing.

"I've noticed some Cree don't accept pork, and I brought it up with them. It's good to understand each other," she says, insisting cultural differences are to be celebrated, not feared. Nancy has also observed that, whereas Stoneys build their sweatlodges in isolated places away from onlookers, the Cree seem not to be as particular about their privacy.

"Why do we have ceremonies? To me, we do it for learning and taking pride in ourselves for what we were taught. Like my grandfather taught us, we just give the best we have in our offerings, the best of whatever we have in our homes, like bannock, meat, and raisin soup. We all pray to one God, and we do our offerings to Him the best we can. I believe in it. It's who I am."

The Indian Summer sun warms our shoulders as we sit behind the Potts's house, at a homemade picnic table. The question-and-answer part of the interview over, Nancy, her husband Paul, and I chat for a while. Friendly dogs play around us, but there is one little pup who keeps his distance, cowering whenever I try to pet him. The fur around his neck hangs in tufts and his skin shows through, raw and glistening.

"He must have got himself caught in a snare," Nancy tells me. "I've tried to catch him and put peroxide on it, but he won't let me near him. He'll be all right," she says, assuring me the pup's own healing powers will pull him through.

When I tease her about not being able to photograph her doing something traditional like making dry meat, because the wooden racks beside us are empty, she laughs but tells me matter-of-factly she could fill them pretty quickly if she were to send someone out hunting for her.

"But, if you really want to see tradition, come to our camp in July when we take the kids out. You'll learn a lot," she suggests. An invitation that sounds even more interesting is her offer to take me to her trapline near Lodgepole, an area special to her because relatives are buried there. Describing the log cabin and the work we would have to do once there, she urges me to come and "use your muscles and do something good for yourself.

"You've just come from the city. Cities block your energy. They're made of things that shouldn't be there. If you believe in spiritual things, you have to be in open spaces like this, amongst the trees, not in the city. There's lots of electricity, a lot of cars, and people everywhere. . . a lot of young girls that are in their time [menstru-ating], and all that energy is mixed up. A powerful place is a clean, pure place, where the things are that the Creator meant for you to have." We make plans for a November bush trip, with Paul chuckling as we discuss all the things we will need.

When I ask how the two of them came to be married, I get a won-derful answer.

"We used to play house together," Nancy informs me, "under the spruce trees with a fire and everything. I was the wife and Paul was my husband and Sophie Cardinal was my little girl. There was this big, long dog up at Tender Lake — our families got together to trap in the spring — and somehow we were packing with it. We tied some rocks together, and the dog packed them. Paul was leading the dog, and I was packing a doll on my back."

We all have a good laugh about the childhood playhouse becoming real and the nineteen babies she and Paul eventually had together, though only fourteen survived. These she nursed at her breast.

"If they cried at three or four o'clock in the morning, I got up with them. . . cleaned them up and fed them. And I stayed up with them. That's how you make your kids early birds. When they wake up, you've got to get up, too. If you attend to them and try to put them back to sleep, so you can get another hour, it doesn't work. You have to stay up with them until daylight."

Equal distribution of attention and love is the other big thing to remember in raising a family, she says.

"Sometimes we do wrong, even if we think we're doing the right thing," she says, recalling how she once upset her family after setting a precedent for buying her children expensive gifts. Upon presenting her oldest daughter with a leather jacket after her graduation, she found she couldn't afford to favour the rest to the same degree. "Now I do little things for them that aren't so costly, and they appreciate it," she says.

Observing the height of the sun in the sky, Nancy stands up. "If I had a tipi, I'd tell you what time it was. When the sun comes straight down, right in the middle, it's dinnertime. But I guess the old people ate whenever they got hungry. They didn't have clocks. The only time was sunrise and sunset.

"Indian time," she snorts, as we gather our teacups. "That's what white people say when we're late, but they're the ones who made it. They should call it 'white-man's time,'" she jokes, as we head into the house for soup.

13

Russell Wright

Siksika (Blackfoot), Siksika First Nation

Jack Royal was a child when he first heard about plans for the world-class Black-foot Crossing Historical Park that now dominates a portion of the Bow River Valley on the Siksika First Nation. The future general manager of the cultural centre, which opened in 2007, may have heard a younger Russell Wright speaking of his vision for this great cultural project since sharing Blackfoot culture and history was the elder's greatest passion.

Russell's daughter Lucille Wright recalls her dad talking about creating a great museum to celebrate Blackfoot culture as early as the 1960s.

"My dad and the late Chief Leo Youngman were founding members of Black-foot Crossing," says Lucille. She doesn't think they were planning anything as elaborate as the resulting 6,000-acre historical park, but both men realized a special facility might be necessary to house ceremonial items such as sacred bundles and pipes when museums were legislated to repatriate such items in 1977.

Old Sun College, home of the small museum Russell walked me through as I interviewed him twenty years ago, was about to close its doors back then, but

Chief Leo decided it would be the resting place for the returned sacred items, and the development helped the school to stay in operation to this day.

The items have found a new home at Blackfoot Crossing Historical Park, at the heart of which stands a stunning 62,000 square foot building accommodating exhibits and interactive displays. Its Vision Quest Theatre offers informative presentations on Blackfoot culture and visitors can wander the park's various historical sites and monuments on their own or with a guide.

Russell Wright, who passed away on September 25, 1995, played an integral part in the twenty-year effort to plan the $33 million Blackfoot Crossing Historical Park, the largest single First Nation cultural tourist attraction in Canada.

A big brown-and-white Appaloosa whinnies to her dun-coloured colt as the intruder enters the corral. The nervous herd bunches into a corner, and a dappled gelding rears in agitation. As the plaid-shirted rancher draws nearer, the horses dance sidelong against the fence, faint outlines of their ribs showing beneath the sheen of their coats. Spirited and handsome, each horse looks muscular and fast — a pleasure to ride if broken and calmed enough for bridling.

"We should have been branding and castrating today," Russell Wright comments, scanning the herd. He hooks his thumbs in his jeans and bends low to fit between the slats of the corral's board fence.

"I used to have over two hundred head of cattle. Right now, I've got forty. My uncle Teddy Yellowfly — he was a steam engineer, the first one from this reserve to be well-educated — he told me to get cattle and horses, 'Then you'll make something of yourself.' I took his advice. I know I should be thinking about retiring, but I think I'll buy more stock. Ranching is what I do."

Russell mentions his plans as we walk from the hot, dusty corral to his cool kitchen for a ginger ale. He lays his black hat on the table and stretches his long legs. Gazing at the pointed tips of his boots, he is reminded of the funny remarks his "cowboy clothes" roused years ago when he first visited northern Alberta.

"I went up to Trout Lake once to learn about community development work, and here were all these Cree — they had mukluks and mackinaws on, really warm clothes. I wore a light overcoat, a suit, and my cowboy boots and hat. They laughed and asked me, 'What kind of funny Indian are you? You look like a cowboy.'"

Russell might have asked them the same thing. After all, what kind of Indians don't ride fast horses and roam the prairies? He laughed along with his co-workers, fellow members of a race as diverse as Mother Earth herself. From Arizona's corn-planting Pueblo Indians to the Northwest Territories' caribou-hunters, aboriginal lifestyles have been dictated by the environment, and it just so happens the flat, open spaces of southern Alberta are more suited to ranching and farming than traplines and moose-hunting.

Russell's Blackfoot ancestors — so named, legend has it, after one of them once walked across a prairie burned to ash and blackened his moccasins — adapted so well to their environment that they once ruled southern Alberta's plains. They excelled at making war and hunting buffalo, their life source. But within three years after their famous leader Chief Crowfoot convinced fellow head chiefs Old Sun and Heavy Shield to sign Treaty Seven in 1877, the buffalo were wiped out and the Blackfoot were reduced to accepting beef, flour, and tea from government ration houses on reserves.[1]

After the Riel rebellion and the death of Chief Crowfoot in 1890, the tribe unwillingly settled into the routine of farming and gardening. But after being pressured by the government to sell large portions of their reserve between 1910 and 1920, the band became the wealthiest tribe in Canada and flourished as ranch and farmland was developed, along with a lucrative coal-mining business.[2] The agricultural era proved to be the most progressive period in Blackfoot history, Russell informed me as we toured the museum at Gleichen's Old Sun College the first time I met him. He showed me what had come before the age of planting seeds and herding cattle as we stepped back in time to the Stone Age.

While Russell recalled ancient "creation" stories, he let me handle some of the stone tools in the museum display. Some had blunt ends for clubbing or hammering, but a few — honed from animal horns — looked extremely sharp. Arrows, some with hooked edges for war and others with smooth points for hunting, lay beside mallets used for pounding berries.

"Domesticated dogs were the only things the people had for travelling," Russell comments, indicating a miniature travois made of skinny poles crossed and tied with sinew.

With the coming of the horse, the next era arrived and with it the greatest upheaval in terms of cultural change. Burgeoning numbers of European settlers and missionaries altered the free and independent Blackfoot lifestyle forever.

"I'm allowed to touch this but I can't open it," Russell said, pointing to a tightly wrapped sacred bundle. The Blackfoot culture reached its peak during this period, as evidenced by the intricate shell, bead, and quill decorations on hide clothing, religious objects, and saddlery in the display.

"Missionaries came with one thing on their minds — to civilize and Christianize us. I buy their Christianization process, because I believe our Native spirituality can be very inefficient. I'm an Anglican. I guess I have no problem incorporating Christianity with Native spirituality, because I have a traditional background. I can make quick translations from Blackfoot to English, and, even if I'm writing a scientific paper, I still see it in Blackfoot linguistics and semantics."

Russell easily blends both religions and called his facility with languages "wonderful — it gives me a link to the past, a focus on the future, and at the same time I can deal with the present."

Walking over to a tipi display, he showed me a handsome backrest made from lengths of willow strung together between two legs of a tripod. "In the tipi, the man's place was around his backrest and he hung his shield, pipe, parfleche bags, and medicine bundles from it. The woman's place was everywhere else in the tipi, and if she wanted her husband out she just took his backrest with everything on it outside," Russell explained.

From the horse and missionary era, the museum moved into the agricultural era as the Blackfoot worked the land. Those prosperous times became gloomier with the advent of the 1960s. The tribe struggled to establish new economic ventures as their numbers grew and the cost of living soared.

"Looking back, the '20s were progressive years, because most families were engaged in some kind of agriculture and, most importantly, we had our language and cultural values. Children were still going through the traditional education system based on wholistic concepts."

Blackfoot education is based on the sacred four and the circle. Four signifies the number of parts in many significant wholes — four seasons, four directions, four human growth phases, four decision-making steps. And these great steps or changes form a circular chain, always coming back to a point and circling again.

As Black Elk, of the Oglala Sioux, once said: the power of the world works in circles, and when the tribes were strong their power came to them from the sacred hoop of the nurturing nation. As long as the hoop was unbroken, the people flourished. Everything the power of the world does is in circles: the sky, earth, stars, sun, and moon are round. The wind, in its greatest power, whirls. Birds' nests are in circles.[3]

A basic tenet of traditional life was: there is oneness in the world the Creator has given humans and it is important that they understand their place in the circle of life. "We understood a whole lot of things had to be integrated to make a whole. A person going through his life changed four times as a child, youth, adult, and elder. Along the way, our people believed in a circular way of thinking — whatever we say will come back to us.

"Early childhood was spent learning the language, followed by youth guidance in the thirteen-to-seventeen age range. There was an attempt to hasten mature thought, not necessarily maturity. In Blackfoot terms that meant inform, teach, guide, and encourage. Anytime you were talking to a young person, you applied these four principles."

Life was considered a circle of continual learning and re-learning, as the Blackfoot understood the human tendency to forget important principles. Within the tribe, every adult and elder was socially required to teach and re-teach young people who would eventually become elders themselves, replacing the ones who taught them tribal history and traditional values.

"The emphasis was on human worthiness — to be worth something to the tribe. This is an ancient tribal philosophy, and it's why our ancestors were so strong. They were strong in the community sense, and they stayed together as a wholistic society." Tribal government systems were based on self-rule through consensus, and "that meant everybody understood what was required of them. Of course there were no written laws. They were orally transmitted, and everybody had to learn them and abide by them. They weren't enforced, just practised."

After the museum tour, I thought I had gained a good appreciation for Blackfoot culture, but Russell cautioned I could never truly understand until I spoke Blackfoot and listened to the legends, stories, and mythology of his people.

"For a long time, our people have orated about a unique, well-functioning, sophisticated culture and part of that was the elders' storytelling. That was their communication and education system. I was born in 1921, one of the last to go through it, before I went into residential school when I was nine."

Russell not only knows many legends, he has also studied the history of oratory. He plans to write a book of Blackfoot legends incorporating traditional values, especially for schoolchildren, teachers, nurses, social workers, and police officers.

"I want youngsters to know about a certain trickster we call Old Man, or Napi. He was half-spirit, half-man. He could speak to nature and to animals, the elders said, but he was also a trickster. He was very mischievous — greedy, deceitful, bad-tempered, vain — everything discrepant to a human being. He was such a bad character, to this day no tribe will own up to whether Napi was of the Siksika, Peigan, Blood, or Blackfeet nation. We're still debating that.

"As kids, we used to ask elders to tell us stories we already knew by heart. We'd say, 'Can you tell us about this or that historical event? What do you know about it?' What we were really asking for was their analysis, their particular interpretation of the event as it related to life.

"When you have a main subject like Napi who can speak to animals, it's fascinating. The stories are examples of life's responsibilities and our rapport with nature and our environment. The stories deal with people trying to co-exist."

Most Napi legends "belong to" or are "specialties" of grandmothers who traditionally taught tribal lessons about family life and persuaded listeners not to mimic Napi. These stories are "comical and sound really crazy," but they conveyed moral messages about life, while some whimsically explained how certain animals, birds, and vegetation acquired peculiar characteristics. Napi is joined by his infamous friend Coyote to teach how not to get along with your neighbour, and the two outsmart, outguess, and humiliate each other in countless legends. In one popular story, Napi suffers terribly when he loses his eyeballs and falls victim to Coyote's merciless pranks.

"Finally, Napi was so mad he grabbed hold of Coyote and plucked his eyes out and stuck them in his own sockets. Now that he could see, he spotted a nearby gooseberry bush and picked two berries and stuck them into Coyote's sockets. That's why coyotes today have pale, greenish coloured eyes."

It was Napi's bad temper that led him to assault a birch tree with his stone knife one day, resulting in the black marks and nicks still visible today. Eventually, it was the trickster's conniving trait that caused his demise, as Russell recounted a legend about the first relations between men and women.

"One day, Napi was out walking and he came upon a camp of all men — no women. He left them, eventually, and found another camp — all women. The women had a woman chief, and Napi was so struck by her beauty that he decided he wanted her for his own.

So, he became a matchmaker. He began to devise a way for the men's camp to meet with the women's camp, and it just so happened the two camps were of equal numbers. Napi planned that each man could have a woman, and he wanted the women's chief to himself.

"Now, the woman chief caught on to Napi's deceitful ways and realized what he was trying to do. She immediately cast a spell on him and changed him into a fir tree. That tree is not too far from the Blackfoot Reserve, somewhere to the southwest of here. It's where Napi ended. He tried to be a matchmaker, but he did it the wrong way. He was going to cheat and try to win the woman chief to be his wife, but that was the end of him."

One story about Napi's race with Coyote explains why certain animals such as bears and mountain lions aren't eaten by the Blackfoot. Another describes the first buffalo jump used to secure massive amounts of meat for the tribe.

Russell's research indicates the subject matter of a story identifies its origination from one of four legendary periods. "Way back into history, we started with stories about Napi and they were about evolution and the formation of the land — prairies, rivers, lakes, foothills, forests, and mountains — how they originated."

After the creative forces spawned the earth, a period of darkness followed. "It's the era I call 'the great menaces.' Legends from that period were about monsters, fierce animals, cannibals — a lot of corruption. But that was a short period, not many legends came out of it."

Stories from the third era reflect the arrival of a mythical benefactor named Bloodclot, who arrived amongst the Blackfoot when things looked darkest. He began life as a bloody mass cast off by a buffalo — hence his name — and, magically, became an infant and grew to manhood overnight. "Bloodclot began to eradicate all evil. He talked to the people and told them how they could fend for themselves. He was hard on them, always criticizing. He said things like, 'What is the matter with you people? I see a lot of able-bodied men and capable women. . .' He was antagonistic in his approach, and he told people how they needed cohesiveness. They needed to stay together, live together, and work together to survive. In the end, he left the people."

The fourth legendary period is comprised of explanations of how the Blackfoot received sacred gifts, ceremonies, and bundles and how the structuring of the "eight great religious tribal societies" was initiated and carried out. The Horn Society was the highest religious order, devising the tribal code of ethics; the Brave Dogs were the warrior protectors of the tribe; grandmothers and matronly women were included in the Buffalo Women's Society, which provided spiritual leadership and family life lessons; and children belonged to the Prairie Chicken Society.

As Russell points out, legends answer questions people have asked for ages — how did the universe take shape? Why was the earth created? Why is there death? Stories established natural laws that govern all things.

As contemporary artist and author Helmut Hirnschall writes, age-old legends reflect an "awareness not only of the creative forces to whom all humans owe their existence but also of the power of the stars, the benevolent or destructive actions of the elements and the forces that make nature the interacting provider for all beings." According to Hirnschall, "The interdependence between animated and inanimated matter was so deeply understood that life was felt in everything and death regarded as merely a descriptive name for another way of life. Such a philosophy has much to give, even if it is presented through mythology." [4]

Russell and his wife Julia, a crafts instructor, refuse to listen to people who discredit legends and say Native culture is dead and the languages are dying.

"We were left a legacy, one our ancestors worked hard at and suffered to leave to us, so we can't default in teaching our children, especially language. Cultural values are built in, and there are Blackfoot terms that have no English equivalencies," Russell stressed. Many descriptives in Blackfoot assume the tribe is one family and, "That's why old people still speak in kinship terms, addressing young people as 'my daughter' or 'my son.'" Russell insists that cultural values can be re-introduced and applied to modern life. He would like to see children taught in a wholistic way in school and to be as cherished by the tribe as they once were.

"When a child was born, it was traditional for the midwife to cut the umbilical cord and the child's aunt or older sister would clean and dry it. Then she made a hide pouch in the form of a turtle or some other animal, beaded it, and sewed the cord inside. The child wore it for the first five years of its life at special occasions when people gathered together. The pouch reminded people the child had many parents and everyone was responsible to help the child grow to become worthy to the tribe. That's wholistic living."

The unity of the family and tribe was broken when children were taken away from their parents and raised in residential schools run by missionaries. Cultural values were suppressed and many children were raised without love and without learning to communicate. Unexpressed feelings turned to rage and led to delinquent behaviour. After World War Two, traditional culture was replaced with alcohol culture.

On the Blackfoot Reserve in the '50s, industrialization and inflated prices caught up with band members who couldn't afford expensive farm machinery. Coal mines in the area closed as natural gas caught on. Ashamed because they could no longer act as providers, men leased their land to white farmers and many turned to alcohol.

In what is known as the "Sixties Scoop," children of this alcoholic generation were removed from their families and placed in non-Aboriginal foster homes. Caught between two cultures, they felt alienated in white society yet were estranged from their indigenous heritage. "Those kids, in the situation they're in, are really cultural orphans," Russell was quoted as saying in a 1988 *Calgary Herald* newspaper article. The Blackfoot tribe was the first in Canada to sign a child welfare repatriation agreement between the federal and provincial governments and to initiate orientation programs integrating returned children into the community.[5] Russell sympathizes with foster parents who have lost children they have bonded with but believes these children are future leaders who must be raised in the Indian way.

"Young people are the most urgent issue. I think we can go back and start to encourage them in our traditional values. As someone once said, 'We need to apply the four Ds and decriminalize our youth — stop addressing them as criminals, deter them from hurting themselves, divert them toward a new direction, and develop them, which means help them to help themselves.'"

Russell teaches young people traditional values and the proper way to approach an elder "with food and a gift" if they want to know something. He urges them to "Make enquiries of old people, instead of asking questions," because, traditionally, to question was to challenge.

"It has something to do with face-to-face conflict — if you question me, you are doubting me. You're not open to what I might tell you if you're already thinking of questions. But if you make an inquiry and ask, 'Can you tell me a story about this or that and explain it?' then you'll get a good, honest answer. You don't just walk up to an elder, especially the new crop of elders, those of us not yet in our seventies, and say, 'I have a problem.' The elder would probably come back speaking English and say, 'Welcome to the club. What else is new? Who doesn't have a problem?' Approach him or her in a respectful way, and they would probably say, 'You don't have a problem. There's just something bothering you that you don't quite understand.'

"The elders quite often tell us, 'You're too busy labelling things, putting on price tags. Time has a price tag. . . you're always putting labels on things, saying things like this is a problem or so-and-so is a problem.' Elders don't do that. They take a person for what he's worth. They say there's no such thing as someone who is good for nothing. We're all worth something. . ."

Russell values the equanimity instilled in him by elders when he was growing up. His grandparents spoke only traditional Blackfoot to him, a tongue that embodies "gentleness and sophistication," but loses this quality the more Anglicized it becomes.

"What always comes back to me is the way my grandparents taught me. They were always telling me stories, always explaining things to me. They didn't say, 'This is bad, this is good.' They didn't differentiate between the two, everything was nice to them — nature, other people, animals — they were all nice. We don't have an opposite word for nice in Blackfoot. It's descriptive, and to say it we have to say a bad thing."

Russell pointed out that Blackfoot etiquette is non-confrontational and elders never debate a subject, they only have dialogue. Traditionally, decisions were made based on four principles: dialogue, consensus, decision, and action. Leaders aimed for harmony, and the majority ruled in decision-making. The wholistic number four came up again when Russell described the material, spiritual, social, and artistic components of a healthy culture.

"Material culture is interesting to look at. We believe objects are inanimate of themselves. This pen here is an object by itself, but when I use it, it becomes alive — animated. It's part of me, an extension of me. So, our traditional concept of possessions is not to hoard them, but to use them. If anybody can find a better use for what I have, let him take it."

The once close-knit Blackfoot society has wandered from this universal principle. Greed and other modern social ills continue to take their toll, with overcrowding and political cliques adding fuel to the fire.

"But we've still got the artistic component — our arts and crafts are known worldwide. And we're starting to see a lot more ceremonies now. I think young people are beginning to realize that here is a religion that really works. Spirituality is the only thing working in penal institutes and drug and alcohol programs. What we really need to work on is bringing back our social culture — the principles I've been talking about. That needs to be applied through the education system."

Indians in the United States have been successful in teaching bicultural, bilingual education, and Russell hopes for a repeat performance in Canada but warns that Canadians — Native and non-Native alike — must first realize that bi-words aren't bad words. Distinct societies must avoid isolation and think wholistically.

"I believe Native people could contribute to the concept of Canadian community, if we ever get that far. That's what our ancestors had — common unity, community spirit. That's how they survived."

1   Hugh A. Dempsey, *Indian Tribes of Alberta* (Calgary, Alberta: Glenbow-Alberta Institute, 1979), p. 16.
2   Ibid., p. 19.
3   T.C. McLuhan, *Touch The Earth — A Self-portrait of Indian Existence* (New York, New York: Simon and Schuster, Inc., 1971), p. 42.
4   Helmut Hirnschall, *North American Indian Myths and Original Paintings* (Vancouver, British Columbia: Plainsman Publishing Ltd., 1979), no page numbers.
5   Mark Lowey, "Vanishing Society: 'I think we're going to lose our heritage'" (*The Calgary Herald*, 11 September 1988), p. F6.

14

Joe Patchakes Cardinal

Cree, Saddle Lake First Nation

"The one thing my dad always said is, 'The journey from the heart to the mind can be a long one,'" the late Joe P. Cardinal's oldest daughter Theresa tells me. By that, he meant that we sometimes let our mind take over — and it's usually racing with intellectual concepts — so we lose touch with kindness and love, those things the Creator wants us to connect with, she explains. Theresa, who has her Masters in Education, is honouring her father's words by naming an upcoming teachers' conference she is helping to coordinate "From the Heart to the Mind in Education."

Joe believed in the power of education to open people's minds and help them toward a better life. Perhaps emboldened by the success of Blue Quills First Nations College, Joe's former residential school that was reclaimed in 1970 after a government lobby and is today operated by his own people, he and four other elders also guided the formation of Edmonton's Amiskwaciy Academy to bring a culturally-based curriculum to Aboriginal high school students.

Joe sat on the board of Native Counselling Services of Alberta for twenty-seven years, and the Aboriginal Multi-Media Society of Alberta (A M M S A) for fifteen — just to mention two organizations he helped to guide. He also served as an elder on the National Parole Board, where he addressed about 2,800 inmates during his tenure.

Joe passed away on December 12, 2004. He was a family man, chief, veteran, visionary and spiritual leader in his community.

Standing over six feet tall, broad shoulders pulled back and spine straight, Joe stands out in the hotel lobby crowd. The stiff, white hairs of his brushcut are carefully clipped, and a dark sweater lends a look of prominence. His face is chiselled rock, softened by wispy crow's feet around alert, inquiring eyes.

Spying an empty table beside a window, he walks across the hotel restaurant with an athletic gait. Evening is descending upon Edmonton, and he enjoys watching the changing light. He orders a huge steak, hungry after a day of meetings with service groups and a legislative visit to chat with Métis Solicitor General Dick Fowler. He and a few of "the boys" presented Fowler with a picture of a wolf, and now Joe asks if I know why they chose that particular animal.

"Because it's strong and powerful," I reply, but it's not the right answer.

"Well, a wolf always looks after its own," Joe explains, his face crinkling into a bemused smile. Plowing into his supper, he ponders overnighting in the city but remembers a morning meeting in Beaver Lake. He opts for a quick bite, and then it is back to Saddle Lake, a two-hour drive east of Edmonton. As an elder with many responsibilities, from leading pipe ceremonies and acting as board member for several organizations to delivering conference addresses, Joe is a busy man.

Born to Patchakes and Honoreen Cardinal at Birch Mountain near Fort McMurray in 1921, the story of his childhood is a familiar one. The self-confidence he exudes today came late in life. Fond, unconstrained boyhood memories as a trapper's son are overridden by dark, confused recollections of missionary school experiences that left him feeling totally powerless and disconnected.

"At first, I didn't know what the hell was happening to me. I didn't know any English, just Cree. All I knew is I was in some kind of jail." His prison was the Blue Quills Residential School, located just west of St. Paul, which he attended until Grade Six. He recalls learning some English and mathematics, but spending most of his time doing farm chores. Joe pauses, focusing his piercing eyes directly on mine. "Do you know a woman in Goodfish Lake is writing her thesis on mission schools, and she found out the discipline system used in boarding schools was copied from Kingston Penitentiary?" he inquires. He has no doubt the research is faultless. Verifying recent media exposures of almost unbelievable ignorance and intolerance of Native culture by early missionaries, Joe recalls how his impressionable young mind was slowly and systematically poisoned against his ancestry.

"When white people came to church, we had been trained to bow to them in the hallway as we walked by to sit in the front row. When I got out of school, I guess I must have been about twelve, I honestly almost hated my parents because I'd learned they were bad people. I remember not wanting to have anything to do with them.

"We were not human, because we didn't know about Jesus. I can't believe how much fear they put into me. Everything was 'Jesus will punish you,' and 'God will do this to you.' All I knew is I could never do anything right."

Joe's teenage years were spent "not feeling very good about myself." An opportunity would arise, he would try to take advantage of it, then his deeply ingrained sense of incompetence surfaced to ensure failure and depression. "But the Creator works in strange ways," he says, explaining that it was in a bloody battlefield filled with gore that he first began to believe in himself.

"In 1941, I joined the army at nineteen. I got to England, and I was scared. I felt inferior to the white man. I'd been led to believe the white race was a super race, and I guess I kind of believed it. But in

Normandy, France, I held lots of guys who were dying. I heard them scream, and I saw their guts spill out. I found myself thinking, 'These guys all scream and die the same way. I must be the same, too.'"

Joe admits the suffering he witnessed emboldened him and changed his life. "I found out I was okay," he says, but more degrading circumstances were to threaten his new found confidence upon returning to Canada. "I came back in 1946. I wanted to join the Canadian Legion, but I wasn't allowed to because I was Indian. It was hard to adjust to the reserve. I could drink beer in the army, but when I came back I couldn't, because I couldn't set foot in a bar."

He found himself a "prisoner of war" on his own reservation: in the late 1940s he wasn't allowed to leave without a pass from the Indian Agent. At the Legion, management told him if they were to accept him as a member he would "spoil" the establishment and nobody would come. Joe wanted to buy a trapline, but the Indian Agent refused him, telling him Indian Affairs expected him to become a farmer.[1]

Isolated from sharing memories and making sense with other veterans out of what he had just been through, bitter feelings welled up inside. "But, gradually, I learned to forget. Those feelings don't do any good," Joe says, warming up to a subject he feels strongly about. Diverting from his life story, he assumes a role familiar to him — that of a counsellor — to discuss the topic of negative reinforcement. His own experiences, coupled with stories from his peers, have made him extremely sensitive to the damage wrought by bad missionary school experiences and racism, but he gently urges people to acknowledge the hurt and move out of the past to become a warrior within themselves. He believes reserves will be good places to live when people begin to open up and talk about their hurts and problems, when they begin to move past the denial stage that they need healing.

"We all have weaknesses. I can't sit here and tell you what to do. You already know. But we have to challenge ourselves," he says, to climb out of the pit of negativity. People must deal with their pain and get help to do so, instead of destroying themselves. If the positive aspects of the self are taken care of, the negative side will die a natural death, Joe believes, counselling that faith "in the Creator and yourself" is the most powerful medicine on earth.

If there is faith and a yearning to know the Creator, life will give you the exact experiences you need to learn to live a good, clean life and accomplish that which the Creator gave each person special talents to do, Joe insists. His battlefield experience of self-realization was an example of this natural law, he claims.

Returning to his life story, Joe says he married Jennie in 1947 after getting out of the army. The couple had eight children and either fostered or adopted many more. To support his growing family, Joe worked at various jobs including farming and trapping between 1950 and the late 1960s. He spent the years between 1969 and 1975 as Chief of the Saddle Lake and Goodfish bands. Ironically, his most memorable battles as chief were not with the government but with the religious institution responsible for making him feel worthless as a child. He theorizes that the priests couldn't stand losing their monopolies over communities as integration occurred and Native people started making their own decisions.

"I sent my kids twelve miles away from Saddle Lake to go to a non-denominational school in Vilna. That made our priest mad. He told me I had no backbone for my people and my kids would turn out no good. He even wanted me to go and take my name off the church registry."

The day he and band councillor Ralph Steinhauer, who would later become Lieutenant-Governor of Alberta, witnessed the full impact of rivalry and distrust between church leaders in the area, Joe feared for the future. "I went to pick up Ralph. We drove up to a field between the Catholic and Anglican schools in Goodfish Lake where the kids played at recess. The priest had gone and put a big fence across the middle. Ralph just cried when he saw that."

Joe gave orders for the fence to be taken down and curtly reminded the priest that his domain was the church and that he, Joe, would direct band affairs, including education. As Aboriginal people assumed more control over their lives and tried to keep pace with changing society, Joe travelled north to places like Fort Chipewyan and John D'or Prairie with Alberta Newstart, a community development program.

"We tried to make people aware of what was happening and help them with things, especially economic development." Joe attended meetings, both formal and informal, to understand community difficulties, and taught skills to members that would help them to cope with the competitive, complicated white-man's world.

Joe has made a life out of listening to people's problems and helping them, with an emphasis on human and spiritual development. He offers "plain old good advice," often stemming from wisdom his grandfather shared with him.

"They called that old man 'Mr. Moses.' He was a chief for about twenty years and his Cree name meant 'Chief More Than Usual.' He was a hard worker and always went to sweats. I'd sit with him, and he'd tell me things. And you know, today, after fifty years, his counselling is still not out of date. He told me I might be a chief someday, but if that happened I should listen very well to others and then I'd know what to say when I spoke. But many times I've abused that. I want to speak first."

A new phase of Joe's life was initiated by chance when he travelled with friends to the Wind River Reservation in Wyoming to pick up his son Eugene who was being doctored by an Arapahoe healer named Raymond Harris. "I didn't know anything about Native traditions. I didn't even know where Wyoming was! We drove for two days to get there. When I met Raymond he asked me, 'Who are you?' I didn't know how to answer that question. I took out my wallet and handed him my status card. He handed it back to me and said, 'You need to learn who you are. Out there (on the fasting grounds) is where you will learn that.'" [2]

Thus began Joe's spiritual life of helping people with ceremony and prayer. He apprenticed with Raymond and eventually began leading weekly sweats and overseeing fasts in his own community of Saddle Lake.

Joe's spiritual and advisory work takes him all over the continent. He recently returned from an AIDS conference in San Diego and says he accepts as many invitations as possible to attend cultural gatherings or workshops sponsored by service groups, usually performing pipe ceremonies and giving opening addresses. His visits with Aboriginal inmates in jails across the province have made him a crusader for Native justice.

"At the University of Alberta, there's twenty-nine thousand students and only one hundred and fifty are Native. Yet, look at the jails and see who's in the majority there. I tell taxpayers to look and see how much money goes to penitentiaries. How about putting education on the same footing? When it comes to Native education, I hope you'll support us, I say, because it is the key. Whether the world destroys itself or not, we have to strive for education."

Many of the inmates he speaks to are first-time offenders whose crimes are alcohol-related. Far from being violent criminals, they regret their alcohol problems and actions. They are victims of an overbearing and alien legal system in which they are often instructed to plead guilty to avoid complications.

Lately, Joe has been getting more calls than ever to speak at non-Native gatherings. He speculates a collective guilty conscience, especially since the 1990 Oka crisis, may have kickstarted Canadians' interest in First Nations but hopes global spiritual awareness will replace natural resource exploitation of the past. "When we talk about environment we have to talk about spirituality. Why did God make this world? Are we going to spoil His gifts — trees, animals, water? Spirituality has to take the place of greed."

Although he has been offered plenty of jobs in Aboriginal communities and with service groups, he turns them down in favour of his "human development work," preferring to "get by on my old age and army pensions." He finds satisfaction in shouldering the responsibilities of being a pipe-holder and upholding vows to walk a moral and selfless path. He must constantly challenge himself to be worthy of the pipe and behave accordingly, always moving in balance and harmony. Most pipe-holders recognize, for example, that if they are provoked into anger by a child or a dog, or any living thing for that matter, they must not handle the sacred pipe for the rest of the day.

Joe's prescription for a better life includes re-examining the wonders of being alive and heightening the senses to aspects of life that may have been forgotten, like beauty in nature. He reminds those who have been deluded into thinking they are worthless, as he was led as a child to believe of himself, that God doesn't make junk. "You're made like a miracle. Your body and mind are important, but you have to develop your spirit. Our spirit is really something. It's like the drive shaft of a car — it powers everything. The spirit is involved with everything, even material things. The Creator meant us to work for things — a house and food. Your work can even be made spiritual when you get a good feeling inside from it. You don't have to go to church.

"Even things like food and spirituality go together. When you eat, you feel good. When you don't eat, when you go out in the bush for four days and fast, well, that's another thing. You look at yourself — an empty stomach versus a full stomach — and it makes you think more. You're like a storekeeper taking stock of his merchandise. When I fast I have to stand back and say, 'This guy, myself, I have to deal with him and I have to challenge him.' I ask, 'How did I do as a family man, or as a teacher?' I have to look at myself and not other people."

Joe stops speaking, pinning me with that intense look again, eyes glinting. "It's you! You're the one!" he exclaims.

Joe guarantees a better life to people who sincerely invite the Creator into their lives and ask for help. God always responds — an awesome power waiting just behind the door, if only it is opened. It is as though God is shy and someone seeking Him has to show Him how sincere they are before He will come in. Joe now knows that the mission-school notion that God is a punishing entity couldn't be further from the truth.

Spiritual values are a Native person's heritage, and it is time to re-claim them, Joe declares. At the same time, he is careful to point out it is not a sell-out to take on some of the white-man's ways.

"We are bicultural, because we accepted so much from the white man. I have a hot-water system, but that doesn't mean I can't follow the ways of my grandfather, too."

1 Ross Hoffman, *Perspectives on Health Within the Teachings of a Gifted Cree Elder*, (Pimatisiwin: A Journal of Aboriginal and Indigenous Community Health 8 [1] 2010), p. 22.
2 Ibid., p. 22.

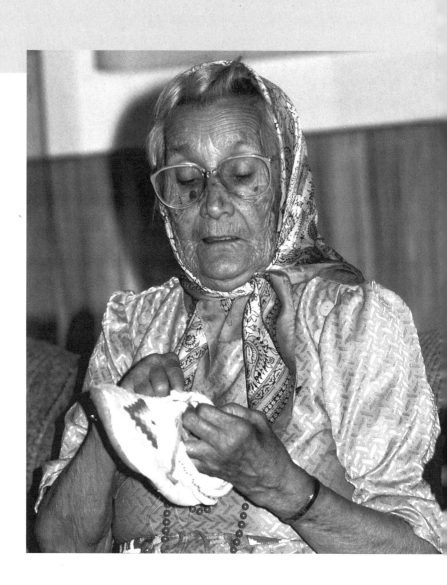

15

Louise Big Plume

Tsuut'ina, Tsuut'ina First Nation

Ever since the late Louise Big Plume let her granddaughter help prepare a turkey dinner at the age of nine, Cara has been cooking the family feast at Christmas. "She was that kind of Isuus (grandma)," Cara says. "She was always teaching me things like how to make pemmican, dry meat and bannock when I was a little girl. I never saw her just sitting. She was forever beading, berry-picking or sewing. The last outfit she made was a girl's traditional cape for my niece and I'm in the process of finishing it."

When Louise's mother passed away in 1969, she passed the tipi the family puts up at the Calgary Stampede to Louise, and now the tipi belongs to Cara's mother. It will likely belong to Cara one day. "My granny was so generous. I always noticed that when people came to visit her she always gave them gifts. Now I do the same," Cara adds.

Louise had nine children, and has thirty-seven grandchildren, 103 great-grandchildren, and thirty-six great-great-grandchildren, as well as numerous adopted children and grandchildren.

Even though the tipis at the Calgary Stampede Indian Village are open to visitors, I've avoided going inside because I feel like a snoopy tourist interrupting a family's privacy. But when I strolled through the village on a sunny afternoon with my niece Jenessa, the wind lifted her hat and it rolled into the doorway of a tipi marked with a Tsuut'ina sign. Stooping to pick it up, I stole a glance inside.

How cool and peaceful the interior looked, an oasis from the sun's glare and the frenetic crowds outside. Everything was orderly: beaded clothing and parfleche bags hung from poles, fur rugs were neatly laid out and a small fire crackled under a kettle. As my eyes adjusted to the darkness, I noticed that it was stems of silver-green sage that an older woman was arranging on the floor. Some children sat toward the back.

"Excuse me," I mumbled, then turned to go back outside. But the woman had noticed Jenessa standing at the doorway and motioned for us to come in. She introduced herself as Louise Big Plume and watched with a slight smile as my niece's eyes travelled up the tall tipi poles to the blue sky peeking into the smokehole and then took in the stone fireplace and cooking tripod standing over it. Louise realized that this was the four-year-old's first time in a tipi.

"I have thirty-three grandchildren and twenty great-grandchildren, just like you," she said, getting Jenessa's attention. "That makes fifty-three in all, correct?" she asked me. I nodded. "Then, uh, there's some more coming — great-grandchildren. Two or three coming yet. This fall or this coming winter or sometime," she said, starting to laugh. "And I know every one of them. I know their names and their birthdays. Sometimes, I can't afford to give them presents anymore. I used to when they were small, but, today, thirty-three and then twenty. That's a lot."

Louise talked of how she has been coming to the Stampede since 1932, and her tipi is the oldest one there. Made in 1912, her father bought the privilege to paint the meaningful design on its exterior and then gave the tipi to Louise's mother before he died. She passed it on to Louise, and one of Louise's children will inherit it next.

I could have listened to this friendly woman all day — it was so pleasant sitting there in the coolness, amidst the fragrant sage. But Jenessa started to fidget and made it obvious she wanted to go back out into the noisy, familiar crowd beyond the canvas doorflap.

I mention that I'm writing an elders book before we leave and Louise agrees to be interviewed. She invites me to her home — a stone's throw from Calgary and within view of the Rocky Mountains. Anytime was good with her, she said, except she was always babysitting and we would have to work around that.

Luckily, when I call her a couple of months later, she's able to arrange for someone to look after the kids. I drive to the Tsuut'ina community and pick her up at the band office. She suggests we talk in the Tsuut'ina People's Museum in the Seven Chiefs Sportsplex, and, once there, we settle into comfortable chairs in the elders' lounge, while Louise chatters about the beaded moccasins and clothing, ancient tools, and wild, stuffed animals displayed in glass cases around us.

"That cougar over there — my grandson killed it and one of the Tsuut'ina boys mounted it. My grandson goes out after bears, cougars, beavers. . . my freezer's never empty during the winter. I ate a lynx once. I've had bear and buffalo, but I like deer best. I just had deer for dinner today." Louise mentions that she used to plant a huge garden when she was younger, but now she makes do with a potato and carrot patch.

"My grandchildren already ate all the carrots out of it before I had a chance to pick them," she comments, adding good-naturedly, "Things like that don't bother me because I live for my grandchildren."

Inside another glass case is an ancient saddle, fashioned from bone, wood, and antler with rawhide-wrapped stirrups and a rounded "knuckle bone" saddle horn lashed to the frame with leather thongs. To me, it's a grand symbol of the Tsuut'ina relationship to the animal that helped compress the forbidden vastness. Humans and the "medicine dog" or "big dog" had come together as one on the prairies.

Endless movement over endless space, they drew the line of the circle complete.

"An old woman left that saddle," Louise says, noticing me eyeing it. "She died about five years ago, at ninety. You know, today we all wear eyeglasses, false teeth — you name it — even false fingernails. Well, my old granny there, she never wore glasses and she still had her teeth. She never even brushed her teeth." I remind Louise that she isn't wearing glasses either and looks pretty spry for seventy-seven, but she shakes her head.

"No, I have to wear glasses for beading and reading. And look at my hands," she says, indicating bent fingers that look like they have done more than their share of work. Back in the Dirty Thirties, her sought-after beadwork put bread on the table while her people eked out a living labouring at whatever jobs they could find on and off the reserve — cleaning houses, digging potatoes, cutting pickets, cutting hay, and selling wood.

"I'd take my work to Calgary, to craft shops here and there. I used to get the hides from Hobbema — I've got some relations up there. One of my grandchildren married a Cree from Louis Bull [First Nation], and I go up there to visit whenever I have time.

"The Cree always bead flowers, but southern people use Indian designs like those," Louise says, pointing to a glass case displaying a pair of "crow-boot" moccasins almost completely covered with white, blue, and yellow beads sewn in a geometric pattern of squares forming a peak called a mountain design.

"You saw lots of my beadwork in my tipi," she comments. "I've made fourteen dresses — all beaded. But with my hands now, I have to quit."

Louise grew up and began raising a family in lean years when older people in the community were given rations and parents received food stamps to buy staples like tea and sugar. She married Stanley Big Plume and had the first of her children in 1936 but says she "raised them on nothing, just whatever jobs we could get. There was no welfare or family allowance. We had to work. We had some cattle." Louise describes the events of her life leading up to her marriage to Stanley, the husband chosen for her by her foster father who adopted her into the Bull Caller family after her own parents died.

"I went to boarding school at Old Agency when I was eight, just eight, mind you. That was an experience. I didn't know one word in English. I couldn't even pronounce my name. We weren't abused, but we were poorly fed, lots of potatoes, no butter, just grease. Most of us girls and boys were really small. We were all undernourished."

In the 1920s, diseases like tuberculosis and trachoma threatened to wipe the Tsuut'ina out. The band was adjusting to the agricultural era but had been so reduced in numbers that the government pressured the chief to sell "unused" land. Historian Hugh Dempsey writes that after a doctor visited the reserve and saw how many children were suffering from tuberculosis, a medical doctor was appointed as Indian agent and the reserve became one big sanitorium.[1]

"After old Doctor Murray came in about 1922, things did get a little better," Louise confirms. "We started to have milk and better food, but before that it was terrible."

During Louise's school years, she was allowed to come home on the weekends "but that was only if we weren't into mischief. If we were into mischief, we were punished for the weekend and had to stay at school." Louise spoke Tsuut'ina when she visited her parents but was punished if she uttered one word of it to her friends when she got back to class on Monday. "That's what really hurt the most, not being able to speak our language. There was a minister there. Oh, he was rough on the children. He didn't abuse them, but he sure punished them for speaking Tsuut'ina."

Throughout her eight years of schooling, the same teacher in the same tiny schoolroom taught Louise. "She was a real good teacher, but still, we didn't learn much. There were too many of us for one teacher in one room."

After leaving school when she was sixteen, Louise spent two years at home, never venturing far from the house unless her mother was with her. "Our parents were pretty strict with us. They wouldn't let us go anyplace we wanted. Today, young kids are let loose. They go everywhere."

The day finally arrived when her adopted father, who had gone blind, took her aside and told her what he expected. "He told me, 'I can't dress you up and I can't teach you anymore. Your mother is having a hard time, too. So you have to try and get married so somebody can look after you.' So, I had to do it. I was married off to a boy I never knew. . . I used to see him, but he wasn't my sweetheart or anything. I had to please my mom and dad because they raised me. I had to do what they said. I liked somebody else, but I had no choice in the matter."

Though I didn't ask Louise what her wedding day was like, I sense it was a lot less traditional than the ceremony depicted in a pastoral mural on one of the Tsuut'ina museum's walls. In it, a young couple stand before a holy man in the presence of four old men, who teach the boy to be a good provider and husband. On the other side, four old women stand serenely and they instruct the girl to be a wife and mother. A caption below the painting explains: The boy and girl feed each other berries because the boy's duty is to provide and the girl's is to feed him. They repeat that they are united for life and will live in harmony within the circle of life. Because the vows are made in the presence of spirits, as summoned to the ceremony by the holy man, the couple cannot make promises they aren't capable of keeping. They tie eagle feathers in each other's hair to acknowledge the eagle will be the guide and protector of their marriage, and as they leave the presence of the holy man they pray and thank the Creator for the life he has given them.

These are powerful matrimonial observances. From Louise's description of her parents, I surmise that her father would have liked his daughter to be married traditionally, but not her mother.

"Dad used to go up behind the house to have a sweatbath, and my mom used to scold him when he came back. She said, 'You're supposed to be a Christian. You're baptized.' She was brought up in a Catholic boarding school, so she was very strict with our religion.

She was brainwashed, I guess. So my dad would tell her, 'I just go up there because it's good for my bones.'"

Louise gave birth to the first of her nine children several years after being married. Six of them are still living but her husband Stanley passed away seven years ago.

"I get by on my pension, but I don't just use the money for myself. It goes to my children. I still help them out now and then." She cooks for two nephews who stay with her, babysits, and teaches the Tsuut'ina language to children at the elementary school twice a week. In the little spare time she has left, she reads. She likes historical novels and scans the daily newspaper, "but there's nothing good in it. In all my days, I've never seen so many shootings and stabbings as now. I read a lot about drugs. Oh, I'm dead set against drugs. Drinking is bad, of course, but drugs are so dangerous. You become a vegetable. I think that's why kids commit suicide. My grandson killed himself three or four years ago. I think he was high on something. He shot himself."

Drugs are easily available, since the community sits so close to the big city of Calgary, and local elders feel they are fighting a losing battle with young people. "You know, you can talk to them until you're blue in the face, they simply don't care. There's too much money today, too many choices, and no thankfulness," Louise says, wishing parents would offer their children more guidance. She coaches her youngest daughter, who is raising five children alone — four of them boys — since her husband died of a heart attack.

"I told her to make sure they come home at a certain time, or just ground them. They went to a movie and she told them to be back by ten o'clock. Well, they were home by 10:30. If she keeps telling them, they'll listen. But if she's not strict, they'll get out of hand."

Louise was alarmed by what she read in newspapers and saw on television about the 1990 confrontation over land between Quebec's Mohawk Nation and the army. "The government will never forget what the Indians are doing. They're going to turn around and get tougher with Native people. It could ruin things."

Some of her own people, about three hundred of them, took a

stand against the Canadian Forces Base in Calgary by blockading a military training bridge leading to their land in 1989. They wanted the Department of National Defence to pay a leasing agreement and to clean up its on-reserve firing range. The band disputed the sale of 948 acres of land they say was expropriated in the 1950s by the government under illegal terms. "Two lawyers came to me to ask what we got in 1951 when the chief sold the land. I remember he sold it without the band voting on it because we had no money. The government twisted his arm. But I don't think we'll get it back. There are too many buildings involved."

Ironically, the army barracks sit on land once the site of Tsuut'ina Sundances. Frank and Mary One Spot, elders who keep the tribe's ancient sacred Beaver Bundle used in traditional ceremonial society, have said the military camp should never have been built on such holy ground.

But the government has a history of violating the Tsuut'ina when it comes to land. Chief Bull Head, who led the tribe until 1911, fought for years to obtain a reserve at Fish Creek near Calgary after the government grouped the Tsuut'ina in with the Blood and Blackfoot Indians on a reserve at Blackfoot Crossing, near Gleichen, east of Calgary. The tribe refused to settle with the Blackfoot, and Bull Head kept his sights on land his scouts discovered near Calgary. The location near Fish Creek had pine trees for building good log cabins, and as the story goes, each tribe member added a rock to the pile to mark the site. Today, it is said, the stone cairn still stands.

The chief kept his people on the move until he wisely petitioned Ottawa in 1881 for the reserve he had chosen and was granted his request shortly after. His people built log homes and planted crops, but even though they were a fiercely independent people the closeness of Calgary had a corruptive effect on them and disease weakened them further. Many clung to traditional lifestyles, hunting in the nearby Rocky Mountains and spending winters camped in the foothills away from the white-man's influence.[2] Louise can only imagine how awful it must have been for her once-proud and plentiful people

to have been herded on to the reserve to face disease and demor-
alization.

"My father said our name is Tsuut'ina because there used to be so
many of us," she mentions. The word means "earth people," which
refers to the tribe once having been as plentiful as grains of earth
or sand, writes Hugh Dempsey.[3] Louise remembers her father telling her about a time when, as a little boy, he was forbidden to play
with another tribal member because the child was a stranger. "My
father's mother came out and told him, 'No, you can't play with him.
You don't even know who he is.' That gives you an idea of how many
people there were, they didn't even know each other."

Louise explains her people come from the hardy northern Beaver,
or Dene, people who live on reserves in Alberta and British Columbia. The Tsuut'ina split away hundreds of years ago.

"The Beaver were always on the move, and one time they were
crossing a big lake way up north. As they were coming, a little boy saw
something sticking out from the ice. It was a horn and he wanted it,
so he started crying to his grandmother. Well, you know how gran-
nies are. She knelt down and started chipping the ice to get that horn
out and the ice began to split. Us Tsuut'ina were on this side and the
Dene stayed on the other side."

The Tsuut'ina "stopped around Alberta" and the "Navajo Indians
— our relations" went farther on south, Louise explains. On the prairies, the Tsuut'ina closely aligned themselves with the Blackfoot and
thrived until the white-man's diseases decimated them. In 1869, a
smallpox epidemic reduced the tribe to less than one hundred. Louise says the flu was the big killer in her time. "After the war, when
the army came back, they were giving Indians grey blankets. The old
people said the flu was from those blankets. That was in 1918. The
Tsuut'ina were all dying."

Louise's mom told her the reserve was in a state of shock as some
families lost two or more of their loved ones in a day. At the mission
school, nurses came from Calgary to administer to sick children.

"I was still too young to be in school at that time, but my husband was. One night he was sleeping, and during the night two boys on either side of him in the dormitory died. He said when he woke up in the morning those two boys didn't move. He panicked and started to cry and the matron came rushing in. He was lucky to have survived. He just got a touch of the flu."

The tribe numbered about 160 in 1924, as many fell prey to tuberculosis, but improved living conditions and health care pushed the band up to its population of nine hundred today. But as Louise and other elders stress, the Tsuut'ina are still afflicted. The killers today — especially of young people — have only changed faces.

Our first visit ended on a dark note as Louise worried about Tsuut'ina youth, but when I visited her another day she was in a storytelling mood. She told me her version of a well-loved legend about the "Old Man," the trickster/hero who made the land and who goes by a different name amongst the Blackfoot and Cree. The story went like this:

The Old Man went out walking as he always did. He had no vehicle and no horses, no other way to get around. When he got to the top of a hill, he looked down the valley and saw a beautiful tipi. He walked to it and found his friend inside.

"Come in, come in," his friend said, so the Old Man went in. His friend called to one of his two wives, both of whom were outside tanning a hide, "Come in, come in and feed my friend."

"No, I'm busy out here tanning a hide," his wife replied.

So, the husband grabbed a stick and prayed over it, and then he went outside and hit his wife over the head. He left one wife tanning, but the one he hit came in to cook.

"Husband, we have nothing to cook. We have no food."

The husband stooped over a heap of bark sitting on the ground beside the cold rocks of the fireplace. After making some movements over it, the bark turned to dry meat, beautifully thin, not too tough, and without fat. The wife boiled a pot of water and threw the meat in to cook. So, they all ate and ate. They really enjoyed the cooked meal.

Finally, the Old Man said, "Gee, my friend, do you know we have the very same mystical powers? Why don't you come and visit me sometime? I'll show you." The friend agreed to come, and they said their good-byes, promising to see each other soon.

The Old Man had no wife and no home, but he began to prepare for the visit because his friend might come any day. He asked the first woman he came upon to be his wife and, luckily, she said, "Okay."

"You might see somebody, some day, coming over that hill there. If you do, come and tell me right away," he told her.

One day, the woman ran to the Old Man and told him she saw something coming toward their tipi, away off in the distance. Old Man dropped what he was doing and went into his tipi to wait.

When the friend arrived, Old Man welcomed him and went about being a good host. He called his wife to come in and cook for them.

"No, I'm trying to finish my work outside!" she yelled back.

The Old Man picked up a good-sized stick and hit her over the head with it, but he only knocked her out and she fell down. Fortunately, he was able to revive the poor woman.

"Now, my wife, come in and cook for us," Old Man repeated. But when his wife entered the tipi, there was nothing to prepare.

"Take that bark there and cook it," he instructed her. She looked at him as if he were crazy but obeyed and grabbed a handful of wood and threw it on the fire. It blazed for a moment but then smoked so much the three of them had to run outside for air.

Coughing and choking, tears streaming from his eyes, Old Man shook his head, "My friend, I'm pitiful. I guess I haven't got any more powers." His friend just laughed at him.

1   Hugh A. Dempsey, *Indian Tribes of Alberta* (Calgary, Alberta: Glenbow-Alberta Institute, 1979), p. 41.
2   Ibid., p. 39.
3   Ibid., p. 35.

16

Vanora Big Plume

Tsuut'ina, Tsuut'ina First Nation

Have faith. Have patience. Share all that you have. Everything happens for a reason.

Vanora Big Plume's words are like sweet medicine to my soul after an exceptionally tumultuous six months. I need to slow down and catch my breath, and sitting with Vanora is just what the doctor ordered.

Everyone should have someone like her in their life. She may not say anything you didn't already know, but she makes you understand life's issues in a way you may not have taken to heart, or may have forgotten. Sitting with her, you realize that the universe is unfolding as it should.

Outside of Vanora's west-facing window, the day is becoming night as the sun slowly slides behind the Rocky Mountains. We're sitting in her little office in a building that houses the Headstart program for pre-school children. Here, she teaches the Tsuut'ina language and the tools of her trade are all around us. Colourful cut-outs of letters are tacked to walls, words dance across white boards, and pictures of animals are displayed to capture the children's imagination. Little booklets containing phrases are stacked on shelves. Vanora opens one for me.

"This one is about animals; here's a dog. The word for it in our language is "klu cha." She shows me more pictures of dogs — dogs eating, dogs sleeping, dogs running and walking — all with the phrases explaining their actions underneath in Tsuu'tina. Her grandchildren, she mentions, drew many of the pictures we're looking at.

"I'm trying to make language units. I've got a lot of work to do, but it's good we have something in writing. We start the students with numbers and animals, then we move on to learning foods and things like that."

Another booklet contains pictures of pemmican, frybread, meat and candy. "Klik-on-eh" refers to foods that are sweet. Most Tsuu'tina words are descriptive. Sweet water is the word used for soda pop. The word for frog is "toshkoshi," which translates into "the one who croaks in water."

"A lot of things we didn't have a long time ago, like oatmeal, bacon and rice, so we just said what they looked like in our language." The word for crackers is "something different made out of pastry." A translation Vanora finds especially interesting is the Tsuut'ina word for popcorn. A long time ago when the people saw dried kernels popping in a pot over the fire, they christened the food "ghost spit."

Vanora misses her brothers Clarence and Rodney, and especially her mother, Hilda Big Crow, when it comes to language issues. "They were my support system. My brother Rodney Big Crow was a spiritual person and he left a big space in this world when he died. But I really have faith and when I'm stuck, I pray to my mom. After I sleep, she sends me the information in one way or another. Or I go to my sister Keitha. I can usually count on her."

Vanora's devotion to teaching the Tsuut'ina tongue is crucial since it is one of the most endangered Aboriginal languages in Alberta, along with Beaver, from which it is derived. Today only about sixty of the two thousand band members in the community speak their language fluently, and most of them are elderly.

An ambitious project to create a new pool of Tsuut'ina-speaking teachers was launched in 2011, when Bruce Starlight and other community elders partnered with the University of Calgary to create a language and culture program. The Tsuut'ina Gunaha Institute utilizes European teaching strategies to teach the ancient language.

"The problem that I saw a long time ago is consistency in teaching, and our teaching methods," said institute director Starlight in a January 2011 *Calgary Herald* newspaper article. "We tried to get the elders to teach the language, but they lacked the science of teaching. Then we had a teacher who was trained by the province, and we found that too rigid."

Starlight was referring to the English-as-a-second-language format, which didn't work, but he's hoping the teaching strategies, student engagement, curriculum design and educational environment of the University will help elders teach the language.

"We still have a language pool that is workable, but every time an elder dies, an entire dictionary is lost. You can't do language without the culture. All your value systems, all your mannerisms — everything you do is tied up in the culture. You cannot separate the two."

Also quoted in the newspaper articles about the new institute was Beric Manywounds, one of twenty-three students who signed on to learn his native tongue. A twenty-eight-year-old filmmaker who documents the experience of his people, he struggled with his identity and place in the world, but has come to understand his language holds keys to who he is.

"Society is lost when you lose your language," he was quoted as saying. "It's offered me all kinds of insight into life, and I'm honoured to have a chance to preserve it."

The pre-kindergarden kids who sit in Vanora's Headstart classes are perhaps luckier than Beric. They'll have a jump start in learning their language at a time when their minds are receptive to new information. If all goes as Vanora plans, they will be fluent speakers who uphold their proud and unique heritage.

Out of all nations in Alberta, the Tsuut'ina have the most interesting past. They migrated from their northern Dene homeland to relocate in the south. Surrounded by the Blackfoot Nation, their ancestors intermarried and adopted many of their new neighbour's ways, but steadfastly held on to their Athapaskan language.

In a video featured on the *Blackfoot Digital Library* website, Bruce Starlight tells a story that occurred when his people first arrived in the south, handed down from his elders.

"There was a battle between us and the Bloods. We fought all day and they couldn't beat us. We had no guns and we had no horses. We were a small group but we knew ourselves to be great warriors. We could fight as though we were ten times our number. That's how we established ourselves."

The late Mary One Spot, whom Vanora knew well before she passed away, explained that her people have religious societies and hold sacred bundles as do the Blackfoot. Spiritual power came in dreams and was called "nagha-nastai" (that which I dreamed). The people sought power in a place thought to be the abode of a spirit, like a high hill, an overhanging bank above a dark pool, a remarkable rock or a lonely lake. From four to ten days they ate and drank nothing, all the time praying and trying not to sleep. If a spirit visited, the nature of the revelation was kept a secret until such time as the power was used.

As in other plains cultures, the family arranged marriages, but it's interesting to note that the Tsuut'ina son-in-law was more responsible for his wife's parents than their own sons were. According to E.S. Curtis, who wrote *The North American Indian*, "A man having good luck in acquiring horses was expected to be generous in giving part of them to his wife's brothers and her father. He was in duty bound to divide his game with the occupants of his father-in-law's tipi. Father-in-law and brothers-in-law, after receiving gifts from a man, would try to outdo him in generosity. In times of stress the duty of providing for the family devolved more upon the son-in-law than upon the sons. He endured the greatest hardships for his father-in-law, encouraged by the thought that when his own daughter was married he would receive the same consideration from her husband. In return for his efforts, his mother-in-law kept a new pair of moccasins on hand for him, and prepared special dishes which her daughter carried to her own tipi.[1]

The mother-in-law would never personally deliver the food to her son-in-law because the Tsuut'ina also followed the belief the two should never speak or be together. According to E.S. Curtis, "Should either by chance enter a tipi where the other is, he or she departs immediately, and must then give the other a horse or a present of equal value in order to make up for the shame of the encounter. It is the duty of those in a tipi to warn an approaching individual that the mother-in-law or son-in-law is present in order to avoid these costly meetings. The only time when these two people in this relationship could remain in the same tipi is when the son-in-law's wife or child is dying. Both then sat with their faces covered and averted, addressing each other when necessary, as son and mother."[2]

Curtis wrote that this taboo didn't apply to father-in-law and daughter-in-law, but Tsuut'ina band member Dan Crane begs to differ. "It was the same. That rule would have ensured there was no inappropriate behaviour between a father and his new daughter, just like it kept the mother-in-law and son-in-law from any temptation."

Back in 1857, the explorer John Palliser estimated the Tsuut'ina population at 1,400, but Vanora says epidemics of small pox and scarlet fever reduced their numbers drastically. One of her grandmothers, Louise Big Plume, said in the 1920s tuberculosis hit the reserve hard, and it didn't help that she and other children were so poorly fed at the residential school. Finally, a doctor visited and saw how many Tsuut'ina children were suffering and he declared the community one big sanitorium.

The food served in the school improved after that, and over the years, the Tsuut'ina became strong again.

Vanora agrees that her people are hardy; her own mother was in her nineties when she passed away. A poignant memory involves her mother's constant efforts to get water for her family. "She used to get a couple of barrels and she'd put those in the wagon. We lived on the other side of the reserve so it was quite a distance down to the river. She'd fill up those barrels at least two times a week. In the summertime she'd keep barrels outside to catch the rain, and in the winter she'd melt snow for water."

Vanora grew up poor and attributes her appreciation for everything she has to her austere childhood. "My dad passed away at an early age, so my mother was kind of our father and mother at the same time. She worked hard for us and that's why we worshipped her."

Vanora tells me the same thing many other elders have mentioned, "We didn't have much but we never thought we were poor at all." Vanora had her brothers and sisters to keep her company, and one of their favourite pastimes was to lie on the grass and look up at the stars.

"I used to lie there and think about an old story I heard. It was about a girl who wished a certain star was her husband. The next morning when she went to the river to get water a handsome man came out of the trees and told her he had come for her. When she asked who he was, he told her he was the star she had wished upon the night before. He told her to close her eyes and together they went up into the sky.

"They lived up there and had a child. The husband told her she could do anything in her new land except dig turnips that grew a little distance from their lodge. One day, though, thinking nothing would happen if she dug just one of the vegetables, she used her digging stick to uproot an extra large turnip. When she lifted it out, she saw a hole, and when she looked down she saw a large camp far below. She began to cry because she could see it was the camp of her own people and she missed them dearly.

"When her husband came home that night he saw she had been crying and wanted to know what was wrong. When she told him he scolded her for digging the turnip, but was kind-hearted and told her he would hunt the next day to get skins to cut into strips to make a long rope. When he had the rope made, he wrapped his wife and their child in a hide and tied the rope to it. He lowered them down through the hole.

"Down below, a man was lying on his back gazing into the sky. He saw something black coming down and he and his friends piled all their robes in a heap and the bundle dropped into it. From inside it, a voice told them to move it away quickly because the rope was coming behind. They pulled it away and a great pile of rope came dropping down with a thud. They opened the bundle and there was the girl who had disappeared from camp. Her parents were overjoyed to see her again for they thought she was dead, and they were so happy to see they had a new grandchild, too."

When Vanora finishes the story, we take a break for a cup of tea and she tells me how she remains positive after suffering a challenging life.

"There are so many things that I went through. Tragedies like losing an eight-month-old baby and then two full-grown, mature boys. In 1997 I lost my son in a car accident. He had three children and another one on the way. And then, two or three years ago I lost another one. He was in Edmonton with his wife — she had a conference up there and he went with her. He had a heart attack and died. So, I think for me to survive all of that I had to have strong beliefs in God. And, as I said before, I know they're all still with me. I can feel it. My mom is with me in spirit all the time. I just ask her for guidance to help me with my children."

Vanora prays constantly for her son who is the Tsuut'ina chief. She refuses to discuss any of the issues he faces, especially the contentious subject of the road the City of Calgary would like to punch through the reserve.

"That's his doings and I have no comment. You know lots of people ask me about his business but I just stay away from it."

Vanora's mother used to tell her: "If people criticize you, don't let it get to you. You have to be really strong to just let it go, but if you're weak, your mouth can go on you. If anybody talks about you, just let it go over you." She passes that advice on to her son constantly, since it's impossible for a leader to please everyone.

She also echoes her mother's advice to "be good to people. Be kind and share what you have." The old people said it's better to give than to receive because if you give, you will always be taken care of. You never know when you will receive something you weren't expecting.

I shared a story about the goodness of giving with Vanora during our interview. It came from Eileen Brass, an elder who spoke at a women's gathering I had recently attended. Eileen told us, long ago, her grandmother lived near a well and was always giving away extra food she had to strangers who came for water.

"We never got two helpings of any meals she made because she gave the leftovers to other people," Eileen told us. Following her grandmother's example, Eileen was as generous as she could be to people, and her kindness was repaid one day in a way she could never have anticipated.

"After being in and out of the hospital, I was told my kidneys were failing and I'd need an operation quickly or I would die." Having not yet comprehended how serious her situation was, "never mind thinking about how I would ever find a new kidney," her son's ex-girlfriend, Rhonda, got her blood tested without telling anyone and had been cleared as a compatible donor. Eileen was overwhelmed. Here was someone she wasn't related to, nor was the relationship between her son and Rhonda intact, yet the young woman had stepped forward to help her — perhaps putting herself in danger in the process. Rhonda went through with the donation and she and Eileen are like mother and daughter to this day.

"I helped her with the birth of her baby and we have an amazing relationship," Eileen concluded.

"My mother would love that story," Vanora says. "She'd say it proves that everything happens for a reason. If something happens that doesn't seem good, don't immediately think it's a bad thing. Look at what happened to my granddaughter. Someone ran into the back of her car when she was parked at a convenience store and she had to return the vehicle to the place where she had bought it. While they were doing repairs they found out there was something wrong with that car and they recalled it and gave her a new one. You see? How would she have known she had a faulty car if she hadn't been rear-ended in the first place?"

Vanora leaves me with some final words to think about. "If something happens that you don't like, don't be quick to lash out. There is a reason that it happened and it's for your own good. Be patient, and the reason will become clear to you. Most of the time, if you wait a little bit, the situation will sort itself out anyway and you don't have to do a thing."

17

Albert Lightning

Cree, Ermineskin First Nation

The sun has just come over the Rockies when Albert, already dressed for the day, wakes his son. Perry dresses quickly and wonders what his father wants him to do. Wordlessly, Albert motions to his pipe bag and Perry picks it up, following him out of the tipi. They walk toward the buffalo paddocks at Stoney Park, in the forested foothills of the Morley Reserve, west of Calgary. At the pole gate, Albert lights some sweetgrass and takes his pipebag from Perry, entering the paddock.

From a quarter of a kilometre away, the buffalo come thundering. The big bull eyes the old man as he approaches and Perry worries his father will be knocked down, gored, and trampled. Albert calmly holds out loose sweetgrass from his pipebag and the bull takes it and chews it. The other members of the herd form a loose semicircle around the two, watching.

"Life was interesting with my dad," deadpans Perry Lightning, grinning. He is Albert's third oldest son, and we sit in his kitchen drinking tea as we remember the old man. He tells me Albert adopted him "right out of the hospital" and he became his dad's oskapios (helper), travelling with him and handling his pipe for him in ceremonies. Of course, he adds, "it's weird" to hear people revere him as some great medicine man "because he was just my dad. He certainly didn't agree with that up-on-a-pedestal kind of stuff — he was a humble person. He just had incredible faith in the Creator."

Perry talked about his father's relationship with people around the world. Many met him at the Ecumenical Conference held on the Morley Reserve for many years beginning in 1971. He attended the Annual Micmac Spiritual Convention on the Shubenacadie Reserve in 1976, in Nova Scotia, and reintroduced the sweatlodge there, also visiting several Mi'kmaq communities encouraging traditional spiritual renewal. When skeletal remains in old Mi'kmaq graves were found — victims of a smallpox epidemic — it was Albert who was called upon to lead the spirit-releasing ceremony. He was invited to many other communities, from Arizona to the Northwest Territories and beyond, as his status as a spiritual leader and wisdom keeper grew.

Albert's oldest son Dick Lightning shares with me that he walks in the wake of his father's reputation. In his travels to various meetings and gatherings, upon introducing himself, he is invariably asked if he is related to Albert Lightning. "I joke with them and say, 'Yeah, he's my brother.' They smile and then tell me they heard him speak or they sweated with him or they saw him in a documentary. . . and then I don't even have to be smart or anything, they like me already," he quips.

I'm gratified to hear Albert's buffalo tipi is still kept by the family, and Perry and his wife Trudy are looking forward to putting it up again this summer beside a medicine wheel Albert built many years ago at Morley.

How do you write about a wizened Cree elder, born at the turn of the century, whose life was a bridge between earthly reality and the spirit realms? Should you speak about the disembodied beings who guided him or of his communications with animals, at the risk of overstepping boundaries, perhaps sullying the sacred?

In respect for Ermineskin Band's Albert Lightning (Buffalo Child), who passed away on April 19, 1991, I refrain from relating all he shared with me. I will say, though, that spending time with him was magical, as he told stories about a little person who visited him and of how he communicates with horses.

Albert had asked to see me after reading a draft of the profile I had written about him for this book, so I went to see him on April 15. Though he seemed healthy, I didn't know it would be my last visit with him. He wanted to talk some more about his visit "upstairs" to the Creator's land, of which he had spoken many times before. He talked at length about the second coming of Christ. He also explained that God had shown him all the spirits that his people were given to live with on earth. He urged me to go out on the land by myself to cry to the spirits for their help so they might gift me with a power to help myself and others.

"When I went up to the world above, I saw the whole earth. I didn't see anybody, but I heard a voice. It said, 'Look down. See the world. Any place you think of, you can see it.' I saw Europe. I saw Israel, where Christ walked for thirty-three years on this earth. I put my feet in his footsteps and I saw him go up [to heaven]. Jesus said he would come back to the earth. He didn't say when. Is the world ready for Him?

"Jesus said I would see the second coming," Albert went on. He didn't say which worldly or spiritual realm he would be observing from, but only four days later he passed away as he sat peacefully in his favourite chair before his living-room window. It is a common thing for spiritual elders to know when they are going to die and then call family members and friends close to transfer knowledge before they go.

Albert's second oldest son Rick once asked me, "How are you going to write about my dad? No one will believe it." He advised me that when the old ones tell legends, they are not just fictitious stories. They are reality to elders.

"You'll think they're just stories, and so will most other people. But to him they happened. He experienced them."

Just such a story about Albert was shared with me by someone years ago and I never forgot it. The exact circumstances are vague, but it went something like this: he and his grandfather were sitting in the bush together in the springtime. They were near a booming ground — a place where prairie chickens gather to drum their wings to attract a mate — and Albert's grandfather perceived they were about to begin their sacred dance. He told Albert he could listen to them drum their wings, but that he should be respectful of their movements and keep his eyes closed. The young boy tried hard, but when curiosity to see the spectacle overcame him, he decided his grandfather wouldn't know if he stole a quick peek, so he did. When the drumming ended and his grandfather told Albert to open his eyes, Albert counted only four birds where once there had been five. He asked his grandfather where the fifth one had gone, and his grandfather answered, "My grandson, the one missing forever from this earth is the one you looked at when you opened your eyes."

I wasn't worthy enough to see the little person Albert says comes to visit him, but I know something, perhaps, about that of which he spoke. I have heard stories and read about the May-may-quay-so-wuk, known to the Cree as little people who live far under the ground, among rocky places, and under the water in marshy areas. Cree author Eleanor Brass writes that "only Indians of good character are privileged to see them and, even then, only on rare occasions. Long ago, it was said these little people were crafters of arrowheads, flint knives and stone heads for hammers. These they traded with the Indians for buffalo meat, hides, porcupine quills, and other things they needed but couldn't get for themselves. These tiny people had mysterious powers and often played tricks on the Indians. Hence, everytime anything peculiar happened, they attributed it to the May-may-quay-so-wuk."[1]

While writing this piece about Albert Lightning and the May-may-quay-so-wuk, I came across a story about sightings of little people in northern Canada on the front page of a Yellowknife newspaper. *The Press Independent* described numerous sightings of "little people wearing traditional caribou skins and carrying bows and arrows sighted at different times over the summer in Cambridge Bay."[2]

Apparently, the little people were usually sighted around dusk. Near the local garbage dump, a small stone house with a plywood roof had been found. The matter had been raised in the legislature and Government Leader Dennis Patterson was quoted as saying not only was he well aware of the activity in the Kitikmeot area of the Arctic, he was "glad to hear the little people have been sighted. I think, perhaps, their existence may help promote tourism."

Many people believe the little people still exist; they are said to live near water and some are helpful while others are mischievous. My friend says he saw two paddling down a creek by his house in a canoe, hauling a dead fish that almost filled the entire boat. Another friend says her mother-in-law always left her little friends offerings of sunflower seeds and sample bottles of whiskey. Arnold J. Isbister of Saskatchewan writes extensively about them in his book *Stories Moshum and Kokum Told Me* describing how they move quickly like small animals, are always in good spirits, and have depth in their eyes like they know everything. I could go on and on about little people, but this is a story about Albert Lightning.

If there was an Indian Nobel Peace Prize, Albert Lightning would be a worthy candidate. Fluent in Blackfoot, Cree, Stoney, and English, he has spent a good part of his life promoting unity and reminding people to honour the Creator and His natural laws. Hundreds of boarding passes, issued to him since planes began to fly, attest to his reaching out to First Peoples around the world throughout his life to share cultural information. He sees no difference between religions and helped plan the first Ecumenical Conference at Crow Agency in southeastern Montana back in 1969. It attracted a relatively small crowd of people from varied racial and religious backgrounds inter-ested in spiritual sharing.

"It took a few years for people to start coming. When it finally got going they began to come from all over, from Florida and farther," Albert says. The conference became an annual summer event until well into the '80s.

I first encountered Albert Lightning at the 1987 edition held on southern Alberta's Morley Reserve. The gathering had not been held the year before, and only sporadically in years previous, but had been revived due to a curious event. In early spring of '87, four buffalo had been struck by lightning and killed at Morley's Stoney Park. Traditionally, a buffalo had been butchered and cooked to feed conference guests at Morley, and Chief John Snow treated the deaths of the buffalo at the hand of the Creator as a natural indication the conference should be held the following summer.

Attendance was sparse. Few people knew the conference had been revived, and only about thirty of us gathered under the arbour the first day. After the sacred fire was lit and Albert had performed a pipe ceremony, he spoke about the changes he saw happening to the world and emphasized a return to spirituality. His basic message was that the next century will be spiritual or it will not be at all.

"Don't put off preparing for tomorrow, do it now," he said, urging people to develop good character. In the spirit world everything is open, so don't believe that bad thoughts and actions go unnoticed. Learn to control them, he said. Memories of Albert's talks during the four-day conference have faded with time, but I remember the essence: when you see the right thing to do, hold on to it firmly and don't look at material conditions or consequences. The Creator has planted seeds of truth in you, so you know the right thing to do.

Albert spoke of natural law and how the truth will never lead anyone astray, but individuals must be strong enough to hold on to their good decisions. People must not look for physical or material results from everything they do. Instead, they should pay attention to their dreams and develop their spirits, feeling good about helping others and putting themselves last. They must see what is real in life, not the unreal.

I remember Albert nodding in agreement with Chief John Snow's words to the crowd: "Although people think the grandfathers have abandoned us, what with all the bad things that have been going on in the Indian world, these spirits have always been with us. It is we who have forgotten about them." Albert made it clear he wanted to share his knowledge of the spiritual undercurrents in everyday life with conference delegates and invited them into his magnificently painted "white buffalo" tipi to see black-and-white, poster-sized photographs of spiritual images he had collected. One, taken at the top of a mountain in the Kootenay Plains area of the western Rockies, showed the distinct form of what looked like a veiled figure standing out in white against a grey, cloudy sky.

"I show these pictures because so many people need to see proof before they will believe. I show them so people might come closer to believing in the spirit world and that the Creator looks out for us," he told the group.

"Even though some people think cameras and tape recorders shouldn't be taken near spiritual ceremonies, I think differently. It's a way of communicating the traditional ways to others who can't read about them or be fortunate enough to take part in such ceremonies. It's time we stop being secretive about our beliefs and experiences and share them with the world, because the world needs it."

Albert talked a lot about natural law. He said that humans' inner natures are an exact copy of the nature of the universe, and deep knowledge of the self comes from nature. Western society's materialism and technology is unnatural to the point that many people are unaware of natural cycles and energies and even fear insects, animals, trees, and birds. As humans become unbalanced, so does their world. Medicine people understand natural laws and work with varying frequencies of energy to accomplish what seems impossible. They know there is a right time and place for everything and what is possible given a certain set of circumstances. They know when to pick herbs and not to waste anything, because waste is unnatural.

On the second day of the ecumenical conference, Albert presided over the traditional marriage of a young couple from Saskatchewan. He was resplendent in an eagle-feather headdress and deerskin shirt, and the bride, standing before him on a starblanket, joked that the elder was better dressed than both she and her husband. In the old tradition, Albert had spoken to Sunny Day Walker earlier about being a good husband to his wife-to-be Sky Blue Mary Morin. He counselled him to provide for his family and protect them, but to be gentle and avoid jealousy.

About forty people gathered to witness the marriage as Albert prayed to the Creator and Grandfathers to bless the couple. He repeatedly spoke to the guests, drawing them into the sacred fold, making them more than just spectators. His serious elder personality was gone, replaced with humourous antics. His jokes about the lighter side of marriage filled the tipi with laughter.

It would be several years before I caught up with Albert again, although his photograph came to my attention several times. In 1989, I saw him in an old picture at Morley's Nakoda Lodge, standing beside Chief John Snow as an honoured guest at the facility's grand opening. In 1990, he appeared in a newspaper photograph of delegates attending a Northwest Territories meeting to discuss ways of saving a diseased herd of buffalo from being destroyed.

Whoever invited him to that meeting must have been aware of his affinity for the huge, shaggy beasts. They may have known his Cree name is Paskwāw Mostos Awāsis, Buffalo Child, and that brown buffalo are painted on the back of his famous tipi and two white ones stand guard on either side of the door. Perhaps this person also visited his home and took note of the imposing buffalo head that hangs over his fireplace and dominates his living room.

I certainly felt the stuffed animal's glass eyes on me when I visited Albert in the fall of 1990. He told me he had gotten the head from Morley, from a herd the Stoneys raise for meat. The head is huge. What a magnificent animal it must have been! As we sat looking out at the cars zooming along the black strip of Highway 2A that runs past his living-room window, Albert spoke of the animals that once darkened the prairies before train tracks and roads were built.

"The buffalo spirit comes to me when I sing and drum and smudge with sweetgrass. It says, 'I ask the Creator to become many so that I can feed the people once again and meet their needs,'" he says slowly.

As he stares out the window and silence fills the space between us, I ponder what the buffalo spirit means in its communication with the old man. Finally, Albert gives me a clue.

"I believe the earth will renew herself and things will go back to the old way of the Indian."

Albert shares no more about his prophecy. He moves on to the subject of spirit travel and how he learned about plant medicines and the soul during each of his four visits to other realms.

"I was stooking hay and then I was going to thresh, but it snowed. I took my coat off and laid it on a stook. I walked over to the next one and I just went. I left myself. I went upstairs. I was away for about seven hours, they told me after. I went to heaven. It's beautiful there, trees and grass. It looks a bit like here but a lot nicer.

"There are other worlds. I've been to four. It's true that when you die, what happens to your soul depends on how you lived your life here on earth."

In the Cree afterworld, there are seven realms and the soul is sent to the one that relates to the penance it must work out. For example, if someone was greedy during their earth walk, the soul must go to the realm of greed, where it suffers while paying the debt of selfishness and hoarding. Eventually though, heaven is the final resting place. To the Cree, there is no hell, but some spirits become attached to the physical world from whence they came because of strong feelings such as guilt, revenge, and love — emotions retained from their earthly existence. The spirit is caught in limbo until it can be helped into the next world.

Albert recalls a long-ago meeting he had with the spirit of a woman who had just passed away.

"I was in a house like this," Albert says, waving a hand to indicate his kitchen. "People were sitting all around. Beside me there was a doorway, and on the other side of the wall there was a bed and a woman lying on it. While I was talking, she fell asleep. People thought she was sleeping but she died. Her spirit came and talked to me. She said she was going to accompany me in my travels and look ahead for me and let me know how things are going to turn out ahead of time. Her spirit is still with me."

Albert's story offers insight into something that I had heard about spiritual power: someone practising good medicine never brings about an occurrence by personally summoning supernatural powers. He or she is simply told ahead of time what is going to happen and then helps it to happen. And, as Albert said years ago at the Ecumenical Conference, "There is a right time and place for everything."

During subsequent visits with Albert, I learn he was born in 1900 at Pigeon Lake, west of Hobbema, and later moved to the Ermineskin Reserve where he ranched. An oval, sepia-toned photograph hanging in his living-room shows Albert and a woman standing shoulder to shoulder, solemn looks masking youthful features. Since Albert doesn't talk much about his early life, I learn from his son Rick that the picture was taken in 1917 and that the woman is Albert's first wife Mary Baptiste. She died the same year, during the flu epidemic.

"I guess, with such tragedy, he had to grow up pretty quick," comments Rick, who, as a child, accompanied Albert as his server wherever he went.

"It's called ohpikihakan in Cree. It's where an old man takes a son into his family to act as his helper, to look after him and do things that are too difficult for him to do. In turn, he shows the young man his secrets for him to carry on," Rick explains.

"I remember being at some place and getting horses ready for a Horse Dance. We were washing them and decorating them and, before I knew it, I was up on this horse and it was dancing in a circle with the others. It was incredible. The horse danced all by itself. But when it was all over, my dad had to pay for me to be in the ceremony. We drove all the way home without food because he only had enough money for gas. I still wonder why he just didn't tell me I couldn't be in the ceremony before I got caught up in it."

Rick describes himself as the challenge in his dad's life. "I was kind of a bad kid. But I don't remember him ever really getting mad at me. He made me read the dictionary when I was little so I'd know lots of words and be able to speak well. He always told me, 'if you can communicate then you've got it made.'

"His Blackfoot name is Iron Shirt. A long time ago, I guess some Blackfoot wanted to kill him and he told them to go ahead. They thought he was pretty brave to challenge them like that so they left him alone and gave him that name.

"People used to bring their horses to him. He had a way with horses. He could train them to do almost anything. There's a story that there was a bunch of people standing around at some gathering and my dad sent his horse into the crowd to pick the woman who would make a good wife. His horse pulled at a certain woman's sleeve and that was my mom."

Albert doesn't ride horses anymore, but he still goes to as many rodeos as he can, sometimes catching the international finals in Albuquerque, New Mexico. And he is a fixture at Hobbema's annual Christmas rodeo.

Preferring his La-Z-Boy recliner to a horse's back these days, Albert can usually be found sitting before his east-facing picture window and puffing on a Player's Filter. Most mornings he is up at five AM to watch the sun come up. Later in the day, he orders lunch at his son's restaurant just down the road.

He is visited by band members or outsiders like me wanting to talk or hear an old story. He usually obliges, speaking slowly and often bowing his head to touch a spot between his closed eyes with a crooked finger as he searches his memory for the right words.

"I'll tell you about the Peace Hills, why they're named like that," he says when I ask for a story during my last visit with him. "A long time ago, near Wetaskiwin, the Cree were living north of the hill near there and the Blackfoot were camped to the south. Two scouts were sent out, one from each tribe, to spy on each other's camp and report back to the headman. Each scout was carrying a long spear, and as they came over the sides of a hill at the same time their spears happened to touch and cross each other. The scouts were amazed by the way their weapons had come together and they sat down to talk. Subsequently, the two tribes agreed to stop fighting against each other, deciding to live in peace, with the Cree staying in the north and the Blackfoot to the south, not bothering each other."

Just as Albert finishes the story, as if on cue, there is a knock at the door.

"Well, I've got to go," he tells me, getting up from his chair and easily climbing the stairs to his bedroom despite his ninety years. When he returns, dressed for cold weather, he tells me his tipi is standing at the Panee Agriplex at Hobbema and he has been asked to lead a ceremony inside of it to induct the newly elected chief of Ermineskin.

As the truck pulls away with Albert inside, I hop into my own car and return to a city that seems to know nothing of the things the old man talks about.

1   Eleanor Brass, *Medicine Boy and Other Cree Tales* (Calgary, Alberta: Glenbow Museum, 1982, reprinted 1989), n.p.
2   Cooper Langford, "Sightings of Little People Raise Questions" (*The Press Independent*, November 1990), p. 1.

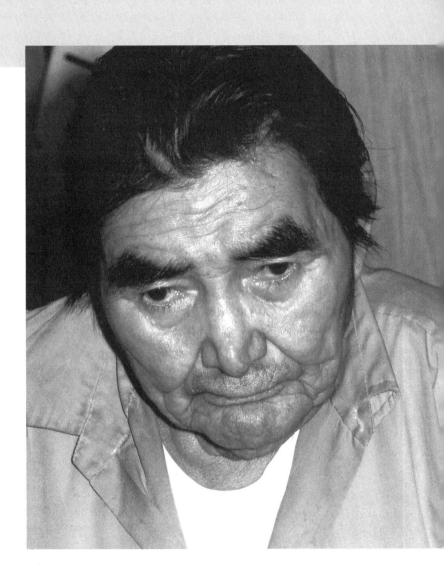

18

Louis Yakinneah

Dene Tha', Meander River (Dene Tha' First Nation)

Louis Yakinneah's eighteen-year-old great granddaughter Vanessa has just landed a job at the health clinic in Meander River. She's still finishing high school but she wants to work and start to support herself. "I passed on to Vanessa something Grandpa Louis used to tell me over and over: things that you need — like your car in the driveway — your neighbour isn't going to come and give you money to pay for it," says Loretta Yakkineah, Vanessa's mother. "He said you have to work for what you need and I think my daughter is realizing what grandpa always said." Coincidentally, Loretta also helps her fellow community members "work for what they need," in her job as an employment councillor for Meander River.

Louis passed away on June 3, 1997, but Loretta, who was raised by him, still feels his spirit with her especially when she gets "stuck." "He was a healer and we always had lots of people coming to our house. I only saw him turn away one person. His way of helping people was through his dreams and I guess this one time he was told he couldn't help that person."

Loretta thinks of her grandfather often, but his memory is especially close every Saturday evening. "That's when Hockey Night in Canada came on and grandpa used to make a big pot of stew and bannock and we'd eat that and watch the game together. He couldn't read or understand English, so I don't think he really understood who was playing or what the score was, but he just liked the fact everyone got together at his house for the evening."

Outside, the mercury dips to minus forty-five Celsius as wind-whipped ice crystals tap-tap against Louis Yakinneah's bedroom window, underscoring his chilling description of a cold and cruel land.

He sits slightly hunched over on his bed in his son Jimmy's home in Meander River. In his quiet voice, he speaks of a raw, challenging life unadorned with material comfort, yet this is not a tough, embittered man. On the contrary, he seems gentle, sad, and kind, and his passage through adversity has given him great ability to feel compassion for others.

The Dene Tha' elder denies he would have traded his younger days on the land for city life, because he agrees with the words of the late Joseph Lafferty of Líídlį Kóé (Fort Simpson), Northwest Territories: "Everything has its place. The feeling is so close to God in the bush. You feel like all the things go exactly as they're supposed to. Everything was just right." [1]

But the climate in which he hunted and trapped in northwestern Alberta extracted a price, and it preys on Louis's health. Years spent working in the bitter cold have weakened his lungs, and his breath is a shallow rasp.

"I don't work now. I just sit at home and eat and rest all day. My chest is no good. If I get a little cold, I get pneumonia. In the summer, I go out and sit in the sun. There were so many times when I was young that I was out and hunting even before the sun came up." When asked about his early life, Louis is silent for a few moments, then says, "If I told you all the stories of how I grew up, you'd be surprised at all the hardship we went through. We were living out in the bush, and there were hardly any people. It was really hard for food.

Food was the only thing in our lives we always had to worry about." Sometimes, there would be nothing to eat in the morning, no food to supply energy needed to walk long distances. "Then my mother would make us a hot cup of tea with a little bit of moose fat in it, just a little piece as big as your little fingernail. Then we'd go out to hunt."

Wild chickens and fish were commonly eaten, and rabbits were good for the stew pot and winter clothing. "If we found rabbit tracks, we'd stay right there and camp. My mother would save rabbit skins to make us coats and blankets," he explains. To make them, she would skin the fur from the bodies the way an apple is peeled, dry the long strips, and then knit them together.

"When we ran out of food and we couldn't get a moose, my dad would go for ducks. Sometimes, we even had to eat baby ducks. We'd have wild onions boiled in a pot with small ducks, and my mom would put a bit of flour in with it."

Louis was born in 1910 "on the muskeg at Little Stoney Creek near Indian Cabins," and his family lived alone in the bush, sometimes joined by relatives. Some of his earliest memories are of checking rabbit snares for his father. "If the rabbit was still alive, it was hard for me to kill it. I didn't know how to kill it — I guess I was too young."

When Louis's father died, the Yakinneah family lost a loved one and food-provider. For little Louis, it seemed life would end without his dad. He had watched his father paddle down rivers in canoes he built from birchbark, tree roots, and spruce gum and return in the evening with something to eat. Who would fish and hunt for the family now?

"After we lost him, I thought we would starve to death. But then my mother said we should stay close to families that have a man so they can help us to eat and not go hungry. I had a lot of brothers and sisters — we were a large family — but people always helped us out." Little Louis matured quickly, and it wasn't long before he learned to use the one trap he owned and then traded his fur for a gun.

"After I got my first gun from the trading post here in Meander River, I was always out hunting for moose. We had to go hunting every day. Every day is your hunting day when you live in the bush. I just about killed myself I worked so hard for my living."

Louis's skills as a hunter and trapper did not go unnoticed. It wasn't long before a couple living west of Meander River called for him to marry their daughter. Sadly, his first wife died of cancer after their only child was born, and the boy was given to an aunt to raise. Later, Louis married again and had three children.

The summer was a busy time for the Dene. "Everyone travelled around making food. We dried and smoked it all. We made baskets out of birchbark to carry it in. In the winter, people had no jobs, we just trapped. I'd be out in the bush for a month and sometimes I ran out of supplies, but I managed to live on tea and meat. We lived in a tipi, and we'd split poplar trees into boards and put those inside around the bottom to keep the cold air out, but it still came in the top.

"Why didn't we ever think about moving south? Well, we knew it was warmer, but how would we have gotten down there? And who else lived down there? Would we be hunting in another tribe's territory?"

Louis, like his ancestors before him, shaped his life to suit the land of his birth. "Even though it was hard, I never did really go hungry. I always had meat for myself and my dogs. I think God watched over us. He must have helped us, especially when my dad died." The harshness of the land, along with its great beauty, molded Louis into a humble, understanding, and religious man who has faith in the ability of nature to provide for his people's needs — for everyone's needs — if it is cared for properly. He wishes people on his reserve didn't have to depend on the stores so much for everything they need.

Jimmy, Louis's son, listens to his father speak and nods his head. But when I ask if he still hunts, he laughs and looks at me incredulously. "No, I'm too scared. Besides, I feel sorry for the animals. I'd rather play bingo. That's where my food comes from," he says, joking.

Though Louis would never mention it, I learn from my interpreter, Maggie Deedza, that the old man is a spiritual advisor and healer. "He helps lots of people. When my sons were drinking, I couldn't sleep. He helped me," she confides. "He has a big heart."

As I write this, I can still see Louis, sitting on his bed wearing a blue work shirt, black pants, and moccasins decorated with flowers wrought in pearly white, bright pink, and red beads. Just as his story of hardship was softened by happy memories, his bare and harshly lit bedroom was brightened by richly coloured holy pictures and relics. I particularly remember the focal point — an ornate crucifix from which streamed long satin ribbons in four colours: white representing God, blue for the Virgin Mary, green for the earth, and red for protection from evil spirits.

1   Lanny Cooke, Líídlį Kóé, *Two Rivers of Faith (Fort Simpson Denendeh)* (Yellowknife, Northwest Territories: CanArctic Graphics Ltd., 1984), p. 17.

19

Dorothy Smallboy

Cree, Mountain Cree Camp (formerly Smallboy's Camp)

Dorothy Smallboy passed away on January 16, 2001 and took with her extensive knowledge about surviving in the mountains. It's been twenty-four years since the first time I visited Smallboy's Camp, now known as The Mountain Cree Camp, and forty-five years since Lazarus Roan and Robert Smallboy led their people from Hobbema to escape change brought by oil money. I speak with Mountain Cree Camp leader and Dorothy's brother, Wayne Roan, before writing this to see how the community is faring. "We lost the school for ten years back when the old ones who brought us here passed away and we worked hard to get it back," he tells me. "Now our Kikino Awasis School is educating fifty-one children and we're proud of our Aboriginal curriculum. Different people come here to teach the students for a while and they're amazed at how quickly they catch on," says Wayne. "The school ensures our young people have a reason to stay here and then find employment in the area."

Wayne says Chief Smallboy told him to put on a Sundance before he passed away and to ensure the spirit and intent of the approximately 180-member *community lived on. "We have a council circle that guides us and we still be-lieve in the pipe," Wayne affirms. The council is negotiating a lease agreement from the Alberta Government to formalize the camp's right to remain where it is. The camp has weathered intrusions from logging, oil and coal-mining companies, and members have to travel further and further to cut firewood, but seasonal ceremonies inspire the people to remain true to the vision of Roan and Smallboy.*

Wayne suggests the animals must be reacting to encroaching development in the eastern slopes of the Rocky Mountains because they are coming closer and closer to Smallboy's. "It's becoming common to see cougars, and the other day a grizzly bear walked right through camp."

The first day of November dawns clear and crisp in the Rocky Mountains. Overnight, six inches of snow has fallen on Smallboy's Camp, and the community awakens to a white world. Tonight, members of the camp established in 1968 by the late Lazarus Roan and Robert Smallboy — Cree visionaries who turned their backs on their oil-rich reserve to return to a rugged and more natural way of life — will take part in a give-away. After a pipe ceremony, each participant will forfeit personal, material objects to show sincerity in thanking the Creator for His provisions and requesting protection through another long winter.

The fading afternoon sun barely lights the kitchen in Joe and Dorothy Smallboy's plywood-walled house, one of the westernmost homes strung along the gravel road bisecting the camp. Lisa Smallboy, twenty-two, scoops flour, baking powder and water into a metal bowl to mix dough, patting it into a circle and carving out neat wedges to fry in oil. A brown grocery bag bulges as she drops golden puffs of frybread into it for tonight's feast.

From somewhere in the yard, a generator kicks in and kitchen lights blaze as Lisa explains why her parents aren't home. "They went to a meeting in Hobbema. They're never home anymore. Mom had it hard before, so she's leaving us at home to do the work and she's travelling all over the place now," she laughs.

Dorothy's youngest daughter Shannon takes advantage of the light and weaves a bracelet on a bead loom for a friend she met last summer. Little Dove, one of the many children Dorothy fostered and whom she adopted, watches the older girl work and then shows off her own handmade yellow-and-black bracelet.

Darkness falls, and the industrious household order is disrupted when a young boy knocks on the door requesting a jar of canned saskatoons for the feast. There is a scramble as the girls pick through Dorothy's well-stocked cupboard, finally locating the prize among almost identical-looking jars of preserved blueberries, saskatoons, and chokecherries.

Joe and Dorothy's youngest son Paul finishes working in the yard and sits in on the kitchen table conversation. When Lisa displays the medal she won for long-distance running at Edmonton's 1990 North American Indigenous Aboriginal Games, Paul jokes that his sister crossed the finish line first only because her competitors were "little girls with shorter legs." Lisa admits to winning by default but is still proud to uphold family tradition.

"Mom used to run in races they had for kids at rodeos. When she won, she got a bag of peanuts," says Lisa. She teases Paul back: "You should talk. You can't even get out of bed in the morning."

The good-natured bantering, smell of cooking frybread, and busy beading fingers speak poignantly of Dorothy in her absence. She once told me I was poor because I had no children, and her meaning hits home as I survey her contented family. She has raised twelve children of her own and had health problems stemming from nursing so many babies, but at fifty-five she is willing to foster more children despite Social Services' advisory that she is too old. "What do they mean? You're never too old to bring up children if you love them," she told me, exasperated with what she considers a pointless government regulation. "We've taken care of so many already. And we were given some pretty sad cases, the worst kids they had, I think."

A case in point is Windy, Little Dove's older sister. When she first came into Dorothy's custody as a two-year-old, she wouldn't eat at the table, running instead to the kitchen garbage can to pick through it for food. She also had chronic diarrhea and bowed legs. Dorothy lavished a mother's love on the child and tied her legs together at night to straighten them while she slept. Exhausted after sitting up nights with Windy for weeks, she finally administered a healthy dose of castor oil.

"It did the trick. She wasn't a sick little kid anymore."

Dorothy's nurturing energy stems from a simple philosophy: "All life is sacred. The Creator owns our bodies and our spirits so we have to take good care of them in His name. But He did give us one thing that's ours — our mind. We choose what we make of ourselves with our minds." It is the job of elders to help people with their minds. Ceremonies help to keep hearts open and curb selfish determination, too. The Creator gifted humans with intelligence, so use it to live a worthwhile life, she advised.

I first met Dorothy in 1988. She was standing in her kitchen, feeding laundry from a mountainous pile into a tiny, apartment-sized washing machine. She stopped her housework to offer me coffee, and we chatted for a while. Anxious about a woman who was going to give birth to her fourth child, she was waiting to be called for the delivery. Dorothy has delivered fifteen babies without mishap at Smallboy's Camp.

"If the mothers follow my advice, there are usually no problems at all. I tell them, 'No driving, no Coke, and no eating oranges or wieners while they're carrying the baby, because they could harm it," she said.

During my 1988 visit, the community was planning a summer's end powwow to mark twenty years since Roan and Smallboy led the dozen or so families away from Hobbema into the Rocky Mountains. The group first settled on the flat Kootenay Plains, southwest of Nordegg, but the close proximity to Highway 11 turned their camp into a tourist attraction. When the Stoney Indians, who lived in and had historic ties to the area, asked them to move, they relocated north. The elders chose a spot near the Cardinal River, south of Edson.

The first year was hell. Winter's cold assaulted Dorothy's twelve-by-fourteen-foot tent as she knitted socks furiously to keep her family's feet warm. Her knowledge of food preservation and sewing became invaluable.

"The only things I took were my cook-stove, my mattress, and my sewing machine. We bought flour and rolled oats, but I made my own jam. We ate berries and wild meat." For warmth, Joe stacked hay bales against the sides of the tent for insulation and built wooden walls the following year to minimize the cold.

"Still, some of the ladies couldn't hack it. . . making fire all winter," Dorothy explained. "I was raised like an Indian so I was used to it. But my husband was a farmer. He had to learn how to hunt."

As Lazarus Roan's oldest daughter, Dorothy spent her life taking care of her brothers and sisters. As a teenager, she cleaned cabins at Ma-Me-O Beach to earn money for groceries. After she was given to her rancher husband in an arranged marriage in 1952, she often spent all day in the saddle rounding up cattle for branding. She took to the rugged lifestyle and hard, physical work of Smallboy's.

"I only remember one winter when we were hungry. It was after we'd moved from Kootenay Plains. It snowed so hard we couldn't get out. We didn't have anything to eat. I guess my dad was telling everyone not to worry. It was just a matter of time before Joe [Dorothy's husband] would run out of sugar and have to make a run to the store. He finally went. Some guys shovelled the snow in front of the truck, and they made it."

The public reacted to media stories about the group's brave attempt to return to their Cree ancestors' lifestyle. Church groups sent truckloads of supplies, but Smallboy's Camp remained poor. Always, there was the temptation to return to Hobbema, only a short drive away. Dorothy confides she never considered returning, but jokes that she would like to collect on all the bets made against the band's toughing it out, because "Nobody thought we could make it."

Lazarus fuelled his daughter's faith in the camp and what it stood for. He had kicked an alcohol problem in his younger years, and

Dorothy watched him flourish in the mountains. His leadership and prophecy kept her firmly rooted to camp life.

"He talked about what would happen if we stayed in Hobbema. He'd pretend he was rolling something with his fingers. . . rolling a cigarette. He said 'tobacco' and 'powder' would be worth lots of money. . . people would go crazy for it. I didn't know what he meant."

Years later, when Leonard Peltier and several other American Indian Movement (AIM) members ran the border to find refuge at the camp following the 1975 Wounded Knee incident, Dorothy realized the substance of her father's vision.

"I remember some guys knocking on our door and asking if they could camp across the road. We didn't think anything of it. We lent them a stove. The next thing I knew there were helicopters and police all over the place. I finally went down to the school to see what was going on. I walked in, and there was a constable there. He said the guys were Americans wanted by the police for murder. There was [confiscated] stuff on the table. . . guns and a pipe and some funny-looking cigarettes and powder. I'd never seen stuff like that before so I asked what it was. The policeman thought I was joking. I said, 'No, we're bush Indians and we've never seen it before.' He told me about drugs. Then I knew what my father meant."

Drugs and gang-related shootings that have plagued the four reserves around Hobbema seem to prove Lazarus right. But since his death in 1977 and Robert Smallboy's in 1985, the stronghold that is Smallboy's Camp has veered away from the elders' strict way of living, assumed a few of the white-man's conveniences and is also experiencing its share of problems.

Even so, Dorothy will never leave. Her father is buried on a grassy hill, amongst spruce trees and facing the Rocky Mountains, a short walk from her house. His grave makes the area all the more sacred to her. At Smallboy's Camp, the curriculum is based on natural law. As Wayne Roan, Dorothy's younger brother, puts it, "All God's creation is a natural element, and the Indian is the interpreter of God's law. We teach that humans are a part of this law but many have separated themselves from nature and being a part of the world. The Indian knows he is one of God's many creations and he is not a separate thing from nature."

In the isolated setting, there is a return to "Indian time," a term Dorothy claims is grossly misunderstood. "I remember I used to get so mad when I was working. Someone would always say, 'Guess she's running on Indian time' whenever someone was late."

Time is not wearing a wristwatch, she explains. There is the sun to tell time. Humans weren't meant to be controlled by something mechanical that says when you should be somewhere or doing something. Time is sacred, a rhythm of life. It is walking with the sun. That is not to say no one stays up late by the light of an electric bulb at Smallboy's, but the pace is slower and the community is more attuned to natural rhythms, like preparing for the changing seasons with ceremonies and preserving food.

And even though hauling water and using outdoor toilets in winter is bothersome, Dorothy is satisfied knowing her children are enjoying a "clean, strong" way of life. She teaches young girls how to preserve food and make dry meat, even if the delicacy "never lasts very long around here no matter how much we make." The boys are taught to build houses and hunt. They grow up at a slower pace, learning their language and the importance of modesty and understanding. "All the kids have Indian names, and the boys and girls are taught to respect each other," she explained. "I'll take the hardship over everything for the sake of my children, just so they're raised the same way I was."

Traditional teachings and Cree culture are intact at Smallboy's, but sitting in Dorothy's kitchen I'm surprised to see a few more modernity's have crept into her house since I last visited, namely a television and a video player. When I pop in early the next day, I learn one of Dorothy's children brought the audio-visual equipment to the house and left it there. Dorothy clears bannock crumbs from the kitchen table and we sit sipping coffee and chatting, while the children watch movies like *The Black Stallion* and *Bambi* over and over again.

"My daughter's youngest son won't eat deer meat because he thinks it's Bambi," Dorothy jokes. She admits to watching a few movies herself once in a while now that she has gone "bead blind" and can no longer decorate powwow outfits and pass away the long winter nights.

"My children buy me all these things. When I first got that gas stove, I burned everything," she laughs. "But we're going to give this house to Paul and Lisa. Joe and I want to build a log house. That's closer to the way I like to live."

The conversation inevitably rolls around to children, and I share my concern about a friend's abortion and the guilt she is experiencing. Dorothy frowns and shakes her head.

"That's bad. Suicide. . . abortion. In our religion, you cannot harm life which the Creator has given."

Prayer is the cornerstone of Dorothy's life. "When I go outside each day I talk to the sky — just saying thanks for the good sleep I had or whatever." She has yet to miss attending a Sundance.

"There's so much in our religion that is the same in the Bible. Jesus fasted forty days, we fast four in the Sundance. To us, one day makes up for ten. The centre pole is the Creator, and we make offerings to Him."

The autumn give-away now taking place, and the summer Sundance, are important ceremonies for giving thanks to the Creator. For healing, sometimes called upon are the spirits of a family that froze to death in the 1930s near the camp because heavy rain had soaked their firewood.

Years ago, Dorothy had need for spiritual intervention to heal internal bleeding. "I could hardly stand up, but I walked around and tried to dance. One of the spirits helped — an old man with a walking stick. Four times I felt a jolt go through me. It was powerful. And the next day I was walking around again.

"There is life after death. How we live our lives in this world determines what kind of spirit we'll be and where we go after we die."

20

Albert & Alma Desjarlais

Cree, East Prairie Metis Settlement

It's late summer and Albert and Alma's front yard is filled with kids. Under a white gazebo, traditional crafts instructor Joyce Hunt is teaching fish scale art, and from inside a tipi I can hear drums as Herman Sutherland shows a group of youths how to play hand games.

As the afternoon winds down, Albert and Alma's son Marcel gathers everyone into a circle to prepare them for tomorrow's sweatlodge ceremony. He tells them what to bring: shorts for the boys and nightgowns for the girls, and everyone should bring a towel. He tells them how the rocks will be heated and water will be splashed on them to release steam. "But if it gets too hot, just say 'all my relations' and we'll open the door for you."

Albert and Alma have been hosting this annual culture camp for several years. As usual, the sweatlodge ceremony is the grand finale for the Aboriginal foster children who attend and, for most, it's their first time. For me, this one is extra special because I finally get to experience the power of love within the Desjarlais family. I've known Albert and Alma for years through their work as elders at the Peace River Correctional Centre, but I've never been to their home to sweat with them. Together, their family sweats every week so everyone knows the songs and they sing loudly and forcefully.

During a soft song, Albert and Alma's granddaughters harmonize and the sound of their blended voices is beautiful. It's so wonderful to see a family in ceremony together and I think to myself, it's true — the family that sweats together, stays together.

"We are a close family," says Alma. "We try and teach the kids our way of life which we went away from for a while some time ago. We also use herbal medicines, the traditional medicines. Our grandkids help us pick medicines and some of them grow as far away as the mountains in B.C. And the fact that they sweat with us and all sing with us — I think that is what brings us together to be a close family."

Albert and Alma are well-known elders who have modelled good behaviour for their family and it has paid off. Together, they had eight children and an adopted daughter. They have twenty-four grandchildren and one great-grandchild.

Their grandchildren are polite and respectful and interested in following in their grandparents' footsteps.

"People are surprised to see our kids follow us so closely, but like I always say, we're not doing this for ourselves, it's for the young people," Albert explains. "Maybe they can get something out of what we are doing here today so these things will guide them as they go through life.

"In the sweatlodge, we are teaching people to handle the ceremony, not only our own kids but whoever wants to come and join us. Joyce, the one teaching fish scale art, she can sing pretty well. I get her to splash the rocks in the lodge. She makes it hot!"

Albert says he can't force anyone into learning to put on sweatlodge ceremonies "but I think Joyce will take it up. She'll make a good elder some day."

James Lamouche, a research officer for the National Aboriginal

Health Organization, has worked closely with the couple in the interest of protecting and promoting traditional healing practices and medicines for the improvement of Aboriginal people's health.

"They are invaluable resources. They've been asked to come to Ottawa by my department and other organizations. In 2007, they travelled to New Zealand to a gathering that included academic researchers and Indigenous elders and healers. Their commitment to each other is amazing, and they are truly dedicated to sharing the knowledge they have openly and freely with others. They're role models. They walk their talk. They're saints. . . at culture camp they allow dozens of kids to overrun their place."

The late Rufus Goodstriker, of the Blood Nation in southern Alberta, said, "There is medicine everywhere and we are just walking all over it." He liked to use wild strawberry for blood problems. "It's an example of a medicine the old people know about. This simple thing out there, the best thing there is. . . are the strawberry strings, leaves, the stem and the roots. Chop them all up and it works on the blood. Of course, I have got the roots I put in, the master root I use. That has a song to it and I talk to it. Because I respect it."

Albert and Alma also respect the many different kinds of plants they work with and are trusted healers. They have been together for more than forty years and their combined knowledge is formidable. They work together as a team and doctor people in the traditional way.

"Sometimes when the grandfathers are talking in the sweatlodge we're counted as one person. Our prayers go together," says Albert. He tells me he met Alma at a dance back in 1965. "Did I know she was the one for me right away? Well, I probably did. I do know, now. It's like we have one mind."

Albert recounts the way the two of them quit smoking. "Alma was at the stove and she was lighting incense and praying. She did this two times before to help me, without me knowing. Then she came and sat at the table. I got my cigarettes out and I pushed them toward her and I said, 'Here, you will have to finish these, I quit.' She said,

'Me, too.' That's what she was praying for, for us to quit, but I didn't know that. We quit right then and there. That was seven years ago."

Albert is a farmer but his spiritual work comes first. I've witnessed one of his sons volunteering to handle the haying when Albert was busy with patients. He admits he and Alma don't get much rest because someone is always driving into their yard looking for help. "It's like that. A lot of people will come to us for medicine as soon as they have problems or are sick. They just know that we can help them."

Albert thinks he and Alma are so successful in healing and advising people because they walk a constant, narrow path and never fall off it.

"You have other medicine people who drink and play slots. To me, I don't really believe in that. If I do that and then try and ask the Creator to help me to help these other people, I don't think my prayers will be answered. The spirits, or God, have to pity you."

Albert says he and his wife enjoy helping people and are happy to hear that someone who was sick has gotten better after seeking their help. "It's not all that easy, but it's part of our job that was given to us by the Creator and we will carry on with it," he affirms.

Since 1985, when his father passed away, Albert has been carrying the family pipe. "I grew up with the sweat, and the pipe that I use to pray to the spirits and lead the sweatlodge ceremony has been in the family since the 1800s. When my dad got sick he started showing me things like how to doctor people. He didn't show me everything but he showed me some of the main things, like what is good for some of the sicknesses people have."

Out of ten boys and six girls in the family, Albert is the one his father chose to learn about medicine and healing.

"But my bothers and sisters believe in it and they come to me when they need help. My oldest brother was sick in the hospital — his kidneys were giving out — and my youngest brother came for help. I talked to him just last night and he said my oldest brother was doing better and he's back at home now. That's how good this stuff is, eh?"

When Albert gets too old to help people, he's going to pass what he knows on to one of his boys. "Each one of them — Larry, George and Marcel — are really good, and my granddaughters who sing in the lodge are following in our path, too."

Albert admits he didn't always follow the straight and narrow, and once served six months in jail for supplying liquor to minors. He stopped drinking while doing time in Fort Saskatchewan in 1962.

"While I was in jail I had this dream. A man came and talked to me. He said I should ask in my prayers to be able to forget about what is taking over me, like this alcohol and bad behaviour. So, right away I started doing that. I prayed twice a day for two years and after that I thought I didn't have to do that so much. It's going to be forty-eight years ago that I quit drinking. I'm so thankful that person came to me because I would be dead by now if it wasn't for him."

Albert quit drinking three years before he met Alma, "so our kids have never seen us drink. I know they respect us for that. Many times I see parents drinking, or they are going to play bingo and they're leaving their kids alone. They don't realize their kids are watching. I tell parents that they are teaching their kids more by what they are doing than by what they are saying to them. Actions speak louder than words."

For seventeen years, the couple has been travelling every two weeks to the Peace River Correctional Centre. The return trip takes them about four hours but they are committed to the inmates there. "We used to lead sweatlodge ceremonies but somewhere in the penal system a rule was broken. The sweat was out in the open and someone threw a dead bird over the fence and that was the end of sweatlodges. It was deemed too risky because inmates might receive things from the outside during those lodges. Now, we're just able to do pipe ceremonies. It did seem like more inmates were staying out of the system when we were able to sweat with them, but we're going to keep helping in whatever way we can."

Arlene Desjarlais, Albert and Alma's daughter, offers the last words in this story about her parents, a tribute to the love her family shares. "My parents have taught us to work together as a family and to come together in good times and in tough times. They have instilled in us that family is important. When my mom was sick in the hospital a few years back, my dad had a hard time seeing her like that. He said it hurt too much. He asked us not to leave the love of his life alone and that he wanted one of us to be there at all times. Not all of my siblings could be there to assist with this task. Val, Marcel, Aunty Sophie and I took turns for the eight weeks of her hospitalization and remained with her twenty-four hours a day. We watched over her, brushed her hair, and showered and massaged her while she was bed-ridden. This care continued until well after she returned home.

"Through all of this we also had someone at home. Mom didn't have to ask; it was expected we would cook and clean for my dad and take care of him, as well.

"We are blessed with the teachings of the pipe, the ceremonies, the lodges, and the songs. Last year, when the house that sheltered the sweatlodge burned, we all felt like someone had died. It was hard to see the flames and hear the roaring fire take the house away from us. My parents lost a lot in there. I remember the next morning the first thing I thought of was the pipes. I phoned Mom to see if the bowls could be found, and they were. I don't know if my Dad will ever get them fixed to be used, especially the one that has been in the family for six generations. One thing my Dad said stayed with me and it is a simple message: 'We already know what happened, we just have to move forward.' Forward, they did go. Many people called and offered help and the house was rebuilt before Christmas. My parents don't have a lot, but they always have something to offer anyone who comes to them. I see how they open their door and their hearts, and never turn anyone away."

21

Dominique Habitant

Beaver, Child Lake First Nation (Eleske)

Up until he was placed in the High Level Hospital's long-term care ward in the summer of 2011, Dominique called me almost every week. Our conversations were eclectic: in the winter he was often in a story-telling mood, laughing about the funny things that happened to him in his younger days of riding wild horses in the rodeo, and trapping. If he'd gotten his truck stuck that day, somewhere on a snowy side road on his way to Fort Vermilion, I'd hear all about it. In the springtime he'd tell me how many new calves had been born into the small herd he kept. As July drew near, he'd always ask me to buy grandstand tickets to the Calgary Stampede rodeo, because as an ex-bareback rider himself, he wanted to see the greatest show on earth once more before he died. Or, he'd ask if I was coming up to the annual Catholic Eleske Pilgrimage he and his wife Madeline always helped out with.

Sometimes he'd tell me how his diabetes was acting up, and that he always got a handle on it when he went back to starting his day eating porridge. After I gave birth to my son, he called more often, and gave me bits of advice on how to raise him. "Let him walk around outside and just watch where he goes," he'd tell me. "Don't interrupt him. Let him discover this world all by himself." If I was feeling a little down, he told me to always pray and believe that the Creator would take care of me.

More than a few times, I asked him to recount the story of the day his snowmobile quit on him in the middle of a northern lake in a winter blizzard. Toward evening, his fingers were numb from the cold and he couldn't even try to tinker with the motor any longer. Even though it still had gas, the machine was unresponsive. As the temperature dropped and his stomach growled with hunger, he began to fear he might be just as dead as his snowmobile come morning. Desperate, he dropped to his knees and prayed to God as the wind whipped around him. Finally, he tried starting the machine again and, to his surprise, the headlight glowed dimly. Giving it some gas, the motor caught and roared to life. Relieved, he rode home as fast as he dared push the machine, and never did have trouble with it again.

One fall, Dominique phoned to tell me about "a ten-pound" fungus he'd spied growing on an old willow tree in a swampy area not far from his home. He knew I liked to burn the Weekeemasigun as incense and bless myself with it, as many people do with sweetgrass. Willow fungus has an earthy, woodsy smell and some say you can cure migraines by breathing in the smoke. Sometimes it's hard to find these white mushrooms growing on trees, especially one that big, so I remembered Dominique's words when I finally made it up to northern Alberta some months later. We spent a whole afternoon tripping over deadfall and scratching ourselves with wildrose bushes to find it in an ancient willow forest but never did. It didn't matter. Dominique made a good fire and we talked and drank tea. He had aged quite a bit since I'd seen him last and it was obvious just getting out of the house and onto the land was doing him good. The stories came fast and furious until the light failed and we had to get home.

Dominique spoke Beaver fluently, and as he grew older, his knowledge of the Beaver language came into play, and not just among his own people. During a few summers in the early 2000s, two girls flew to Canada from somewhere in Europe to spend afternoons with him learning the fast-disappearing language.

Dominique is always happy and his laugh is unforgettable. In the late '90s we had a Francophone boarder staying with us at our house in Peace River. The *first time he took a phone message from Mr. Habitant, he misheard his name and wrote on a piece of paper "Mr. Happy Time called." I laughed when I saw it. Dominique is Mr. Happy Time to me.*

Dominique Habitant's hair is frozen white in the minus forty-five Celsius weather and his breath billows about his head as he chops down skinny spruce trees. Whacking the branches off, he neatly stacks them on the handle of his upturned axe. The spruce poles he's cut will form the roof, and the branches the floor of his snow camp — a pit hollowed out of the deep snow and sheltered by tall trees.

In the dugout, Dominique's friend Tommy coaxes flames from a pile of cut birch. The wind blows and a shower of icy crystals falls from branches above him causing the fire to smoke and sputter. Dominique laughs as his best hunting buddy scowls and bends over the wood to try again. Tommy and I are in charge of boiling tea water and roasting a split chicken on a stick while Dominique works. He has cut the spruce poles and stuck them in the snow so the ends reach out over the pit. Across these, he stretches canvas to form a roof over one side of the dugout. Spruce branches are interlaced over the icy floor — everything designed to keep heat in.

"This is where I would make my bed," Dominique explains, unrolling a bearskin over the spruce boughs underneath the roof. "We used to use some blankets and canvas for sleeping. With a fire going all night, it's warm in here. Then you can lie back and listen to the coyotes howl. You never had a hotel room as good."

Today, Dominique hauled dry logs from his Eleske First Nation home to camp, with a chainsaw to cut them, but trappers on foot years ago didn't have such luxury. A supply of good wood was crucial when the sun went down and, cold and tired, they needed to get a fire going fast.

"In the summertime, we made sure to leave wood leaning up against trees so it'd be there in the winter. Or you could peel the bark off a tree so it would die and be good and dry by winter," Dominique says.

It is surprisingly warm inside the snow pit. As we sit on the bear robe drinking tea and munching chicken and bannock, Dominique remembers an old trapper's joke.

"In the winter, two trappers were sitting by the fire. One guy said, 'Where I set my traps, there's so many rabbits, their tracks just overlap on each other's and there's no more deep snow. It's all trampled down from their footprints.' The other trapper just laughed and said, 'Hah! That's nothing, you should see my trapline. The rabbits are so thick there, they're piled up in three layers, and the last layer — their fur is still brown!'"

Amidst laughter, I ask Dominique if he killed as many beaver and moose as he says he did in his younger days, or does he tell tall tales, too? He shakes his head and laughs some more, assuring me that he is not fibbing. The conversation switches to trapping.

"If you and your family were out on the trail, the Hudson's Bay would send out dog teams with supplies like groceries and medicine and stuff like that. We sent back moosemeat for the Bay manager. Then, in the summertime, you had to pay for your groceries when you had money from working and selling your fur. Away back, people used to travel all over this land. The Beavers went straight west from here for the winter and then they came back to Mile 16 in the springtime. They hung all their fur robes and winter stuff up in trees." Dominique mouths a Beaver phrase that sounds like dow-oon-nay-a-la-tay, which means something like "they hang things there." He explains the term was used in reference to his people.

"The people stayed around here to pick berries, and they went around Fort Vermilion to make dry meat. They left again in October to go west again, hunting and trapping. They just kept making a big circle."

When I ask Dominique why his people are called Beaver Indians, he laughs and answers, "Well, I guess it's because we're always so busy. There used to be a lot of us. We speak a language like the Slavey, and we talk just like our relatives on the Blueberry Reserve in B.C."

Later, I read in a history book that the Beavers were known as

Tsattine, or Dwellers Among the Beavers, maybe because the Indian name for Peace River, which the Beavers lived near, is Tsades, or River of Beavers. At one time, the Beaver Nation included at least five different bands and they hunted in the area along the Peace River from Fort Vermilion to the Rocky Mountains and as far south as Lesser Slave Lake. Smallpox and other diseases took their toll, and today there are small pockets of Beaver: Dominique's band on the Child's Lake and Boyer River First Nations, at Horse Lake (near Grande Prairie), and in northern B.C. Historically, the Cree drove the Beavers north of Lake Claire and out of their vast hunting grounds, until a truce was finally struck between the two tribes. The River of Beavers was named the Peace River after it was designated as the boundary separating the northern Beavers from their southern Cree opponents.[1]

At fifty-eight, Dominique seldom goes out on his trapline because a foot injury, sustained when a horse stepped on it, makes walking difficult. He keeps busy helping farmers during harvest time and doing odd jobs, seemingly satisfied. But as a younger man, he built a reputation for himself as an excellent hunter and trapper.

"I remember my father tying a ptarmigan's foot around my ankle. He said I'd be able to walk far and fast when I got older and it's true. No one could keep up to me."

Few things, least of all cold weather, threatened Dominique when he was in his prime. A daring spirit and a passion for horses were responsible for some of his wilder adventures. He loves to tell the story of how he tamed a wild stallion, hobbling a mare from the free-running herd as bait. When the male came to sniff the mare, Dominique snuck up from behind and roped him, isolating him in a grove of trees and feeding him every day. Finally, he removed the hobbles from the horse's legs and broke him to a saddle.

"Oh, he was mad. But I broke him and he was the best horse. I could ride him forever and never get sore — his gait was so smooth." Years later, he traded the stallion for a wagon.

And then there was the time Dominique snuck out at midnight

to ride a bucking bronc that no one else dared go near. "But the cinch came undone and the whole saddle flew off, me included," he chuckles.

Dominique was a hardy fellow and could stand more pain than most. Once, determined to rid himself of three aching teeth — one an eye-tooth — he downed some painkillers and yanked the offenders from his jaw. He endured the excruciating pain, which grew as the drug wore off, because he didn't want to bother with seeing a dentist. He admits, though, that sometimes the exertion of living off a harsh land pressed him to his limit.

"I'd be coming home from hunting, hungry and so tired. There were no roads, and in the deep snow I could hardly lift one foot after the other. A few times, I thought about how easy it would be to just fall to the side of the trail and forget about everything. But then I'd remember how much Jesus suffered when he died, and I saw how little my troubles were. Then I got the strength to go on."

Dominique is comfortable talking about spirituality and the powers given his Beaver people by the Creator for survival. He mentions Ah-Ko-Keh, a powerful medicine man, who once saved his people from enemy forces. "Some Dogrib people had come down from the north, and they surrounded a Beaver camp. The people could hear them in the bush all around. Everyone was scared. Shots could ring out any time, and the enemy would take over. So they called for the old man Ah-Ko-Keh to help.

"Ah-Ko-Keh got a birchbark bowl — a big one. He spread out a moosehide and put the bowl on that. He started singing and everyone went into the tipi he was in. After a while, the bullet shells started to roll into that bowl, one by one, until those guys had no more bullets. Then the people heard someone blow a horn. They heard that on both sides of the camp. But after that, they didn't hear any more noise. Those people must have left back for the north."

Dominique thinks Ah-Ko-Keh may be the old man called Sijoli mentioned in a book written about Father Jungbluth, a Catholic missionary who learned to speak Beaver from the old medicine man.

The author writes: "Old, blind Sijoli. . . a patient man. . . smoked his pipe and stared into nothingness." But when the young student told Sijoli his people should be learning to read and write, the old man reacted instantly, asking how those skills would be of help in killing a moose or a duck to survive? The young priest had trouble answering.[2] Father Jungbluth met Sijoli in Eleske in 1936, and the medicine man must have died shortly thereafter.

Dominique tells stories about a man who could slip out of his clothes and fly up to sit on the branch of a tree. His helper animals were the skin-shedding snake and the eagle. Others had healing powers and could lay their hands over cuts to make them heal cleanly.

"I think a long time ago the people lived better. There was no swearing or words like 'hate' among the Beaver. I never heard people say bad words until about twenty years ago. In the bush, you have to think about God. If you want to have food, you pray to God.

"A girl had to be full-grown before a man came to take her away and they got married. As long as that man was a good hunter, the parents gave their girl away. The girl was the boss of herself, the man was the boss of himself. If you married, you married for life because the prophet, God's man, had given you his blessing. You didn't even know about leaving each other. I guess more than ninety years ago, as food got scarce, one good hunter would take three or four wives.

"A good-hearted man, a good hunter, was the one people would make as their head man. If he said something, it was worth thirty people saying it. If you weren't a chief, you only spoke for yourself."

Dominique was taught to live a pure life by his parents, Adeline and Joseph, who raised twelve children in a cabin at Stoney Lake, about twenty-five miles south of Eleske. His father traded for the Hudson's Bay and also ranched beautiful red-black and silver-black foxes for the company. He wanted his son to have medicine, but the responsibility meant the boy had to remain pure and make sacrifices. According to tradition, or requirements determined by the spirits, he had to avoid certain foods, activities, and relationships. He had to live differently than other people in the community.

"Even my clothes were washed apart from everybody else's. But then I got married and let it go."

Dominique left the bush for less than a year to attend the Fort Vermilion boarding-school. The experience is imprinted on his memory.

"I remember night-time at the mission. They put us in a steam room. Oh, it was hot! We rubbed each other's backs, and then they would spray us with a cold-water hose. Some of the kids would just cry. But then we went to bed. In ten minutes, everyone would be asleep."

Back at Stoney Lake, Dominique grew strong as he hunted, trapped, and played through the seasons.

"In the summer, we'd go hunting ducks. When they lost their wing feathers in July, you could find them hidden beneath the grass. In the fall, we'd eat marrow and dry meat. We'd even play a game with bones. We'd put a big one out on the prairie, and then we'd blindfold someone and they'd have to feel for it. Whoever found the bone and broke it open with an axe got to eat the marrow."

He remembers pretending he was a great hunter — mimicking his father and playing with miniature bows and arrows. He got a great kick out of stealing his mother's grease bags. "Mom would cut the bladder out of a moose and wash it real good. Then she'd blow it up and work it and it got bigger and bigger. She'd fill it up with grease. But sometimes I'd steal it before she got that far and chase kids with it. We'd make farting sounds at each other."

February was the time to trap muskrat, when the little animals were fat. Dominique would stand beside the rat nest, rabbit fur wrapped around his legs and neck to protect him from the cold, while his father checked the trap set inside. As his father pulled out the rats, Dominique would take them and swing them by their tails in the snow to dry them off. He set traps himself but couldn't seem to find their nests like his father.

"Then I got smart. I followed a weasel. It knew where the nests were. I got a pole and I could feel the rat house under the snow, where it was soft. Muskrats cut through the ice and push the grass up to make a frame, then they fill it up with mud and twigs and stuff. Sometimes, their houses are four feet high."

After Dominique's father died, his mother used to walk the many miles from Stoney Lake to Eleske. "It used to take her about ten hours, and she always had a big dog with her. We moved on to the reserve when I was about ten. After dad died, it was pretty hard," Dominique concedes. When he was about sixteen, he says he met with his father again, above the earth.

"I thought I just fell asleep and dreamed, but when I woke up I heard someone crying. It was my mother." Apparently, his body had gotten so cold she had given him up for dead. "I saw my father kneeling down and my sister and brother in church. They looked young. Maybe we turn young when we get to heaven. But my father wouldn't talk to me. Mass ended, and all the people left to go home. I followed my father to a big house — a beautiful, three-storey house. When I went to go in, something grabbed me and told me it wasn't time to go into my father's house yet. I was pushed out and I sailed through the air. On earth, I could see a little white spot. As I got closer, I could see it was my body lying there. I went back into it."

Dominique says his people know about the Creator from spirit travels and dreams. "White people have the Bible, but the Beavers didn't write anything down. God came to us in dreams. He told our prophets — the ones who have the drums — to tell us to how to live."

A vision Dominique experienced years later at forty-five helped him kick alcohol abuse. In his dream, he saw horses he once owned, long since dead, hitched to a wagon with a polished and gleaming harness. Underneath the wagon, he saw an opening into the ground. He followed the steps leading downward, only to find he had entered what he surmised was hell.

"It looked hot inside there, no flames, just red. People were crying, and a snake about a foot wide came out of a hole in the wall. I was halfway down the steps into the hole when I saw a man and a woman coming down. I had holy water in my hand. I sprinkled some on those two people, and they made it past the snake. But they were going to hell, and I couldn't help them. I knew I didn't belong there."

Dominique's wife Madeline and his children also deserve credit for helping him become sober. "During the time he was drinking, I'd take the kids to church and we'd pray the rosary that he'd quit," Madeline says. Her parents helped her when Dominique was away drinking and advised her to leave her husband to himself. "I knew if I tried to make him quit he'd just go against me," she explains.

These days, Dominique and Madeline are highly respected in the Fort Vermilion area. Madeline takes care of the church in Eleske and plays an important role in coordinating the annual Eleske Pilgrimage to the grotto built by the late Father Meriman, a missionary who largely influenced the couple's spiritual faith. A few years ago, Dominique was given a drum made by a woman in Meander River, north of High Level, and people came from Chateh, Fort Providence, and Fort Chipewyan to attend the special presentation.

"They told me not to keep my words to myself anymore and that I'm supposed to talk to people about God. Then they talked about my life — the things that happened to me — in front of everyone. That's something to go through."

Although Dominique dreams about going back to live at Stoney Lake, it seems an impossibility because the land his family's cabin used to sit on now belongs to a farmer.

"Maybe I could go back and grow wild rice in the lake, or something," he muses, adding it would be better than staying on the reserve "tied to a pole with the government feeding us like a dog. Everywhere I go now, on the land around here, there are signs saying Keep Out, No Trespassing, No Hunting." Rare, bitter words for Dominique.

Stoney Lake would be a good place to retire, away from electricity, television, and noise, he says. "Someone could find their special gifts if they stay away from people and live in the bush. There's nowhere to go and your mind is peaceful.

"In the bush, you can keep yourself clean. The angels like it clean, and if you keep your soul clean they come closer to you. I think they come closest to us in the winter because the land is pure and white then. It is a time to turn thoughts inward, because the spirit and physical worlds come close and communication with those who have passed on becomes easier," he says.

Instead of cursing the winter, Dominique advocates using the cold season as a time to be quiet and share stories and spiritual practices. The right attitude makes any situation bearable, he says. "If you're sincerely working for the Lord, if you don't live just for yourself on this earth, then you'll always be in the right place. God will put you where you'll be happiest."

Maybe returning to Stoney Lake and growing wild rice is not such an impossibility for Dominique, because living in the bush, where he once trapped muskrats with his beloved father, is where he belongs.

1   Hugh A. Dempsey, *Indian Tribes of Alberta* (Calgary, Alberta: Glenbow-Alberta Institute, 1979), p. 71.
2   Shirlee Smith-Matheson, *Youngblood of the Peace* (Edmonton, Alberta: Lone Pine Publishing, 1986), p. 49.

22

Fred Marcel

Chipewyan, Athabasca Chipewyan First Nation

As Chief of his Chipewyan community between 1954 and 1982, the late Fred Marcel shepherded his people through unprecedented change. The elder's concern about the effect of pollution on wild animals and fish from pulp mills on the Athabasca River was obvious in 1990, but what would he have to say about the impact of today's oil sands development if he were still alive?

Fort Chipewyan, home to more than 1,000 Cree and Chipewyan, is located 300 kilometres downstream from the largest oil sands project in the world. The development has eliminated 602 square kilometers of Boreal forest and emits 29.5 million tonnes of greenhouse gasses annually. The process involves strip-mining bitumen, a tar-like, sandy earth also known as "tar sands," then processing it into various petroleum products. This process produces 1.8 billion litres of liquid toxic waste every day, which is stored in man-made "tailings ponds." These ponds currently hold enough toxic waste to fill 2.2 million Olympic-sized swimming pools.[1]

In 2006, Fort Chipewyan's family physician, Dr. John O'Connor, reported alarmingly high rates of rare and aggressive cancers were killing local residents. As of 2010, band elders reported that cancer had become the leading cause of death in the community. Fear and grief consume Fort Chipewyan as fishermen are finding tumour-laden fish in Lake Athabasca and residents continue to lose their family and friends to cancer.

Athabasca Chipewyan First Nation leadership has called upon the Canadian government for an independent public health inquiry for over a decade but has yet to receive it.

When Fred Marcel was born in 1916 at Jackfish, south of northern Alberta's Lake Athabasca, his father wondered what lay ahead for his son. To the fifty-two-year-old Chipewyan trapper, everything was changing.

A year earlier, at Fort Chipewyan, he had seen the Oblate Mission's Brother Charbonneau sitting in a noisy metal box that moved by itself and smoked like a fire made of wet wood. He had asked around to find out what the thing was called, as he watched the priests use it to haul fish from Goose Island to town, and Brother Leroux had answered, "It's a Ford." And, when he had travelled to the Hudson's Bay Company after a long winter in the bush, the manager had told him he'd better have money next time to buy guns, kettles, and cloth, instead of bringing in fur to trade. Yes, things had changed steadily since that first white man, William Stewart, the fellow his great-great-grandfather must have met — came to make peace between the Cree and his people in 1715 so that the Chipewyan would take their fur east to York Factory.[2]

The trapper was anxious for his young son to grow big enough to accompany him hunting and help check the trapline. At least the boy had more of a chance to grow up than babies born fifty years ago when, his grandmother had told him, five out of seven newborns died.[3] As he peered into his baby boy's round face, he imagined Fred would be good-natured and handsome — a good catch. What kind of girl would he marry? The trapper fancied himself proudly walking down the church aisle at his son's wedding, but first things first, he

thought, as he walked to the mission to ask the priest about baptis-
mal preparation for his baby.

The trapper's son grew up to be a respected member of the community, so much so that the Fort Chipewyan Band made him their
chief. The old man lived to see his son marry in 1942, but, sadly, he
did not live long enough to see his son wear the black, gold-striped,
government-issue suit as chief in 1954. Today, Fred wonders what his
father would have thought of the many fast-paced changes he had to
face during his twenty-eight years of leadership.

"It was hard for me to go and meet with the politicians and work
with the government when I was chief. I had nothing to work from.
I never even had the chance to go to the mission for school," Fred
recalls. Often bewildered at government meetings, he was obliged
to sign final agreements. Developmental and social schemes took
place around Fort Chipewyan whether he or his band liked it or not.
Helpless in the wake of steamroller tactics used to secure natural resources by greedy newcomers, the Indians' way of life in the isolated
wilderness settlement on Lake Athabasca was crushed.

Fred was only four years old when the 1918 epidemic of Spanish in-
fluenza killed hundreds of his people, buried in shallow mass graves.
He saw how the decline of the world fur market, which had made
Fort Chipewyan the "emporium of the north," affected his people.
He witnessed the depletion of fish in the lakes and the loss of trap-
ping areas in the face of government regulation and development.

In the days before the fur trade, when the Chipewyan led a nomadic life following the caribou herds north into the barrenlands,
Fred would have been made a temporary chief, needed only in times
of war or to lead the hunt. But as a chief in the mid-1900s, he led his
people in a fight for a good education system. He realized the traditional ways of living off the land were a thing of the past.

"When I came back from the hospital — I had TB treatment for
two years in Edmonton — the people were waiting for me to take
the position of my mother's brother as chief," Fred explains. Chief-
tainship amongst the Chipewyan had been based on heredity in the

Laviolette-Marcel family since the treaty signing, but Fred felt he could only accept the title if he was elected to it by the people. He asked for an election and won.

"Before I left for the hospital, there were no treaty Indians in town. When I came back, there were quite a few Indians, because the government was pushing them to move in for education."

Some families continued to live outside of town after Fred became chief, and he was kept busy trying to get adequate housing and education for those who did. Since he understood the peoples' attachment to the old way of life and the land, he didn't urge them to move to the settlement.

Fred interrupts the interview, excusing himself from the kitchen table. He returns from his bedroom with a long, black metal tube, and removes a rolled paper from inside. He carefully spreads the official-looking document across the table.

"This is the original treaty signed by Chief Alexander Laviolette in 1899," he says, pointing to a signature. In exchange for vast Chipewyan hunting grounds, Alexander secured land reserves, treaty money, education, health, and social welfare benefits for his people.[4]

Fred flicks a corner of the document with his forefinger and thumb, considering it worthless. Alexander hoped it would mean a better life for children to come and so he signed in trust, but land claims and battles for aboriginal and treaty rights indicate the obligations bound within the treaties have been disavowed by government.

"The government promised a lot of good things. There were a lot of promises made to the Indians. There was a record of them, but they didn't come out with what they said," he says wistfully. "We got free school, free health care, and things like that, but even today the government is cutting back on education."

The Fort Chipewyan Band struggled as change swept over them. It was uncommon for government officials to ask for the Indians' input regarding matters affecting them, and they fought to be recognized.

"In the early '60s, the government told us we would be better off if our education was looked after by the Northlands School Division instead of by the Department of Indian Affairs. They went ahead and took down the crucifixes from the school and that was a big thing for the old people. They wanted the children to be taught religion. They came to me right away, and I went to see the Indian agent. We had a vote, and nobody wanted Northlands School Division here. We fought Indian Affairs, but they didn't want to take it back."

Finally, Fred joined the Indian Association of Alberta, and with that organization's backing he was determined not to lose the next round of battle. At an explosive meeting, the Indians delivered an ultimatum to the government to "put our children's education back under the authority of Indian Affairs within eight days or we'll take them all out of school." On the morning of the eighth day, a telegram arrived from Ottawa saying Indian Affairs would take over again.

Another of Fred's stories — this one about gambling — is indicative of the insensitivity and confusion brought on by law-enforcers in the community. One night, while still Chief of the Fort Chipewyan Band, he joined a few men in a friendly game of poker, playing for ten cents a chip. An RCMP corporal heard about the game and showed up to collect the cards and money and inform them they would have to appear before the magistrate. When the corporal picked Fred up the following week to take him to the barracks, he asked why the chief had allowed himself to be charged for gambling.

"'Well,' I asked him, 'where do you go if you live here in Fort Chip? You go to Peace River, Fort Smith, Swanson Mill, and you go to Uranium City for curling. Why do you go?' 'Because I like it,' he said. I told him, 'Well, us too, we play cards because we like it, and we don't hurt anybody. It's just a small amount of money, and we never knew it was against the law.' We played cards for something to do.

"He looked at me for a second, and then he tore up the statement. He gave me back the money and told me to tell the other men not to come to court. That was crooked work. . . if I hadn't been there he would've told the magistrate to fine the men."

Fines were high and jail sentences long, Fred remembers. Many laws were alien to his people, yet most RCMP displayed a general disinterest in the Chipewyan and their culture. Episodes of misunderstandings between the dominant society and First Nations are plentiful in Fred's mind, but he hasn't grown bitter. However, he has spoken out against recent government decisions to build pulp mills on northern Alberta rivers, fearing that water and forests will be destroyed. He has seen numbers of fish and wild animals decline through the years and thinks environmentally unsafe development will wipe them out. The fact that things haven't changed regarding the government's insensitivity toward his people angers him, but otherwise he is a peaceful man who likes to talk about more carefree times.

"When I was young, I trapped and hunted. I was free to go wherever I wanted and I had my own dogs. I had good dogs from 1940 to '43, and I'd go for any race," he recalls, laughing.

At an even earlier age, he attended Tea Dances with his parents that sometimes lasted for days. He loved to listen to the drummers play and sing while the people moved around the fire and to hear the stories the old people told hour after hour.

"Sometimes, we'd use a big, private house for a hall to have old-timer dances. We'd heat it up with the wood stove, and we'd light the gas lamps. Emile Mercredi would make our music with his fiddle. We'd jig, polka, two-step, foxtrot. . . everyone wanted to slow waltz. But there's nothing now. They don't know about music. They dance any old way, eh?

"We had dances at our house at Jackfish, too, especially at New Year's. The women cooked all day on December 31, and then the men shot off their guns." Jackfish, Fred explains, is traditional Chipewyan land, included within the band's reserve boundaries, on the river system south of Fort Chipewyan and east of Embarras Portage.

Church services were also held regularly at the Marcel residence. "I remember a priest gave my dad an old .44 rifle, and some shells. He used that for his bell. He'd fire two shots and everybody was waiting. Those that lived across the water would get in their boats and start their kickers [motors], or people would come walking. We'd say our beads and sing lots of hymns."

On Sundays, the Lord's law was strictly observed. "We didn't do anything — no work, just church. And even in the bush, my dad would stay home, he wouldn't work. I know before the missionaries came there was a different religion. But the Chipewyan are strong Catholics. As far as I can remember, the Chipewyan have always been spiritual people."

1 Ian Willms, Fort Chipewyan lives in the shadow of Alberta's oil sands, This Magazine, November 2011.
2 Archange J. Brady, A History of Fort Chipewyan (Athabasca, Alberta: Gregorach Printing Ltd., 1983), p. 25.
3 Ibid., p. 13.
4 Ibid.

23

Mary Gallant

Beaver, Bushe River (Dene Tha' First Nation)

In the late 1990s, when I lived on a big farm near Peace River, I used to host women's retreats once a year for the Dene Tha' Wellness Department. Director Mable Giroux and ten or twelve women would travel from Chateh, Bushe River, and Meander River to my home, and for the weekend we would cook together, tell stories, participate in talking circles and make crafts. One year, the late Mary Gallant was in the group. I was happy to see her and asked if she remembered the time I interviewed her. "Yes, and you were late," she admonished me, and then burst into laughter. She was the oldest of the women who came for the retreat that year and I had to admire her for getting out of her comfort zone and opening herself up to a new experience. "Oh, she loved coming to your place," Mable told me many years later when I saw her in High Level. "She mentioned it was so good for the women to get away together like that. She went through lots of hardship in her life, and she knew lots of women in the community — especially the single moms and widowed wives — who were in the same boat. She understood one of the best ways to get through sadness and hard times was *for women to come together and support each other, and that's why she liked those retreats so much."*

As an elder to the Dene Tha' nation, Mary was outspoken to the end of her life. Mable recalls visiting her in the hospital and holding her hand at her bedside. "Mrs. Gallant looked at my hands — I had long nails with polish on them — and she said, 'These hands need to be doing some work.' Coming from a woman who hunted her own food and sewed her own clothes for most of her life, I guess she had the right to say that to me," laughs Mable.

THE SUMMER OF 1928

Mary was beginning to ache from crouching for so long. The neat rows of black soil, dotted with green, seemed to stretch to eternity. She threw another thistle inside the wooden box and stood up to stretch her legs. In the distance, she noticed a nun hurrying toward the garden.

"It's probably time to start baking the bread," Mary thought to herself. Some of the other girls had also noticed the approaching nun and were standing up. Sister Bernadette was shouting something, but Mary couldn't quite make out what she was saying.

"She's calling you," Mary's classmate Sophie said, accusingly. "Now what would she want with you? You never do anything wrong."

Mary ran across the potato rows toward the nun. "Your mother's here," Sister Bernadette said, breathless. "She's got something very important to tell you. Hurry up! She's in Mother Superior's office."

Almost running to keep up with Sister Bernadette, Mary wondered why her mother was here. Her visits had been infrequent since Mary's father had died a year and a half ago. Even though the farm was only ten miles away from the residential school in Fort Vermilion, her mother was too busy caring for Mary's younger brothers and sisters and doing chores to make the trip often. Now she had something important to tell Mary. What could it be? Apprehension crept over her.

Rounding the corner to the school's entrance, Mary saw her mother's team and wagon in the driveway. Sitting in the seat was a young man she'd never seen before. He sat hunched over, head down. As they approached, he snapped his head up, eyes resting on Mary for a brief second, then quickly looked down again. Mary's stomach churned as she suddenly realized why the young man waited outside. By the time she and Sister Bernadette reached the Mother Superior's office, her heart was beating wildly. With a half-hearted greeting to her mother, she lowered herself on to a bench and sat looking down at her hands. Her voice cracked and sounded like someone else's as she answered her mother's questions about her health and school grades. Then, silence.

Finally, her mother spoke. "This guy has come here for you. You're to marry him."

"I don't want to," Mary interrupted. Surprised at her own rudeness, yet unable to keep quiet, she protested, "I only turned sixteen last month, and I don't know this guy. I don't know him."

Her mother continued as though she hadn't heard Mary. "His name is John Kidney and he's a Beaver Indian from Eleske Reserve. Your father said you're to marry him. You can't throw away his words."

THE SPRING OF 1989

"They gave me two hours to decide whether to say yes or no," recalls Mary of that summer day in 1928. "Mother Superior asked me, 'Are you going to take your mother's word or turn her down?' It was bad, very bad if you disobeyed your parents in my time. But I didn't know this guy and I didn't want to marry him. I had never even spoken to him before."

Sitting at the kitchen table in her home on the Bushe River Reserve, the seventy-seven-year-old grandmother recalls how unprepared she was for marriage. She had been in the convent since the age of nine, placed there by her father to learn English, and all she knew of life was prayer and a little book learning. She could scrub pots and pans and help bake enough bread for three hundred, but the thought of caring for and feeding one husband was unthinkable. Mary knew she couldn't disobey her mother and turn down the husband chosen by her beloved father when he was still alive. Yet she hated the idea of spending the rest of her life with this stranger.

"Finally, the sister said, 'Make up your mind because it's getting late.'

"I looked at my mother, and I hated to disobey her and I hated to think about going to a guy I didn't know. And my mother kept saying, 'Your dad has said so before he died.'"

Mary realized she would soon be expected to leave the convent to make room for younger students. If her parents hadn't chosen someone for her, the missionaries would have given her away to someone else. There was no other choice; jobs for young girls were unheard of in 1928.

"So, I finally said yes. We got married right there in the priests' residence, and I went home with John."

Mary still remembers the first meal she cooked for him. "It was rice and raisins. Well, it was good. My husband was supposed to enjoy whatever I cooked, so he ate it."

The newlyweds didn't say much to each other as they settled into their life on the Eleske Reserve. Mary spoke French because John could understand it, but not speak it, and he responded in Beaver, which she understood but could not speak. The limited communication suited them, and just how little they shared is evident in Mary's comments about their first child.

"It took me three years to have a baby — three years to decide whether I wanted a family or not. John never said anything. I never said anything. I just don't know how to describe that. He never talked about anything like that, about children. Besides, he never took a child in his arms, he never did."

Despite the delay in beginning their family, Mary eventually gave John five children, only one of whom survived. A neighbour taught her to bake bannock, cook, and tan hides, and she was urged to learn her husband's language, which she did. She even taught herself how to lace snowshoes with babiche (rawhide lacing) by unstringing an old pair to learn how they were made.

After the birth of their last child, John died of tuberculosis. Mary is still amazed that she and her oldest son avoided contracting the disease. With the death of her husband, Mary's life on the Eleske Reserve came to an end, but the next chapter of her life began more joyously when she met her second husband Henry Gallant.

"This was someone I chose," she says, proudly. "We made our decision to marry together. He was a Dene trapper, and we stayed with our family out in the bush until our oldest girl was nine years old — old enough to be put in school."

Mary wed her sweetheart in 1941, and he took her north to live on his trapline. He built a log cabin some distance from the Meander River town-site, and they worked to live off the land. While Henry trapped and hunted, Mary looked after her babies, gathered and cut wood for fires, snared rabbits and squirrels, gardened, and prepared food.

"I made sure there was always something cooked for a meal. I baked bannock over a fire, or sometimes I fried it. When we were in the cabin, I baked bread. If my husband killed a moose or a caribou or anything, I dried it and smoked it. Ducks and rabbits — I boiled them and made soup from the broth. In the summer, we picked saskatoons and dried or canned them. There were lots of low bush cranberries. I always picked lots of them and made jam." Dried or canned milk, powdered eggs, sugar, and flour were the only foods not provided by the land.

Mary has difficulty explaining two things — how she managed to raise her children on the trapline and why, despite having to do without so often, she always felt contented and sure of her family's welfare in the bush.

"We were so poor at times. We lived off the bush, and we toughed it out." There were days when there was no meat to cook and empty stomachs growled, winters when the children barely had enough clothing to keep warm. But through times of despair, she kept the light of her faith in the Creator shining brightly, "and the Lord looked after us." The family was close and prayed together every day, thanking God for what they had.

Today, she lives comfortably enough in a house without plumbing, yet grows wistful describing a time in her life when she owned few material goods but was surrounded by nature and the affections of her husband and children. Every day was a confirmation of what life really is — love, not heaps of possessions. She worked hard, without argument, beside her husband, and they carved out an existence from the land. Mary says everything "fit together" back then, and life wasn't without its special treats: freshly roasted porcupine meat, jam made from wild strawberries, boiled whitefish broth.

The family lived in a tipi during the summer and a cabin in the winter. Some nights, it was cold enough in the cabin to freeze water in the pail. Still, the children were seldom sick, and when they were Mary searched for remedies outside. She picked wild mint for colds, and cut ratroot (wild ginger) for sore throats and the inner bark from the tamarack tree to treat a sore or cut. She boiled the bark of young poplars to make a medicinal tea to soothe stomachaches and diarrhoea.

Family members each did their share of work around the camp or cabin. Mary grew a garden in the summer and Henry took each of his sons, one by one, into the bush to teach them trapping, snaring, and shooting skills. His sense of humour kept everyone laughing; he was quick with a joke and loved to pull pranks on people, especially on the old man who lived upriver from the Gallants.

"We were staying in a tipi, and this old guy came down the river. It was evening, and he asked if he could camp with us for the night. He looked like such a big man with all his warm clothes on but when he took some off, my husband kidded him about being so skinny. In the morning, Henry brought him a basin to wash himself with. The old man put soap on his face and his eyes were closed. When he was full of soap and rinsing, Henry took the basin and the old man dipped a handful of dirt. He yelled at my husband, but Andrew was just laughing. He told the old man, 'Clean your dirty face.'"

In 1948, Mary moved closer to the Meander River town-site so her oldest daughter could attend school. Henry stayed out on the trapline and brought home what he killed. Mary didn't enjoy him being away, and the separation took its toll on the family's unity. Things continued to get worse after the Gallants moved to Bushe River just outside of High Level in 1963. Henry had difficulty adjusting to working at menial jobs and resorted to alcohol, which eventually killed him ten years ago.

Hard work fills Mary's days now, as it always has. She was working outside on a hide, removing the long hairs that ran down the moose's back with swift strokes of her sharp blade, when I first met her on a Saturday morning. As she piled wood for a fire and measured water into pails, she ignored me, then told me matter-of-factly, "You said you'd be here at ten o'clock. I waited for you. It's way past that now. I have a lot of work to do."

Sheepishly, I gathered my equipment and climbed back into my car. I had assumed she was a typical old person who had a lot of time on her hands. Wrong. She was busier than two women half her age. A few days later, I worked up the courage to phone her again. I apologized, confided that I'd learned a lesson about respecting other people's time and asked if we could try again. Fortunately, she invited me over. At first, she responded stiffly to my questions and thought it strange anyone would be interested in her early life. But, by the end of two hours, she was like my own grandmother, explaining in detail the pranks her second husband played on his friends and describing the joys of bush life she would never experience again.

"I used to get a hide ready to tan in a day. I'd take the flesh off in the morning then I'd turn it over and make a fire underneath it to dry it. I scraped the whole thing before sunset. I was about twenty-eight, and I had muscles. Now, I take a whole week to scrape a hide. I feel useless," Mary continues. When I tell her she still does more work than most men I know, yet manages to look young, she makes a face.

"Aaaaaaah! I have a lot of wrinkles," she snorts derisively, then bursts out laughing. "But, I guess when I die my body is going to lay there for a long time, so I might as well move around a lot now. If I sit, I'll just get weaker and weaker."

24

Arnold Orr with Charlie and Emelia Noskiye

Cree, Chipewyan Lake Settlement

Arnold Orr passed away on December 29, 2000.

Probably the nicest thing about Chipewyan Lake is its size. From the sandy beach, you can scan the entire bowl of water from end to end. At sunset, when the sky is pink and the lake is quicksilver, you can spot black loons howling with laughter at the timid light of the early evening stars.

In the dimming sunlight, looking across the water, you might see Arnold Orr or Charlie Noskiye out in their boats, silhouetted in the fading light as they check their nets. Both elders have always lived in this little northern Alberta paradise, accessible only by airplane in the summer, since no all-weather roads lead to it. They will tell you the little lake is teeming with clean, uncontaminated fish and if you put your net out it will be full in two hours. Charlie's wife Emelia says that over the last two years even the ducks have been more plentiful than ever.

Charlie is a master hunter, and Arnold's skill at building things is unparalleled. Charlie likes to talk about how he killed ducks in his younger days, crawling along the lakeshore and flinging a well-aimed stick to break their necks. Then there are the bears he felled using hand-built, weighted wooden-pole-and-bait traps that caved in to crush prey. Arnold tells his share of survival stories, too, but takes special pride in showing off the drums and miniature snowshoes he crafts. His trademark dovetail design can be seen on the corners of log houses and sheds in Chipewyan Lake, and two films, *Birchbark Canoe* and *Forty Yards of Canvas*, document his almost forgotten building skills. As well, Arnold is one of few people who still build river craft from birchbark and spruce wood, and his masterpieces are on display in Grouard, Edmonton, and German museums.

As a youngster, while Charlie went away summers to hunt with his family, Arnold stayed behind in the settlement with his father who guarded the community stores, which closed for the season.

"The ones who went out in the summer were good hunters. That's why we didn't have to go," says Arnold. "My father didn't care to hunt, so we stayed here and planted a garden." During the long summers while everyone else was away, he learned to craft canoes, snowshoes, toboggans, and drums from his father. He also watched a man named Felix Atkinson build log cabins around Chipewyan Lake and then headed into the bush to cut willows to try and copy the older man's building technique by making miniature models. By the time Arnold turned sixteen, he had learned to cut fine dovetail corners and had graduated from building toys to crafting the real thing.

About one hundred residents live year-round in Chipewyan Lake, having traditional ties with members of the Bigstone Band in Wabasca and the Fort MacKay Band. The lake gets its name from the Chipewyan family which first settled there to net whitefish in its waters. Historians say the Cree began pushing indigenous Dene tribes farther into northern Alberta in the mid-1700s as they searched for food and furs. Arnold's ancestors were among the first tribes to meet British traders on the Hudson Bay in 1600 and grew to depend on the knives, guns, and utensils they received in exchange for furs.

A trading post was established after a Frenchman named Auger canoed northward from North and South Wabasca Lakes along the Wabasca River to discover Chipewyan Lake. As Arnold explains it, when Auger came to the mouth of the Chipewyan River he noticed two moose standing on either side of it. Probably deciding the animals were portents of the rich game he would find if he followed the tributary, Auger paddled in a northeasterly direction until he came to a creek that eventually emptied into Carrot Lake, just northeast of Chipewyan Lake. The explorer eyed the area as a fur emporium and also discovered Island Lake to the south. Arnold estimates Auger's discovery was made a long time ago because, "At that time, there was only sand and a little bit of grass growing on that land in the lake. Now, there are big trees growing there."

In 1915, when Arnold was born, his people were still living off the land, but later began to depend more and more on the Hudson Bay store for supplies, especially as the area gradually became over-hunted and trapped out.

"Every spring the people used to buy a supply of tea, tobacco, and other groceries to last all summer. They bought on credit, but they weren't allowed very much. Toward fall, most people had run out of supplies and they used to have a hard time. Sometimes, they ran out of everything, even flour, and it was early winter before the stores reopened."

Charlie confirms, "There weren't too many moose around a long time ago, so we'd go after caribou or rabbits or beaver. We had no income in the summertime and you can imagine how rough it was." Some of the old trappers used to leave Chipewyan Lake after spring trapping season to hunt whatever they could to fill their stomachs, and didn't return until November.

As youngsters, both Arnold and Charlie hunted ducks and snared rabbits for their families. Says Arnold, "In the morning, we had to get up. We weren't allowed to sleep all day. If a child was called two times and he didn't get up, he would lose his blanket. Today, children sleep as long as they want and that's why they don't know anything about hunting for something to eat. The people raised in the old ways are more lively even than these kids — older people get up in the mornings and they know how to hunt." Arnold remembers all too well shivering through his own hasty trips into the bush to trap beaver in the late spring to get back with a good supply of fur to trade for goods before the store closed. After he married and had six children of his own, he felt more pressure than ever to secure supplies to last through the long summer.

"In the springtime, when there was still snow on the ground, we used to leave here with pack dogs. Sometimes we could start out with dog teams if the ground was frozen. We had no rubber boots, just moccasins, and we went packing in the ice-cold water, searching for fur so we could buy something to live on through the summer. But we couldn't kill too many beaver — the limit was around ten or twelve. There were hardly any beaver around then, not like today when you can see them swimming around in Chipewyan Lake. They're all over now."

Charlie impresses upon me how different the land was when he grew up, unblemished with roads and cut-lines. Hunters travelling in dense bush had to memorize landmarks and mark their trails. Traplines and permits were unheard of, and "You just had your area and everyone respected that."

Although there were plenty of well-worn trails around Chipewyan Lake, Arnold was on his own years ago when he struck out north toward Wood Buffalo Park. To get there, his son Elzear says he had to pass many baselines, each twenty-four miles apart, carrying a map in his mind and a heavy pack on his back all the way.

"They just knew the bush back then. Someone would come to the mouth of a creek, name it in Cree, and then by word of mouth you knew where you were going. You watched the sun for your direction and kept an eye out for landmarks," explains Elzear, who interprets his father's Cree for me.

When Elzear mentions that his grandfather Snowbird lived to be about 117 years old before he passed away in the 1950s, I decide long life must run in the family, noting Arnold's black hair and agile youthfulness. Elzear assures me his grandfather's old age wasn't accidental. "Look at how they lived. Walking and hunting and chopping wood every day. My grandfather lived on vegetables he grew in his garden and ate all the fresh fish he wanted. People went to bed with the sun and breathed unpolluted air."

Elzear predicts his father will live another twenty to thirty years because he exercises and eats healthy food. He is independent and outside much of the time, working in his yard in the summer carving snowshoes and bending wood to make drums, often stopping to chat with his pet squirrel Virginia. He hauls his own winter wood supply with a snowmobile and still likes to go out trapping when he can.

"He's ready to work, always. He won't play cards and he doesn't want to listen to my country music. My mom's sick in the hospital in Edmonton and he wants to go to the city to see her. We told him he wouldn't last a day down there," Elzear says.

Both almost eighty, Charlie and his wife Emelia keep active outdoors, too. He sets nets and traps. She picks berries and cuts meat for drying and pounding. They often travel across the lake from the settlement to their "real home" — their cabin — because it is quiet there.

Charlie remembers people settled "close together and helped each other when they lived on the other side of the lake from here." In a co-operative effort that took only days, they designed and built flat-roofed cabins for heat efficiency when warmed with open, mud-plaster fireplaces.

"Stoves took about two days to make. First, we cut grass and dried it. You needed four poles for the main frame and more to fill the spaces between them. We mixed the grass with mud and plastered over the poles sticking up from the floor." The result was a wide, rough-surfaced column recessed for a fire, over which hung a metal hook for hanging cooking pots.

Resettlement across the lake occurred when a preacher built a school on the south side and asked parents to move. Charlie and Emelia mention how scared people were of early missionaries, "because they would take our children away to Wabasca to school."

The Noskiyes and Arnold are concerned about those who went away to school and, having returned to Chipewyan Lake, no longer raise their children in the old way. The elders blame welfare for making people reluctant to work and say it is almost impossible to get labour crews together in the summer to accomplish community projects.

"My father and about five or six others who had families brought up their children properly, not like now," says Arnold, who observes, "Most children raise themselves today. When youngsters run around outside and make noise after dark, I always think to myself that it's not good to raise children like that."

Arnold attempts to interest them in woodcrafting when he visits schools, teaching basic carving skills and how to make snowshoes and birchbark baskets.

Says Elzear, "One summer, he taught a boy how to make a birchbark canoe, but they didn't quite finish it." A series of snapshots Arnold has depict the laborious step-by-step process of forming the frame on the ground and fitting the bark to it.

"There's a lot of carving involved. You have to carve each rib from spruce," explains Elzear. The wood is easy to bend after soaking in hot water, but it has to be kept moist throughout the process or it will crack, making it necessary to work in the shade and keep the unfinished canoe covered.

"This kind of canoe hasn't got a nail in it — it's just spruce, spruce roots, bark, and spruce gum to seal it. If you've fitted everything just right, it should float," Elzear remarks, making a very complicated process sound easy.

Though Arnold thinks it's good that youngsters learn about woodworking, it is the Cree language he really wants them to retain.

"There are some families here who have children who don't speak Cree. When I talk to these children, they just stare at me and don't answer because they don't understand me. The mothers of these children were raised here, but I guess they talk to their children in English instead of Cree. It's their fault the children have lost their language."

Arnold was sent regularly as a child across the lake by his father to visit and learn from the elders living there. Now, it is heartbreaking for him to see how young people "don't really care for the elders today. They don't want to talk to them. They've lost a lot by not visiting because elders have a lot to tell young people. Young people seem to have a lot of other things to do." Charlie agrees with Arnold and he has tried to think of new ways to talk to young people about their culture, but with no results.

"I just can't find any answers. I think they've gone too far off from the way we used to live," he says.

Like many elders, the Noskiye couple and Arnold refuse to tell stories about subjects or events they didn't actually witness or experience firsthand lest they pass on incorrect information. However, Arnold explains why Cree people avoided looking into each other's eyes when they spoke to one another long ago.

"If you looked directly at someone, it was a sign of disrespect. There was a man here who would look at you from a distance, but when he got close to you he'd always put his head down. Women used to wear scarves to cover the sides of their faces so they couldn't look at anyone."

Elzear mentions his father has been studying the Bible for the last four years, though others in the community have turned their backs on most of the trappings of organized religion after friends and non-Native Christians repeatedly tried to evangelize them over the years. Up until about 1963, the traditional Tea Dance and Wikkokewin (Ancestor's Dance) were held in Chip Lake.

"Then people who'd been living in Wabasca came back and brought the Pentecostal religion with them," Elzear explains, indicating his community has, at times, seemed to be a target for missionaries hoping to transform residents' lives by making them Christians.

From his biblical readings, Arnold says he gains spiritual nourishment and wisdom. He is quick to point out how far away many people have strayed from living in the way God's people were meant to. The most important human endeavours — loving, caring, and helping each other — have to become first in people's minds again, he advises.

"Love is what you have to hold on to, just hang on to that. Don't let it slide from person to person, keep it steady."

Explaining why some old forms of worshipping no longer make sense to him, he describes an idol he once discovered deep in the bush.

"When I was small, I remember finding a little stump about two feet high. It had a face and arms carved with an axe and one old man used to worship it and leave tobacco and other stuff there, even a new gun. I think he was worshipping something of the earth. If all the old man's worship went to that statue, what about God?"

Arnold thinks some dreams and spiritual experiences can be false because "they are only of this earth and won't take you to heaven like the Bible will.

"I learned to read syllabics when I was a small boy, and I remember my father used to have a big black book — the Bible. One day, I went and started reading it, but then I just left it like that. Now, many times today, I'm really sorry I didn't read it and stick to it. The answers are all there."

25

Eve Nanooch

Cree, Fox Lake First Nation

I'm making my way up to Fox Lake in the northeast corner of Alberta. The last time I travelled this way was in 1991, more than twenty years ago. The Secondary Highway just east of Slave Lake is paved now almost to Fort Vermilion, and even the remaining stretch of gravel road is wide and easy to travel. The weather's been rainy and the ditches are swathed in fuchsia fireweed. I'm certain I'll see a moose in a roadside meadow, or a bear browsing the saskatoon bushes, but I see nothing, not even a black crow flying overhead. Maybe it's too hot for animals to be on the move this late afternoon.

The road from John D'or Prairie to the Peace River, where I have to drive my truck onto a ferry to reach Fox Lake on the other side, is another story. It's rutted and washed out in places, and there are a couple of abandoned vehicles along the way. I think of elder Betty Letendre, who told me one winter in the early 2000s her truck went through the Peace River ice as she tried to get to a meeting in Fox Lake. Everyone assured her the ice road would be safe so she sat in shock for a few moments in the cab before scrambling out the window and *onto the truck canopy to make it back to shore. With no way to contact anyone, she started walking this isolated road back to John D'or Prairie, stopping along the way to make a fire and have a smoke to calm her nerves, but she couldn't stop her hands from shaking long enough to light it. Thankfully, people found her, but not before her toes froze so badly they required amputation. I felt apprehensive driving this stretch at the height of summer; how must Betty have felt walking it and slowly freezing in the darkness of a winter night. She knows her life was spared for a reason, and, horrible as the experience was, she says it helped make her the person she is today. Suffice to say, she's a sought-after elder in Edmonton.*

So, getting to Fox Lake is tricky, but it's an amazing place. The people in the community are as friendly as their land is beautiful. If I can free up six months of my life to learn Cree, I'll come here and be totally immersed in the language, because even the little kids rattle it off easily. For now, I set up my tent for the night in Leon Nanooch's big yard, where there's a handgame tournament going on, but early the next morning I leave the lively drumming and guessing to visit Henri Nanooch, Eve's third oldest son.

The talented artist remembers me and we sit drinking tea in his kitchen. He's still painting, and today he's working on a mural for the local Child and Family Services building. I ask about his mother and am surprised to hear she passed away only five years ago in 2006. She was born on December 14, 1912, so she would have been ninety-four when she died.

"She was in good health right until she went into the hospital," Henri says, thumbing his mother's funeral program. "I always picture her sewing. She was forever making moccasins, or pouches, or liners for mittens. If she didn't have hide, she'd sew things with stroud (a kind of felt). She had so many children I think she was just always thinking about making enough things to keep everybody warm through the winter."

Looking at her picture, I'm taken back to the first time I met her at a long, outdoor Catholic mass held during the annual pilgrimage at Little Red River, the historic site just downriver from Fox Lake where the Hudson's Bay store once stood. I sat behind the serene, steady old woman, wondering how the seventy-six-year-old could sit still as a statue on the hard, backless bench, while I and everyone else fidgeted like monkeys. Her head, crowned with the black beret *she wore when she went out, was bent over her hymn book as she sang in Cree along with the priest, in deep concentration.*

AUGUST 1991

Small and nimble-looking, Eve sits straight-backed on her bed as we talk. She is a forceful woman of few words, especially when she announces "ekosi" (that's all) upon tiring of the interview. When Rosemary, who translates Cree to English for me, later describes her grandmother as a yapper who loves to talk, I decide I must have been treated to the elder's shy side.

I quickly gain an appreciation of the elder's respect for her Creator and the sacredness of life. Early in our conversation, the subject of abortion arises, and she sternly states that babies are a gift to women from the Creator and every mother must accept her children. To kill a baby is to defy the Creator, Eve says. She is a firm believer in the high moral standards of her time, explaining that if a boy and girl from different families were seen talking, it meant they would marry soon. Parents and grandparents watched out for young girls in their families and virtually protected their virginity until marriage. Her words about traditional family life sound much like those of Ojibwe elder and lecturer Art Holmes, who wrote the book *The Grieving Indian*. At a Grande Prairie workshop, he spoke about the prescribed living arrangement in Ojibwe lodges: parents lived by the door of the tipi and the grandparents sat next to them, while the children slept, ate, and played toward the back. If a young man wanted to court a young woman, he first had to pass by the scrutiny of her parents and grandparents.

Eve informs me that self-control was, and still is, the best birth control. She worries that the availability of abortion generally makes people more irresponsible in their sexual habits. The birth of a child is a joyous event, and in Eve's time the raising of many children meant the tribe was getting stronger, though it also meant never-ending work to feed and clothe a large family.

"I had all of my babies on the trapline. Two other families usually watched me and helped me. I raised fourteen children, but I also lost two girls. And I had five miscarriages. If I was lucky, I would have twenty-one children altogether today," she says. She was sixteen when she became the wife of Joseph Nanooch, whose father had come north from the Wabasca Lakes area of Alberta.

"I used to be a little bit wild in my younger days," she explains, describing how she used to run away from her husband when they were first married because she was lonesome and wanted to return home to her kookum (grandmother). Striking out alone and on foot from Nanooch Lake, she would travel in a northwesterly direction toward Pichimoo Lake, a distance of about two hundred kilometres through rugged bush country. The running finally stopped, and she settled into her role as Joseph's wife; it wasn't long before she was pregnant with her first child, Mary. She says the exercise she got while carrying her babies resulted in her having short and easy labour periods. She never gave a second thought to walking long distances and working while pregnant.

Eve states matter-of-factly that the women did all the work in her time. "The man comes home from trapping and hunting, and he just lies there. We had to do everything." This is the first time I've heard an elder speak so straightforwardly about the inequality of workloads between men and women in earlier times.

"Women had to tan hides, snare rabbits, and always cut wood with a two-handled saw, two of us working together, and we had to haul it. It's not easy when you have a big family and you're always on the move."

As the seasons changed and the Nanooch family travelled to various food-gathering sites, in the days long before the government permanently settled them on the Fox Lake Reserve, Eve worked ceaselessly to set and strike camp. "You had to get new poles [for the tent] and new spruce boughs [for the tent floor]. You'd just get everything put up and then you'd have to move again the next day. And always a mossbag [with a baby inside] on your back, whether you were walking or on horseback." Wagons weren't used by her people until around

1949, and although there was "food all around us" to be hunted or picked, the more laborious task of preparing it fell to women.

Eve's son Henri remembers his mother sewing a huge tent to shelter the family in the summertime when they moved to Nanooch Lake, about eighty kilometres southeast of Fox Lake Reserve. "Somewhere, there's a picture of that tent and there's all these heads poking out of the doorway. I bet that tent was about eighteen feet by fourteen. We were the biggest family in the area." Eve and her husband named their last child Napew (Na-pay-o), a Cree word meaning The Man, because he managed to live the first few days after his birth without much nourishment. Eve gave birth to him in the bush and had no milk for him, yet the little boy survived without until the couple could get back to the settlement.

Eve is thankful to the Creator for being blessed with so many children and having good health. "The first time I was ever in the hospital was last fall [1988]," she says. Henri explains leukemia had turned his mother's blood to water, and nine or ten bottles of blood were pumped into her. Her condition was listed as critical — she even had to be fed intravenously — but she pulled through. It wasn't long after she was released from the hospital before she was tanning hides and making moccasins again.

"The only other problems I had were with my teeth, but I never went to a dentist," she comments.

Eve's husband Joseph, who died in 1986, was a well-loved and respected spiritual leader, continually sought out by people for his advice. Henri says his father came from a long line of gifted individuals, and mentions his father's father travelled in spirit to "check out" spots in northern Alberta when he decided to move from the Wabasca area to Nanooch Lake, nor far from present-day Fox Lake.

When Joseph was alive, he used to put up a Wikkotowin, or "a celebration with one another." Joseph made the feast and dance so the people could give thanks to the Creator for all that is given to the people.

The Wikkotowin is a memorial ceremony held to honour family

and friends who passed away recently, or ancestors who died many years ago. It's held in a rectangular lodge made of heavy poplar poles covered with tent canvas, and is more than fifty feet in length.

I will never forget my first glimpse of a Wikkotowin lodge, made luminous by crackling fires shooting sparks up through the open roof into the chilly August night. Sitting toward the back of the lodge, I was far away from the Manito-kan, the sacred "kind of like God" pole decorated with ribbons, around which the ceremonial feast was placed. I was told a little bit about the ceremony, but not enough to fully appreciate the meaning of what took place that night. It lasted from around midnight until late morning. We ate twice during it, always giving some of our food back to the hard-working servers who then placed it in the fire as a sacrificial offering to the Creator and the spirits of ancestors. Throughout the night, elders, adults, and children danced slowly and prayerfully around a procession of fires, shuffling to the beat of special, two-headed drums played by singers. Dancers meditated on departed relatives, and, during several of the rounds, dolls containing hair or something else to represent the departed ones were carried. The northern lights often dance above a Wikkotowin. They are the spirits of those who have passed on to the next world. No one stares up at the shimmering lights because such behaviour is disrespectful and the viewer also might entice the spirits to come down to him or her.

Joseph Nanooch's thanksgiving ceremonies were similar to the Wikkotowin, but more joyous. As a pillar of the community, he made sure the people prayed and lived lives befitting what the Creator expected of them. He healed them with his spiritual knowledge and natural medicines. "That's why we were never sick," notes Henri, whose father was the grandson of a Cree who once had four wives, but, as the story goes, he embraced Christianity in the 1800s and was compelled to turn away three of them.

Remembering her grandfather, Rosemary says she fell into a deep depression when he passed away. "I always remember the time I was in the hospital before I had my baby. I was really scared. I was getting panicky, but then I phoned my grandfather. He told me not to scream or cry and not to be scared. He said everything was going to be all right. I heard his voice telling me this, and I settled right down. Everything went okay." She still misses her moosum, remarking that her kookum is not quite the storyteller he used to be. And though her grandmother is a soft touch toward children, she is outspoken when it comes to advising parents on how to raise them.

"She tells you right away what she thinks. She's always warning me about giving my kids too much sweet stuff. Sometimes, it's like she doesn't think of you as an adult. . . she thinks you're still a kid."

Rosemary recalls a humorous story about her grandmother's way of coping with modern-day inventions. "I'd ordered a one-piece sleeper for my little girl, you know, the kind that have the feet in them. I dressed my little baby in them for the first time and then I had to go out, so I left her with kookum. When I got back, she'd cut the feet out of the sleeper and put socks on my little girl's feet. I guess she never had anything like one-piece pyjamas in her time."

Eve's life was nothing near as easy as her granddaughter's, but she takes exception to the view people have about early Indians being poor and having nothing.

"We had everything. Well, you just had to go out on the land to get it. We ate healthy foods — meat and lots of fish." Goldeye, pickerel, and jackfish were abundant in the Birch River, running southwest from Lake Athabasca, and moose were plentiful. "We didn't need any pills. If we were sick, there were lots of herbs. There's a plant for everything. There's even herbs for children. The Creator has provided us with everything we need to live a good life," she says. The moose, for example, provided food, glue, and storage containers, among other things.

"We put water in the intestine, then drained it and dried it. We put food in it, and it kept pretty good in there."

Summers were busy times as Eve worked along with other women to dry fish, meat, and berries for the winter food supply. "We picked lots of low bush and high bush cranberries and blueberries. We dried lots of saskatoons because they don't lose their sweetness. We always made lots of jam, too."

She saved feathers from ducks that were hunted year-round to stuff warm quilts for the winter. "You always had to be well-supplied with everything by fall for the winter. You couldn't be lazy in those days," she says. Henri remembers eating lots of potatoes, carrots, and turnips grown in gardens his mother grew "all over the place."

Before horses came to the Fox Lake area, Eve owned pack dogs to carry her household goods from camp to camp. "I remember I always packed the dogs with two washboards — two because they were made of glass and I was afraid one might break." Later, the family owned horses and eventually purchased a wagon from the Hudson's Bay store.

"That made things better, but I still remember we couldn't all ride in it. There were so many of us, some had to ride on a horse."

26

Charlie Blackman

Chipewyan, Cold Lake First Nations

"More and more the things my grandfather told me are coming into play," says Ron Janvier, Charlie Blackman's grandson. "We can tap into the power of our higher selves, and make miracles happen. We can strengthen our mind and spirit in the ways our elders urged us to, especially by fasting and praying out on the land. These undertakings are written about in new age books—astral travel, animal communication, making water into medicine—but it's what my grandfather talked about a long time ago. He told me we have no control over ourselves. Not one molecule is ours. We belong to the Creator. If you are helping someone, it's not you. It's God working through you.

"I'm sixty-five now, and I still like to travel all over the place, but when I was fifteen I went around the country everywhere, finding work and rambling, as a young man does. One day I decided to go home, and I didn't tell anyone. When the bus dropped me off, there were my grandparents waiting for me. Things like that happened so many times. They could look ahead and knew when people were coming, or certain things were going to happen. Everyone

*loved them. They helped a lot of people with their medicine. I am blessed be-
cause they raised me. They're with me in spirit."*

THE SPRING OF 1917

With each sloshing step Charlie took in the thawed muskeg, he wondered when his father would decide they had enough fur for this trip.
He was tired from dragging his feet through deep water, and all he
could think about was heading for home.

A warm breeze rustled his hair. At least it felt better than the cold
bite of winter's wind, Charlie thought wryly. He looked forward to
summer, but he could hardly tolerate the wet spring that ushered in
the berry-picking days. Now that Charlie was growing older, the seasons were flying by. It seemed days ago, not months, since he and his
dad headed north toward Primrose Lake to trap for the two months
before Christmas.

How proud he had been to buy those blue curtains at the Hudson
Bay store for his mom after their return. He'd been happy to hand
over the seven marten they'd cost him. Smiling to himself, he remembered how she had gotten dad to hang them right after Charlie
gave them to her Christmas morning. She hugged him and said he
was the best son a mother could ask for. After breakfast, his aunties and uncles arrived and what a feast there was! The crackling
skin of mom's fattest goose was delicious, and when he asked for
three helpings of raisin pudding he had gotten them. Later, they
all piled into a caboose and headed off to a fiddle dance that went
so late he finally fell asleep on a bench, waking up only when his
cousin Winston pushed him off the seat on the ride back home. How
surprised he had been to see daylight streaming into the caboose
windows.

And here it was April. The only fur any good now was rats and
beaver. As far as he could see, the water was at least a foot and a half
up the skinny trunks of black spruce and scrub alder. Tattered brown
leaves floated around him, and sometimes he played a game of tug
of war with the mud that pulled at his moccasins. Charlie began to

think he actually preferred winter's cold to this oozy, mucky spring. Right about now, he would have gladly traded a slightly frostbitten face for warm, dry feet wrapped in rabbitskin. Though he had tied his moccasin thongs tightly that morning, the soaking moosehide had stretched and become loose in the water, making walking awkward. He felt the familiar and unpleasant sensation of cold water squishing between his toes.

Charlie figured they still had a lot of walking to do before reaching the cabin. Once there, he hoped to surprise a moose or caribou at the nearby salt lick and they would enjoy fresh, roasted meat for supper.

He slogged on, knowing full well that if he so much as mentioned slowing down, his father would say, "Well, it doesn't matter if you're tired. Just the same, you've got to keep going. When you get home, you won't even remember how played out you were."

Adlard Blackman was tough as a bear and moved effortlessly through the muskeg. From fifty paces behind him, Charlie imagined his father smiling to himself as he listened to chickadees herald warmer weather. The boy focused on his father's back, determined to catch up with him, but his burst of energy soon dwindled and he slowed. Looking down at the whirling water around his churning feet, he became lost in thought again. He wondered if his father would let him keep some of the money for this catch of furs. Now that he was getting older, he was starting to go out on his own to hunt and trap. He caught as many marten and white fox in his traps as his father did — well, almost as many — and trapped his share of muskrat in their grass lodges. Yet until last Christmas, his father had never given him any money for animals he had killed, spending it all on clothes and grub for the family.

Charlie imagined the feel of a new rifle in his hands, the one that sat in the polished gun case at the trading post. With that rifle, maybe his Chipewyan people would start calling him Dene Nakaholtherie — The One Who Makes a Good Living. He would shoot many animals if only his dad would let him buy it.

Charlie looked up to check for his father and was surprised to see him only a few yards ahead, leaning against the trunk of a fallen spruce.

"I'm sick, son," he heard his father gasp. Alarmed, Charlie rushed to his side. "It's like everything is moving around me. My stomach's not good."

Charlie looked around, wondering where his father could lay down on the muskeg. "There's an island that way," Adlard said through clenched teeth, pointing eastward. Charlie braced himself as his father leaned heavily against him. Slowly, they began walking, and just when it seemed Adlard was mistaken about the island Charlie noticed a thicket of willow and birch clustered on a small rise. It would be dry there.

As his father sat almost doubled over in pain, Charlie bucked a dead spruce with his axe and started a small fire. Then, he cut and tore out a patch of long, dried grass, using his knife and hands. When he reached dirt, he dug a shallow pit, lining it with dried leaves, grass, and spruce boughs he gathered. He didn't know how long his father would need to rest, but he wanted him to be comfortable. If only they could have reached the cabin!

THE SUMMER OF 1990

"We stayed on that island for four days," says Charlie Blackman, using his cane to push himself up in his living-room chair. The eighty-five-year-old former chief of the Cold Lake reserves, now known as Cold Lake First Nations, has clear memories of trapping and hunting with his father as a boy.

"I dug a little hole, just like a bear would, in the side of a hill. My dad was sleeping in there and I made a fire. Pretty soon, he drank a little tea. Then I killed a moose. We put the front quarter right there by the fire and it cooked. He ate a little bit and pretty soon he felt better. We started walking in the water again. It was a long way to come back home."

Charlie's beloved father was the centre of his life when he was younger. Together, the two travelled countless miles in the bush of Alberta and Saskatchewan. An industrious, strict man, Adlard led a prosperous life.

"He bought cattle and horses. We had over a hundred head of cattle and over fifty horses. He had everything. He never lived to be very old. He died when he was fifty-nine, in 1939. He used to work hard. . . hard! That's why he didn't live long."

A large, framed sketch of Adlard hangs in Charlie's living room, portraying a handsome, moustached face underneath a wide-brimmed hat. With a kerchief tied around his neck, he looks like an early Canadian settler.

"He was kind-hearted. If someone came to visit he always had to give them something — a horse or a cow," says Charlie. But Adlard was stingy when it came to forgiving his growing son's disobedience and dishonesty.

"My grandfather Louis was blind. I used to steal chewing tobacco from him. I cut a little off the plug and then put it back. He must have noticed the tobacco got smaller and smaller."

When Adlard learned of his son's dishonesty he gave his son a sound whipping. "I never stole again. I cried so hard," Charlie says, shaking his head.

"Long time ago, my father said I could take a horse to go see my friends. I had to be back by the time he said or 'You'll be walking,' he told me. I went to see our neighbours and they told me to stay overnight, so I did." The next morning being Sunday, Charlie rode his horse to church and tied it outside, but when mass ended he was surprised to find his horse missing.

"I had to walk six miles back and then I went straight to the barn. There was my saddle so I knew Dad had brought the horse back." Charlie's father had wasted no time enforcing his punishment, but the walk home from church wasn't the end of it. "My dad said, 'Next morning, you go to work, but you walk.' So I did. I got up real early, and I got there before breakfast."

Of course, as in most families, grandparents softened disciplinary blows to their grandchildren, and Charlie's grandfather was no exception.

"I used to love him. He cried, too, when I got whipped for stealing. When he died, I lay down on the toboggan and I just cried. We went away from where we lived after he died."

As the old story goes, Charlie's grandfather's grandfather was an orphan baby saved by an old couple who found him in the snow in the 1700s.

"Long time ago, people used to pack and travel all over. The people left this old man and woman behind; they killed a moose for them and then they went away. Pretty soon, the old man went to see if they left anything behind. The old man heard something and he pushed the snow away and there was a baby. Somebody packed this baby — his mother and father died — and they put him down. The old man ran back and asked his wife if they could raise the baby and she shouted at him, 'Go, run and get it!' They made a bed and they fed him and that baby got fat. That's what his name was — Fat Orphan — and he's where we came from. I'm fifth generation from him.

"You know, our name's not really Blackman. My grandfather's brother was dark and the white people called him Blackman," Charlie adds.

Almost a baby himself when his father first strapped him to a toboggan, Charlie recalls his first trips on the trapline, riding behind his father's dog team. "I must have been pretty young. He used to go trapping, and I stayed in the tent alone. I chopped lots of wood, and he made me stay there. Sometimes, he didn't come home for a long time, late at night. If he didn't come home, I thought maybe something had happened to him and I cried and sat in the tent. And then, soon as he came back, well, I was glad right away again, you know. Pretty soon I started to trap a little bit myself, and one time my dad shot a cow moose and then the calf ran away, but then he came back and he stood there. My dad held me up and, with the gun, he made me shoot that calf. I shot and he fell down. Oh, I was happy because

I thought nobody ever killed a moose like that before. I was about ten, I think."

Adlard crafted a pair of miniature snowshoes so his son could "tramp down the snow and make a route for the dogs." With Adlard pushing the sled from behind, the two often travelled northeast of Cold Lake to Saskatchewan's Primrose Lake, where the animals were plentiful.

"I killed some fur just like my dad, and he showed me how to fix [skin and dry] it. Then I killed something and I packed the meat on my back and I was happy. So I wanted to go again."

It wasn't long before Charlie was venturing out on his own, trapping as much fur as his father. "But in those days, we're not the boss. What I killed, I didn't get anything [paid] for it. My dad got it all."

Charlie fast became a skilful hunter, but, as he tells it, killing the animal was one thing — getting it out of the bush, another. "One time we had no meat for the dogs, no nothing. My dad got up in the morning to hunt, and he told me to set traps for rabbits. I stayed home, but in the evening I packed up and took a .32 revolver, that's all I had — and a box of fifty shells. I remembered about a salt lick where there were always animals, so I went down there to see. When I got there, I saw three caribou. I lay down and pretty soon one came about ten feet from me and I shot. He fell down, and those other two — I shot and shot — but I only got one.

"I went back to the camp and hitched up the dogs to pull that caribou on the ground. So I tied a rope around the caribou's neck and hooked it up to the harness. We started off all right, but then the caribou went in a hole and it stayed there. So I went back to get the toboggan and hitched up the dogs to it. I took my knife, and I started to cut up the caribou to make it lighter. Pretty soon I heard my dad holler, 'What did you do, kill a bear?' 'No,' I said, 'I got a caribou down here.' Well, he came down there so fast and, oh, he just pulled the skin and stepped on that caribou and the hide came off. We put that meat on the toboggan and went home. Then the dogs ate. We ate too!"

Charlie's stories of successful hunts and trapping expeditions are endless. Hilarious tales of how he and his father outwitted a troublesome game warden who continually attempted to confiscate meat and furs contrast sharply with more sober stories of racial discrimination and cattle rustling on the part of white newcomers to the area. His disputes with the government continue, and when politicians slapped a ban on fishing in Cold Lake around 1987, Charlie attended a public information meeting to find out why.

"'Because the fish are spawning,' a guy told me. I told him I'm over eighty years old and I never saw fish spawn at this time, only in spring or fall. 'What I know is white people are spawning; they are taking over. Us, we're poor and we fish every day for our food,'" the elder responded.

Since there was no man-against-nature content in Charlie's stories, I surmise that coping with the earth's forces was nothing compared to the upheaval caused by the white man's rules and regulations. In fact, when I ask a question about how the Chipewyan dealt with freezing winters, the question is brushed off.

"It was sixty below [Fahrenheit] sometimes. We had no overcoats or parkas, just some kind of a jacket or sometimes my mother would make a moosehide coat. We had no overshoes. We would kill a rabbit and put rabbitskin in our moccasins — with our socks, and our feet never got cold. In the spring, you get wet walking in water all day. You take extra clothes and dry the wet ones at night. We always took a little skin [moosehide] so when we broke our moccasins, we could sew them. Then, ready again!"

Summers, Charlie helped his dad in the fields, growing wheat and other cereal crops. "I drove the horses, and my dad ploughed. How many days did we have to do that? Then, we started disking. Our granaries were full of grain. Every year, we hauled it down to St. Paul, three big loads of wheat. My dad sold two loads, and with the third he made flour, enough to last all year."

Charlie claims the land around Cold Lake is excellent for farming. "I know this land. I was born three miles from here," he says, indicating the north end of the reserve were his house stands, near Highway 28.

When Charlie married Lenore Jacko at twenty, his bride became his new hunting and trapping partner. Adlard arranged the marriage, but until the wedding day the couple had hardly spoken to each other.

"I'd seen her, but I didn't talk to her. Maybe we said 'hello' to each other, that's all. But after we got married, we went wherever we wanted. We killed a moose in the bush. We made dry meat, pemmican, and then moosehide for moccasins. We lived together for fifty-seven years."

From the way Charlie's daughter Matilda describes her mother, Lenore must have brought order to trapline living. "She was so neat and clean, really fussy about the way she kept things. She passed away in 1981, and, even today, if I try to rearrange something different from the way she had it in the house, my dad won't let me."

Matilda says people flocked to her mother. "She couldn't turn anybody away. If my dad killed a moose, there she'd be, cutting up meat for people, even if there was none left for themselves. Really, I think people maybe took advantage of them."

Lenore is responsible for Charlie's interest in traditional healing. She first learned about natural medicine from a Cree woman from Frog Lake, southeast of Cold Lake. "My wife helped this lady a lot. She interpreted for her because she only spoke Cree. Pretty soon, the old lady started to give away her medicine. They always travelled together, never stayed home. She taught my wife how to kill a cancer," says Charlie.

"Mom had cancer, and here she's helping people to cure cancer," Matilda interjects. "Once in a while, she'd choke when she was eating something, but we never thought it was cancer. We didn't know she had it until it was too late."

Charlie says his wife could foretell the coming of visitors before they arrived on the doorstep, requesting cures for every illness from diabetes to arthritis. "She says, 'Somebody's coming today,' and, sure enough, someone comes. She knows, but not me. I'm not like that. They always have to phone me first," Charlie says, laughing at his own joke.

At first, he only gathered the plants his wife needed but soon began learning about their curative properties as well. The couple helped anybody except those they considered closer to death than life and people they suspected would disrupt treatment by drinking alcohol.

"If you are drinking, what's the use of taking medicine? Alcohol just kills it," Charlie says.

Matilda explains her father lost interest in healing after her mother died, and it has only been two or three years since he started helping people again. Now, he is travelling across Canada and the United States with his "medicine suitcase."

"Last fall, we met a woman from Vancouver Island in Chetwynd. She was so pale, and the doctors had no hope for her. She had cancer, and my dad made a medicine for her. A few months later, in the winter, that woman's mother wrote to me and said she wanted me to thank my dad for her. She said, 'I don't know if it was the prayers or the medicine, but my daughter's well and happy. She's away skiing in Austria, right now,'" says Matilda.

Some of Charlie's patients seem to think, at first, that his medicine is worse than the ailment, especially one woman who pleaded with him to stop her excruciating headaches. He agreed to help her and heated some rocks to begin the treatment, but when he covered her head and invited her to inhale the smoke wafting from some powder he had placed on the stones, she became uncooperative.

"Oh, she didn't like it. She coughed and everything. But I said, 'Never mind, stay there,' and, pretty soon, there's no more smoke. Then, I put water on the rocks and made a steam and she was sweating. But then she got up and said, 'My head is all right,' and she told us later she never got a headache again."

Charlie concedes anyone can learn about plants but cautions that knowledge alone does not make an effective healer. "I'm not bragging about what I told you, but God wants it. If He says no, I can't do it. I can't help the ones who don't believe I can help them through

God. But if they have faith, I tell them, 'You'll be all right.' I say, 'God made medicine for you. Here, take it.'"

Charlie eyes my notebook full of scribbles and unexpectedly hauls himself up from his chair. "You like to eat fish?" he asks. "Matilda is cooking some. It's from Cold Lake. Everywhere I go, I eat fish, but it's not like the fish from here." The whitefish are succulent — fried to a golden brown — and Charlie, Matilda, my friend, and I polish off a stack of fillets along with chunks of puffy bannock, washed down with strong tea. After supper, the old man begins the story of how he survived the flu epidemic of the early 1900s.

"My dad was out in the bush, hunting by a little lake on the re-serve. He heard a little noise, and he found an old lady. She was a trapper, and she slipped on some ice and broke her hip. She had to lie there all night. My dad wondered why she didn't come back and went looking for her. When he found her, she was just shaking. He made a big fire and cut hay so she could sleep there. He made her a hot tea, then he came back for the horses and took her home in a wagon. That old lady told my dad if there was a terrible sickness or something, nothing would happen to his kids. 'Hurricane, tornado. . . your family will miss all that.' Well, you know that flu? A long time ago, lots of people died, but us. . . nothing. I was sick, all right, and my dad was sick, but nobody died. All around here, over ninety peo-ple died. My father-in-law was digging graves day and night. It was chilling to do it.

"Maybe I was ten or eleven. It was 1918. People would start to feel sick and they would be dead within hours. The ones that didn't get sick went from window to window and the people inside told them, 'This many died, that many died.' My dad went down to check on my relatives and they were all dead — my aunt, my mother's brother, my aunt's cousin."

Before too long, Charlie announces he is tired and I leave him to a good night's sleep. Tomorrow, we are off to a Treaty Six meeting on the Joseph Bighead Reserve in Saskatchewan.

When we arrive at the powwow grounds the next day, Charlie sits on a bench under the arbour as passersby stop to shake his hand or sit and talk. Some are old enough to remember the years between 1949 and 1962 when he was chief of the Cold Lake reserves; others know him only as an old-timer. The meeting is late starting, and we leave before any speeches are made. Reluctantly, I say goodbye to Charlie and promise to look for him at the annual Lac Ste. Anne pilgrimage near Edmonton in a couple weeks.

Somehow, I find Charlie's white trapper's tent amidst thousands of campers attending the religious gathering, first held in 1889 when about four hundred people came to the lake to pray for rain. The lake is believed to have healing powers, and many come in wheelchairs and on crutches to bathe in the water.

Charlie sits on a wooden box, chin resting on the curved handle of his cane, speaking to a middle-aged woman. Her scalp shows through thinning hair, and she seeks medicine to make it grow thicker. Charlie instructs her to buy chewing tobacco as an offering for the medicine.

"I'll send her some bear grease," he tells me, after she has gone to make the purchase. "Until then, she can wash her hair in strong, black tea. That helps, too."

Matilda offers me coffee from a thermos and we listen to rain falling lightly on the canvas over our heads. Charlie explains he has missed the pilgrimage only five times since 1920. In those days, everyone came to Lac Ste. Anne in wagons and there were horses tied everywhere; at night, it was quiet except for the barking of dogs.

"I missed it whenever I had to be around for Treaty Days on the reserve. I stayed back to hand out rations," he explains.

Too soon, the woman comes back and I leave Charlie and his "patient" alone. I look back and catch a glimpse of the woman holding a small tin of snuff in her outstretched hand, giving a traditional tobacco offering in return for "medicine from God."

27

Cecile Chambaud

Dene Tha', Meander River (Dene Tha' First Nation)

Cecile passed away at the High Level Hospital on September 30, 1990 at the age of eighty-nine. I am blessed to have been touched by this little woman's lively spirit. I spoke to her in January 1990, during a particularly vicious cold snap in northern Alberta, but her joyful personality warmed me through and through.

The stove in Cecile Chambaud's little house in Meander River, seventy kilometres north of High Level, is spewing heat, and she throws another spruce log inside it. She settles in a living room chair, dwarfed by a huge tapestry of Jesus hanging on the wall above her. The Messiah's eyes are cast downward, and it looks as though He is watching over one of the smallest sheep in His flock. Cecile's daughter puts steaming coffee cups in our hands, and we settle in for a visit. Out the window, smoke from neighbours' chimneys rises straight up in the frigid, still air.

At eighty-eight Cecile is high-spirited, with a fully intact, impish, and infectious sense of humour. Her good-natured spirit has touched the hearts of many, says former nurse Helen Valstar, whom I met at a Sundance several months after Cecile had passed away. She describes how Cecile's joking affected the medical team at the High Level Hospital.

"When Cecile came in every once in a while for treatment, we didn't want her to leave. The nurses and doctors just loved her," recalls Helen. "If we could have kept her in the hospital all the time, we would have. There's something special about her. . . she laughs all the time."

I like to compare Cecile to a monk I met as a young woman travelling in Nepal. One night in the monastery where I was studying Buddhism, word came that a Tibetan priest who had lived in a cave for twenty years was passing through our area and had agreed to address my group of western students in the morning.

As we filed into the meditation hall the next morning, the little man sat at the front of the room. He smiled at us and leaned forward on the dais, slowly scanning his audience and purposefully making eye contact with everyone. He didn't say anything, but I felt a peaceful wave of pleasure, as if there was a warm shower running inside of me. He was powerfully loving, and I felt purposeful and hopeful in his presence. He spoke for an hour or so, but I really can't remember what he said; I only recall how he made me feel.

Cecile didn't give me life-changing advice or intrigue me with stories of medicine power, she just made me see how beautiful she was with her simple, unassuming life as a northern woman. As the embodiment of unconditional love and kindness, she accepted everyone

With long black silky hair threaded with only a few white strands, Cecile's eyes hold a youthful light. Today she is wearing a brown skirt that almost reaches her ankles and thick, blue gym socks underneath miniature tie-up moccasins.

"A long time ago, my dad took the stomach of a bear he'd just killed and pulled it over my head. He did it two times and that's why I don't have white hair." She says her father "knew something," which means in Dene Tha' terms that he had spiritual powers.

"I remember when I was twelve or thirteen, Adam Salopree (a neighbour who also lives in Meander River and who appears in this book) lost his mother, his father, and his brother all at the same time. The ground was frozen and they just left them there, under a tarp. Adam was just a baby so my sister had to raise him and breast-feed him. I felt so sorry for that little baby," she says in a high-pitched voice that sounds like a young girl's. Cecile's parents also died when she was young, so she understands the loneliness of losing loved ones. But, she notes, at least she was lucky enough to have known her mother and father before they passed away, whereas Adam has no memories of his parents at all. After Cecile's parents died, her aunt cared for her.

"I really missed my mom when I was a little girl. I missed her so much that I went to a tree and talked to it. I don't know why. I guess I just didn't have anyone to talk to."

Cecile was raised around Bistcho Lake, just south of the Northwest Territories border in northwestern Alberta. Despite the haunting stories of spirits and monsters who make their home in Bistcho Lake, it was a place young Cecile wanted desperately to return to after catching her first glimpse of an RCMP officer in uniform.

"We heard about treaty money being given away in Meander River, so we packed everything we owned on our backs and came over. There was a log house where the church is now, and that's where the RCMP were giving out money. We crossed the river [Hay River] and came up the hill. When I set my eyes on the RCMP dressed up with his big boots and hat, I started crying." To a little girl used to seeing dark-skinned people usually dressed in soft, brown moosehide clothing, the sight of the tall, light-skinned Mountie wearing a stiff-looking uniform and big boots was astonishing. "I kept crying, and my father had to take me back across the river and I stayed there. When I woke up the next morning, I was still scared and I wanted to go back to Bistcho Lake."

Years later, as Cecile passed into womanhood, the arrival of her monthly period frightened her a little, but she allowed herself no tears this time.

"My mother had sent me to set snares and my period came. I didn't cry, so I wouldn't lose a relative," Cecile says. She had been warned that if she was sad and sobbed when she discovered the first sign of her body passing into womanhood she would cause a relative to die.

"I was told when it happens I should just stay where I was, so I just sat there in the bush. Finally, they must have noticed I was missing, so someone came. I was scared to look up and then when someone came for me it was a woman. She took me by the hand and explained what was happening to me." The woman led Cecile home but stopped short of the settlement. "She made me a little camp, and I stayed there for eight days all by myself. My father kept me supplied with wood," Cecile says. When she emerged from seclusion, she had passed through a Dene Tha' initiatory rite of becoming a woman.

Menstruation was the sign of a potent power particular to women and from a sense of responsibility to the community women felt obliged to be cautious and to avoid causing harm at those times. They would seclude themselves while menstruating and would refrain from handling men's tools and crossing hunters' paths.

Perhaps Cecile's experience was like Catherine Wabose's, an Ojibway woman of the mid-1800s who told Henry R. Schoolcraft, an ethnologist and explorer, of her solitary vigil at the onset of puberty. She drank only snow water for ten days and heard a voice on the sixth night saying, "Poor child! I pity your condition; come, you are invited this way." She walked to the point outside her fasting lodge from which the voice came and saw a shining path, like a silver cord, leading forward and upward. She followed it and, at intervals, met spirits — including the principal guardian she would have for the rest of her life named Bright Blue Sky — who tested her, named her, and ultimately granted her long life and skills to save life in others. Catherine did, indeed, become a respected medicine woman when she grew older.[2]

About one and a half years after her puberty rite, when she was fourteen or fifteen, Cecile became the wife of a young man named Baptiste Chambaud.

"For the first two nights I was scared, but my new husband 'knew something' and he put his coat around me. After that, I wasn't scared of him anymore." Two years later, Cecile gave birth to the first of twelve children she would eventually bear. "You had to go away from the family tent when you were going to have your baby, too. We were superstitious. They made a little place for you, with a tarp over spruce boughs and the ground covered with dry grass. There was a pole for you to hang on to, and when you had labour pains a woman held you with her arms around you from behind to help stretch you up. You sat up when you had your baby." After giving birth, mothers stayed in separate camps away from other family members for a month.

Cecile says her husband Baptiste took good care of her until he died in 1967. "Lately, I think about him lots and I have tears." She smiles sadly and takes a picture down from the wall. It shows a tall, handsome man dressed in work clothes, with his arm around tiny Cecile.

Even though she likes her warm house and appreciates how easy it is to buy food from the stores, Cecile says if she could turn back time and be with her husband on his trapline, with only a fire and a shelter made of spruce branches and sticks to warm them against minus forty Celsius temperatures, she would do it without hesitation.

Disappearing into her bedroom, she emerges with a faded, pass-port-sized photograph held like a precious thing in the palm of her hand. Handing it to me, I see the images of a pretty girl and a young man kissing in a coin-operated photograph booth.

"This is my daughter, Cecilia Chambaud. She left home about twenty-five years ago, and I never heard from her again. She'd probably be in her late forties now," Cecile explains, sadness heavy in her voice. "I think she's still alive. Maybe she's gone to another country." As she holds the little picture, the room is quiet except for the crackling of the fire. "Maybe if she could somehow know I'm still alive, she'd contact me," Cecilia says, her eyes reflecting a loving mother's concern over not knowing whether her daughter is alive or dead. Before the tears start to come, the picture is put away and

Cecile sits down and asks me if I want to know anything else about her life. I ask her what advice she would give a young person growing up in today's world.

"Don't work until you sweat," she says, after pausing to think for a few moments. "If you do, you'll get old fast. Go to bed early and get up early, then you'll live long. Don't wear make-up and wash your face all the time, then you'll always look young.

"I don't feel too well about young people today. Going to school is good, but they go all over the place. All the young girls do is watch TV, and they're losing the old ways. Now, they don't know anything about what it means to become a woman. They think the old ways are funny."

Cecile explains she taught her own daughters how to clean, sew, and tan moosehides. "I taught them everything I know. I never went to school." There is pride in her voice as she tells me she is a true Dene woman. "When I sign my name I just make an X," she announces matter-of-factly.

Cecile gives me a few more tidbits of advice. "You should always think young and be pure. Don't think about men yet. Never do anything that you think, in your heart, might be wrong. Listen to the voice inside. That's God telling you what to do. If you listen, then you'll know something."

1   Abel, Kerry Margaret, *Drum Songs: Glimpses of Dene History* (McGill Queens Press, 2005), p. 21.

28

Adam Salopree

Dene Tha', Meander River (Dene Tha' First Nation)

"My late uncle always said to me, 'You eat three times a day, and so you should have a fire ceremony three times a year, too — in the spring, in the fall and at the time of the new year," Roy Salopree of Meander River tells me. Adam taught his nephew many songs, and I'm told he also travelled north to teach songs to the Dene of the Northwest Territories and help them to regain traditional knowledge before he passed away in 2003. Roy, an accomplished artist, is a spiritual leader in Meander River, following in his uncle's footsteps. He urges the people to put tobacco, moose grease and tea on the fire, and says it's the next best thing to having a Tea Dance.

"It's hard to get people together for a Tea Dance today," Roy concedes, not like in the old days, when people would come from miles around to attend. "When Adam would call a Tea Dance in Meander River a long time ago, we'd hold it on an island and you had to cross the Hay River in a boat to get to the grounds. I would be the one taking people across and I'd start about three o'clock in the afternoon. I'd still be taking people across at three in the morning. Then the sun would come up and until three o'clock the next day I'd be taking the people going back home to the other side."

Darlene Hooka Nooza, also of Meander River, told me she and her brother were raised by Adam. "He was our grandpa and he always provided for us. His hunting ground was around Bistcho Lake. He never hugged us a lot, but we knew he loved us just by the way he cared for us," she said.

THE WINTER OF 1916

On a frosty October morning, Alexis Salopree sits on a log outside his tent with two of his sons, aged six and seven. The air is crisp and mist cloaks his breath as he speaks. Ice crystals catch the sunlight, dazzling the children's eyes as they fidget a little, excited by the prospect of playing in the white stuff that has fallen overnight.

Their father stresses the significance of the new snow. It signals the coming of a harsh season, the thing for which the Dene have prepared throughout the long summer and fall. Supplies of dried meat and berries have been wrapped in moosehide and cached in trees. Fur coats and mukluks stored last spring will be unpacked.

Reaching for the bucket at his feet, Alexis explains it contains melted snow from this first snowfall. The boys grow attentive, even solemn, as their father invites them to drink from the pail. They wait patiently as he lights his pipe and, eventually, repeats a story he learned from his own father many years ago when he was a child. He tells of an honest hunter who worked hard to make himself strong and who never backed down from a personal challenge. His muscles were hard from using them to run far and lift heavy things. His dogs were fast and obedient because he treated them well, and he never hesitated to help others.

"And he was smart. He moved against the wind and didn't let his prey catch his scent. He knew how to save his strength, never tiring himself too much. He knew the ways of the moose and other animals. He knew when he was in his boat on the river that the little birds with yellow legs kept track of the moose and could show him where to hunt. He could run hard when he needed to, and when the moose tired he made the kill. This man was lucky, but he also knew real hardship. He understood what it was like to chase hunger away with old tea leaves or lichens pulled from the ground."

Alexis finishes the story and asks his sons if they want to be this honest hunter. They nod their heads up and down vigorously and Alexis smiles. Before the sun has climbed much higher in the sky he and his sons collect their rifles from inside the tent and walk toward the bush surrounding the camp. They disappear amongst the frost-coated branches, leaving only their footprints in the snow.

THE WINTER OF 1991

Adam Salopree paints wintry vignettes of his childhood on this cold day in January. Stories of learning to hunt with his stepfather Alexis Salopree are easily retrieved from his memory; it's as though he hasn't dusted them off for years and is happy to have the opportunity to do so. Eyebrows rise and fall and grizzled brown hands gesture as he animates his memories. His voice changes pitch, conveying the wonder a young Dene boy must have felt growing up in the northern Alberta wilderness of the early 1900s. In the telling, he seems to re-discover and appreciate the precious gifts of knowledge given him by his parents. "The first flakes of snow. . . my dad would put that in a pail and it's given to us to drink so we can walk on the snow and never go through," Adam says. A floundering hunter in deep snow tires quickly and goes hungry.

Adam's father knew about medicine for hunting, and he had a good supply of practical knowledge about animals and the bush. This he taught his sons, just as his own father had instructed him. What he passed down to his sons was as valuable as powerful weapons. To northern hunters of long ago, the most effective tools for hunting were those they could carry around in their heads as they memorized land formations and the gathering places of animals.

Some Dene could rely on their dreams and spiritual travelling to help them locate and obtain food and clothing. They could "see" where their path would cross with an animal's on the physical earth and then could go to that spot and make the kill easily and respect-fully.

Dene medicine has been described by the late George Blondin, an elder born in Fort Franklin, Northwest Territories, as a way of know-ing or as supernatural abilities used to surmount life's difficulties, before the white-man's technology reached his people. In his books *When the World was New* and *Yamoria the Lawmaker: Stories of the Dene*, he recounts stories of people who could, for example, melt iron, look into the future, retrieve lost objects or run tirelessly all day with the help of powers given them by the spirits of animals, humans, or forces of nature like lightning or rain. Raised outdoors, children gained knowledge as they became receptive to vibrations or energy exuding from plants, rocks, animals, and other natural phenom-ena. Medicine was just as important as common sense and training were for survival. Children were encouraged to spend time alone in the bush so that animals might give them a power that would bring about success in the hunt, heal illness or shield someone from evil intentions of others.

Aside from helping their children seek power, parents also trained their children to be strong. Explains Adam: "Fathers used to bring their young sons for hunting in January to teach them in cold weather. They don't put any wood near the camp, just to teach the boy how to make fire and toughen him. He has to go with his bare hands and no jacket to get wood. This boy soon has tough hands and tough skin."

The leathery skin and thick nails on Adam's hands attest to this early conditioning. He is healthy and active at seventy; his sleek, black hair looks like it belongs on the head of a much younger man, although his bushy white eyebrows and knowing eyes look like those of a wise old sage.

"We never went to school, but we were taught Indian ways. My father was strict with us, and when we were young boys we never went walking around or visiting. One time, there were two of us outside. . . the sun was going down. . . we decided to visit our neighbours. I heard my father in the tent say, 'Where are those two boys going?' and he told my mother to call us back. The sun was still up, but he made us go to bed. He said, 'Those who get up early will have a long life.' The next day he woke us up early to go hunting."

Adam was only a baby when his real parents died. He says one of his brothers, upon learning his mother had passed away, "just dropped where he stood and died right away." Adam wonders if he would have been able to withstand the grief of losing almost all of his family if he had been older. He looks sadly at the floor as he tells of later visiting his family's gravesite.

"One time, we were trapping near Bistcho Lake and I saw the grave where they were buried, near a big tree."

Adam mentions his real last name is Jim and his birth father was from Fort Providence in the Northwest Territories. After his parents' death, he was adopted by a woman who was nursing her own baby and had enough milk for him, too. He was raised by Alexis Salopree, whose name he has taken for his own and who raised his family according to the strict moral codes of the day.

"There were five of us boys and one girl in the family living in a tent. The girl had to stay on one side of the tent and my mother put a curtain up so she had privacy. She had her own place to go to the bathroom and no one must watch. We learned respect. In those days, a girl must not run around by herself and she must follow her mother. If her mother stays home, then the girl stays home also. Fathers used to talk to their children and teach them to be kind. Mothers taught them how to respect things. I don't think there is that kind of closeness between parents and kids anymore so the kids are mixed up."

Parents raised their children with survival in mind, Adam repeats, stressing the severity of the harsh subarctic conditions of northern Alberta.

"Kids raised long ago were very strong. When we moved from camp to camp, I remember even the littlest ones had to walk, wrapped up in their rabbitskin jackets. In the springtime, there was water running everywhere. All the kids walked in their moccasins, and even though they were wet and cold they didn't mind. They didn't get sick. Today, most kids are raised on cow's milk. Maybe they have strong minds, but not as strong as if they had their mother's milk.

"We lived in a tent all the time. We always had fresh air. Life in the wintertime was hard. I remember mothers used to take a moose-hide — scrape it and take all the hair off — and cut the skin into little squares and roast them over the fire to eat when we couldn't get any animals. And when you scraped a hide in those days, you saved the skin that came off and rolled it into a ball. You made soup with that and it kind of went like Jell-O."

When families ran out of staples like flour and sugar in the wintertime, the men would gather together to make the marathon trip into Fort Vermilion, in north central Alberta, from Bistcho Lake, located in the northwest corner of the province. Some of the men had dog teams, but others had to walk.

"It took a month with dogs and even longer on foot. The women would follow our trail part way, and when we came back a month later they'd meet us almost halfway. They would tramp down the snow and make it easier for us to get through." Adam stresses how strong women were in the old days and how eager they were to help their husbands.

"Not today, they're pitiful. They can't even walk a mile and they're already tired," he jokes.

Women gave birth to many children and parents had to work together to feed them, Adam says. Most worked every day in the winter just to keep their families and ten to twelve sled dogs from starving, especially in years when there was little game. In the winter, hunters depended on nets set in Bistcho Lake to provide fish for dog food and trap bait. Adam says there were lots of big fish in the lake and, besides being a source of food, it was a wellspring for legends handed down through the generations.

"That lake is more than forty feet deep in most places and it's about thirty-six miles across. People say there's a monster that lives in it, and my mother said she's seen it. It looks like a big black fish, and it has things that look like horns on its head. They say it's brought bad luck to a lot of people who've seen it."

Despite the legends, Dene elders at Meander River, Bushe River, and Chateh in northern Alberta speak fondly about the Bistcho Lake area as their traditional homeland. It wasn't until Treaty Eleven was signed in 1901 that many began to move into the settlements in which they live today. The elders also have happy memories associated with gatherings held at Christmas time and in the warmer months, when the pressure to obtain food subsided and "we could pick wild rhubarb and berries and drink sap from birch trees," Adam says.

Tea Dances were often held, and families who lived in isolation on winter traplines looked forward to the times when they could swap stories and dance to Dene drums alongside old friends. Adam remembers his father singing and praying with his drum.

"He used to sleep and dream to get his songs. I still have my drum too, and I've been singing and dreaming since I was sixteen," he comments.

"The songs that we sing today have been passed along to us from old prophets that lived long ago, and some are the songs of animals that we live on for food and that sometimes give us their power — we sing their songs." The spirits of these animals are honoured in thankfulness for all that they give to the Dene.

Since he was young, Adam says, "God used to talk to me," and in his quiet way he shares some of his beliefs.

"If people pray when they're young, it seems like God gives you the power to respect other people and all things in the world. If you pray later in life and you're a very good person in all kinds of ways, then when you die your spirit goes right up to heaven and God welcomes you. He takes you right away."

Adam explains that the spirit separates from the body at death and has two directions to go. "If your spirit doesn't go to heaven, if you did wrong and didn't pray, these are the people who just wander around this earth and they suffer a lot. They have to stay in an awful place like purgatory until they're ready [to go to heaven]. In the Indian

THOSE WHO KNOW *Dianne Meili*

way, prophets can see these wandering people in their dreams. They are like shadows and they are cold and they suffer. The ones who are still around, some people can see them at night, too." Many Dene, especially the older ones, wear red ribbons attached to their clothing to keep them protected from wandering spirits at night.

"If people are really bad, God can't take them and they are reborn on this world. They come back to a woman when she's pregnant." These spirits must live earthly lives again and again until they learn to live according to the Creator's laws and can be accepted by Him, Adam stresses. He shakes his head and wonders how people who understand the continual birth-death-rebirth cycle, and the endless miseries that it brings with it, can be foolish and blind enough to do bad things in their lives and choose to keep coming back to this earth.

Adam finishes talking and offers to sing. His voice merges with the sound of his drum, rising and falling with the cadence that makes Dene singing so distinctive. His last, high note hangs in the air like the smell of smoke from a campfire. Silence fills the room, and no one — not I, nor Maggie, my interpreter — feels like talking as we hold the sounds of the song in our minds. Though Adam sings in a language I don't understand, his song touches my soul and I sense it has special significance for him. Finally, he breaks the silence and explains he felt deep emotion while singing. He confirms the song is special; it is the one his father sang for his mother before she died.

"You are doing a good thing by visiting the elders. I tell you to always remember the Creator and that He sees everything you do. You can't hide anything from Him. Always remember the Creator," he urges, and then we say our goodbyes.

29

Killian Wildman

Stoney Nakoda, Bighorn Reserve (Wesley Band)

Killian Wildman passed away on April 3, 1995.

Peering down the shaft of the spear he has just crafted, Killian Wildman checks it for straightness. Satisfied, he props it against his chair and begins cutting strips of tanned hide. His collection of tools and weapons, crafted from bone, antler, wood, leather, and stone, won't be thrown or pounded as his ancestors would have used them — they will likely be purchased by tourists browsing Jasper and Banff gift shops.

"He gets up about seven or eight o'clock in the morning to do his handicrafts," granddaughter-in-law Rachel Simeon told me as we looked at some of Killian's beadwork. "It's his life now. If he stops, he'll probably get sick."

Jim Guilloux, principal of Bighorn School, has bought several of Killian's pieces and displays them on his living room wall. He appreciates their handmade quality and the work that went into making them, since he, too, spends long hours crafting masterpieces, but his medium is clay. When he toured Killian through his pottery studio, the elder was fascinated by what he saw.

"I opened the peephole in the kiln and showed him a red-hot pot inside. Well, he thought that was pretty neat," Jim said. Picking up a well-formed pot, he told me Killian had made it in minutes after being shown a bit about hand-building. "That man's so good with his hands, he'd make a great potter," Jim speculated.

This morning, though, Killian's hands are preoccupied with carving antler and cutting leather in his backyard. It is a beautiful day for working outside — the blue sky is cloudless, and the sunlight deepens the colours of the tall green grass dotted with yellow dandelions at his feet and the grey-and-white-topped Rockies behind him. The tiny Bighorn Reserve, Killian's home since moving from the more southern Kootenay Plains, looks picturesque from his backyard. The land is bordered by mountains and defined to the east by the North Saskatchewan River, yet the valley's natural beauty is marred. Around 1969, massive destruction began when crews started work on the $43-million Bighorn Dam to the north. Killian watched as bulldozers knocked over Indian log cabins, dug up Indian graves, and destroyed traplines and traditional hunting grounds. A twenty-seven-mile-long artificial lake was carved out of the valley, and mammoth steel electrical towers were erected along the river.

The Stoneys weren't even told about the government's plans to build the dam. Killian mentions the ravaged land was never chosen by the Stoneys as a good place to live, in the first place. The Bighorn Reserve was foisted upon them after the government spurned repeated requests for land at Kootenay Plains, the Stoneys' ancestral hunting and wintering grounds.

The Stoneys faced insurmountable problems while trying to gain what was rightfully their's. Combining Killian's observations with facts from the late Chief John Snow's book *These Mountains Are Our Sacred Places* — which documents the unjust way his people have been treated by land-stealing, insensitive federal and provincial governments — the story is almost unbelievable. It is every bit as frustrating and racist as those behind other land-claim battles being fought today. The Wildman family joined the Abrahams, Beavers, Houses, Hunters, and others in returning to the Kootenay Plains in 1894, led by Ta-otha (Peter Wesley), whose name translates to mean "Moosekiller" in Stoney or "The One Who Provides" in English. No one knows what ultimately sparked his desertion of the Stoney Reserve at Morley, but Chief Snow writes that it may have been due to unbearable conditions and domination. Forced to depend on meagre rations amidst a scarcity of animals and new hunting regulations, Ta-otha couldn't step off the reserve to find game without first receiving a pass from the Indian agent, a stipulation enforced after the Riel Rebellion.[1]

Grandson Moses Wesley thinks Ta-otha may have become angered over the jailing of John Abraham after he killed a cow to feed his hungry family without obtaining Indian agent permission. Whatever the reason, Ta-otha rejected the supervision and culture of the white man and returned to the freedom and great outdoors he so dearly loved.[2]

The Stoneys believed they had a right to land in the Kootenay Plains, especially since the Queen's representative commissioner and Treaty Seven negotiator David Laird had concluded that the Stoneys should receive more land. But when Moses House petitioned the Indian Affairs Branch for the title to the land his Jacob's Band were living on, Ottawa astounded him. Officials disclaimed Laird's recommendation and advised him that if a reserve were to be granted, an equivalent area would have to be surrendered from the Morley Reserve, just west of Calgary. Despite this negative response, in 1910 title searches were conducted on lands at Morley and in the Kootenay Plains and it seemed as if the reserve would be granted. But when Indian Affairs got down to brass tacks and requested a blueprint of the survey to the land in the Kootenay Plains, the Department of the Interior balked and postponed survey plans.[3]

Then, in 1911, the Department of the Interior was reorganized and the administration changed. Under new policy guidelines, officials denied Jacob's Band their request. "Again, my people were left land-less in their ancestral homeland," Chief Snow writes.

If the Stoneys thought things couldn't get any worse, a white squatter in the area proved them wrong. Killian recalls his people helped Tom Wilson build a ranch to graze his horses and exchanged furs with him for food, calling him friend. According to Chief Snow, Wilson warned the chief forest ranger in the area that the Indians would destroy all the game in the mountain corridor. Ranger Helmer, already alarmed by the reduction of Banff National Park's boundaries, urged the government to put the Stoneys' land aside as grazing land for wild animals. Later, Wilson would relocate to Peace River on land the government gave him in compensation for his Kootenay Plains ranch, while the Stoneys got nothing.[4]

Helmer's fears ignited public criticism about the Stoneys' mountain settlement. An excerpt from Banff's *Crag and Canyon* newspaper stated, "In two years there would not be a hoof left. . . [if] this protected area is going to be thrown open to a race of people who do not consider the tomorrow."

Finally, in the late 1940s, the government offered the band a parcel of land to the north. Killian remembers that a school and band hall were promised at Bighorn as a ploy to get people to leave the Kootenay Plains area. The Jacob's Band, whose name had been changed by then to the Wesley Band, accepted the proposal, understanding that the Bighorn land was a waiting place while negotiations for a Kootenay Plains Reserve were finalized, but they never were.[5]

More than eighty years ago, Killian was a little boy living on the land his people would later lose. His memories from that time are carefree, and he concerned himself with nothing more than shooting his slingshot at trees to improve his aim.

The Kootenay Plains was long a gathering place for many nations who appreciated that the valley stayed almost snow-free in the winter, and the weather was mild. But when it got cold, Killian kept warm in the moccasins and coats his mother sewed him.

"We just left the fur on when we made moccasins; even the women's dresses were like that for the winter," he says. "Men didn't wear pants, just a short cloth around them. One time, when we were fishing on Cline River, a fish got inside my friend's [breechclout]. It was flopping around back and forth inside in there, and he couldn't get it out," Killian says, laughing at the memory.

"We wore hats made from the feathers of some kind of grey bird we used to find in the mountains. If you came near that bird, it would whistle. By the time I was fifty, there were no birds like that left," he says, his sad words translated by Rachel Simeon. "When I was small, we didn't bother eagles. Now that I'm old, I see they wear eagle feathers in powwows. We just let them be. We had to use a slingshot to kill birds, but when the white man came with his guns he shot many more than us. By the time I was fourteen, we were living in white-man's tents in the summer. "Later, I built a house for my family," Killian recalls, explaining that he and his wife had seven children and that she passed away in 1985.

"There were a lot of cabins at Kootenay Plains. We used logs, but the roof was mud. When it rained, the water came in. Fires kept us warm, and we had candles and lamps — we made them ourselves with grease and some string."

As a former hunter and trapper, Killian remarks: "At one time, there were no elk here, just moose. The elk came from the north. My father-in-law from Morley Reserve said he used to see buffalo in the mountains."

Killian's grandfather fought and was captured by the Cree, while his own father was a medicine man and, as a child, Killian recalls being shooed away from healing ceremonies. After oil was discovered at Nordegg about forty-five years ago, "The whites came and we made friends with them. Doctors came here and, after that, white people came to get our medicine."

The Kootenay Plains were sacred grounds to Killian's ancestors, and many a Sundance lodge was built there. "Before I lived here [at Bighorn], before they made me my house here, there were many ceremonies. I used to go, but I'm not so strong now. The Sundance was powerful, but not anymore. Now, it's different. People used to help each other finish the Sundance, but there's a new beginning and they don't help each other."

Killian observes that the young people are "going away from the Creator" while the "old people think more and more that God is coming back."

1   John Snow, *These Mountains Are Our Sacred Places* (Toronto, Ontario: Samuel-Stevens, Publishers, 1977), p. 63.
2   Ibid.
3   Ibid., pp. 69–75.
4   Ibid., p. 75.
5   Ibid., pp. 78–80.

30

Victoria McDonald

Chipewyan, Fort McKay First Nation

The Fort MacKay of Victoria's birth back in August of 1915 is a universe away from what greets me at the community's 2011 Treaty Days.

"Look, these rez houses have professional landscaping," my friend notices as we enter Fort MacKay, driving toward the massive band office housing the Group of Seven Companies that serve the oilsands industry. Over the course of two days, I receive cool swag — an umbrella, T-shirt and water bottle — all stamped with the Fort McKay First Nation logo showing two Indians paddling a birchbark canoe, and enjoy an all-you-can-eat lobster lunch, endless bottles of water, pop and juice, and a wrap-up concert featuring the Barenaked Ladies. My friend makes an authentic rawhide drum, for free, in the popular cultural village where women smoke meat and fish and serve cups of tea, and teams play handgames all day.

Clearly, the humble cluster of red-painted houses along the Athabasca River, and the Hudson Bay Company dating back to 1820, are memories only a handful of Fort McKay elders recall. The river those logo Indians are paddling up today sparkles with diamonds and the streets of their homeland glitter with gold. The Treaty Days are subsidized by oil money and I have been treated royally, but I can't help but notice the overflowing garbage cans and half-eaten plates of food abandoned by people, especially the youth. Cheap trinkets and glow sticks sold from booths are broken and left lying on the ground. Fort McKay's cup runneth over and consumption is rampant.

Back in Victoria's day, treats were few and far between and no one wasted anything. The strings of blueberries her father picked and strung to dry in the window were delicacies she remembered with pleasure.

Victoria married Phillip McDonald in 1931 when she was sixteen years old. They had fourteen children, but four of them died. Phillip passed away in 1977. Every spring the couple would hunt together; in a good season Phillip would shoot eighteen to twenty animals and Victoria would skin them.

Before the road was punched in from Fort McMurray to Fort McKay, Victoria and her sister Ellise delivered the babies born in their community. Midwifery was one of the most memorable accomplishments of her life.

Victoria kept busy to the end of her ninety-two years before passing away in Fort McMurray on January 2, 2007. "When sewing and beading became too much for her eyesight she just switched to giving us knitted socks and slippers instead of moccasins," says her son-in-law Rod Hyde.

Stories My Granny Told Me is a book of legends and poetry about Fort MacKay published in 1980 by students. In it, there is a picture of Victoria McDonald fleshing a beaver. The big knife she is using to separate flesh from fur looks dangerously sharp, but you can sense the skill and confidence in her hands.

Ten years later, Victoria has a few more wrinkles and her hair, still pulled neatly back into a bun, is a little greyer. But her hands look busy as ever. Fingers fly as she stitches white silk fringe on to the blue cloth leggings of her granddaughter's fancy dance outfit, which must be ready for a powwow only hours away. Valuable sewing time is lost as Victoria stops to discuss her younger days in the Fort MacKay area, yet she waves away my suggestion to come back at a less hectic time. Sewing is second nature to Victoria, and she works while we talk. Though her beadwork is beyond compare, she speaks wistfully about the ruffled curtains she used to make for the two-storey, red-painted log house she once lived in on the banks of the Athabasca River. She says she used to love fashioning those draperies, throwing thrift to the wind and stitching them from lavish yards of bright cloth purchased from the trading post.

"Lots of women had nice curtains at that time. I remember, too, all the houses here were painted red. The Indian name for Fort MacKay was Red Clay. That's what everybody put on their houses." Victoria recalls that river travellers coming around a bend of the Athabasca River immediately recognized Fort MacKay because of its brightly coloured homes. Most of the elders living in Fort MacKay, including Victoria, were born about eighty kilometres west of the reserve at Moose Lake, where the hunting and fishing were good. A few people still live there. Speaking slowly in English, Victoria describes Moose Lake as a paradise, where fish, moose, and ducks were plentiful. She says the Chipewyan depended on the waters of the rivers and lakes in the Fort MacKay area for drinking water and travel.

"We lived on the river. It was our life," she says, jabbing her finger in the direction of the Athabasca flowing a few hundred yards west of her house. The river looks like a giant's pathway, smoothly carpeted in white and gleaming in December's afternoon sun, unblemished except for two large brownish spots of open water.

"That river used to freeze right over, right away, in the wintertime. Not anymore. I'm seventy years old, and I've never seen open water like that," Victoria says. She blames two upriver oil refineries, Suncor and Syncrude, for discharging oil into the water. In 1983, Victoria's daughter Dorothy, Chief of the Fort MacKay Band, took Suncor to court after learning the company was responsible for an oil spill that had occurred the year before. She won the case, and the company was fined for the incident.

Victoria is becoming angry as she speaks about environmental destruction in Chipewyan to daughter Dorothy, on hand today to interpret. "She's saying how they used to get their water and lots of fish from that river, but she won't eat fish from it now," Dorothy explains. "She gets really mad when we talk about pollution. She wants everybody to write letters to the government and publicize these problems for her about the pollution because her English isn't too good."

Victoria leans toward me and speaks haltingly. "I want my daughter to write to that Native-Perspective radio show so everyone will know about what they put in the river. The water used to taste good from that river."

Sadly, the natural resource once central to Victoria's life, a symbol of days when life was much simpler and wholesome, has become a source of fear. The thought of a pulp mill being built downriver near the town of Athabasca to pour more chemicals into the water makes her livid. She and daughter Dorothy, who is president of a Native environmental group in Edmonton called The Mother Earth Healing Society, will never stop fighting to save the land. Victoria points out other changes in the land that alarm her.

"I notice the trees are thinner. In the bush, trees are dying. They don't have as many leaves as before. And there's no berries. Long time ago, in the summer, there'd be nobody here. Everyone would go to Fort McMurray to hunt. They used to stay on the river. When they'd come back, they'd stop at the place where Suncor is now to pick berries. Cranberries and blueberries. I remember we picked so many. We used to sell them for ten cents a pound. The women would dry them on a tarp in the sun or thread them together and hang them. Now, there's no berries like that."

Victoria switches the topic from environmental illness to social disease when I ask her what she thinks her grandchildren's lives will be like in ten years. "People won't live very long. There never used to be any accidents long time ago. People never smoked or drank. Now, there are always accidents because of drugs and alcohol. Long time ago, people did get sick, but we knew how to heal ourselves. We heated rocks up and covered ourselves with blankets and steamed ourselves. Now, maybe the white man will just come along and take everything," she says. "There will be planes, trains, and cars every-where."

Perhaps hoping to brighten her mother's mood, Dorothy suggests Victoria tell me the story of the first airplane to fly over the area. The older woman nods her head and begins:

"There were a bunch of us out in the bush with my grandfather, and we heard this big noise. When we saw the plane, the first thing we thought of was maybe the war was coming, so we were all scared. We were crying. My grandfather told us to go and hide in the bush. He said he was the oldest and he'd stay behind and die," Victoria laughs. Dorothy says she can't imagine how the noise must have sounded to bush people who had never heard anything like that be-fore. "It was one of those planes with two wings, and it must have just roared."

First encounters with the white-man's new ways of transportation weren't always alarming to Victoria, who tells fond recollections of her first paddle-wheeler ride on the Hudson's Bay Company's *Atha-basca River*.

"It was a really big boat. Tall. Really nice," Victoria recalls. The steamboat carried passengers and supplies along the river from Atha-basca Landing (today's town of Athabasca) to Fort Chipewyan and points farther north. With improving methods of transportation and the European demand for furs, Victoria's life became easier. She and husband Philip, whom she married at fifteen, raised their family of fourteen in a big, two-storey log home in Fort MacKay. It had a cookstove on the main floor and another wood stove upstairs for warmth. Vegetables and the meat Victoria canned were kept in a cold cellar in the basement.

"In those days, we never needed or wanted anything. We had a good life, because the trapping was good. We always had food. All of the men would bring their furs to Fort MacKay, and we'd have a big New Year's dance. We had a good time. No alcohol, just dancing."

Too soon, the interview ends and I leave Victoria's house. Through a turn of events, I end up later at the Fort MacKay school to photograph a powwow demonstration, the very one Victoria's granddaughter will be dancing in.

As the students enter the gym, my eyes immediately pick out a pretty fancy dancer dressed in blue regalia. The white fringes on her leggings flash with her quick, hopping movement. Across the gymnasium, Victoria is sitting on a metal chair, watching the grand entry. My eyes meet hers and she smiles back. Did I really ever doubt they would be done in time?

31

Abbie Burnstick

Cree, Paul First Nation

Twenty years after meeting Roderick when he was a child, I'm sitting with him in a restaurant on a quiet weekday afternoon to remember his late grandmother. He's a father now, devoted to his daughter — who sits in the booth with us sipping orange juice and giggling at some of her dad's childhood stories.

"My grandmother made me who I am today," Roderick says matter-of-factly, before sharing anecdotes of what it was like growing up in his grandmother's house. I knew Abbie to be a strong woman of high morals, but when he tells me she once dumped a bucket of ice cold water on him when he wouldn't get out of bed at sixteen — insisting that he "never waste a day" — I realize the sweetheart who served me tea and bannock was something of an "iron lady."

When Roderick and his brother were about thirteen they found a full case of beer on the side of the road and brought it home to Abbie. She surprised them by cracking one open, taking a drink, rolling a cigarette and smoking it.

"We were sitting on her porch and she talked to us. She told us what this alcohol could do. She told us we had to respect it and if we didn't, those bottles of *beer could take our lives. After insisting we respect liquor, she told us we could pour out the rest and take them to town with the rest of our bottles."*

This is a story about a groundhog I'm going to tell you," announces eighty-eight-year-old Abbie Burnstick, pressing one slippered foot into the floor to move her rocking chair back and forth.

"A long time ago, there was a mother groundhog and she had little ones. Those little ones, they stayed in a hole. And the mother, oh, she would go outside, but she didn't want her little ones to ever leave her, so she left them inside. Now this was in the time of May. Everything was so nice. Everything was so juicy to eat. The leaves were green and the branches were tender. She would be out there eating away, and her little ones, they stayed home. They didn't even know it was springtime. The mother was hiding it from her kids."

Abbie's doleful expression and dragging words emphasize the sadness of mother groundhog's selfish ways, but she pitches her voice higher to describe baby groundhog's wonderful discovery.

"So, one day, one little one came outside. He came up out of the hole, and when he got outside, oh, talk about nice! The sun was shining. The trees were beautiful and everything was so green. He put his paw to his mouth, and he couldn't talk. He couldn't believe what he saw. He ran back down the hole to his brothers and sisters. 'Oh,' he said, 'Our mother is not home. Now I know what she is doing. She's out there eating. Everything is so nice, so juicy! The leaves are all out and the sun is shining. Why don't you come out and see for yourselves?'"

Abbie rocks faster as her story climaxes, her chair creaking. Grandson Roddy, who has been listening to the tale, suggests she slow down in case the noise drowns out the sound of her voice on the tape recorder. With all the guilt of a cookie-snatching child caught in the act, Abbie claps her hand to her mouth, then grins sheepishly. Sitting perfectly still, she delivers the finale.

"So the rest of them all climbed out of their den, and, yes, here it was springtime. They were all surprised to see it had been springtime, and all this time they had been in the dark. The little groundhogs left the hole while their mother was still away. They ran away from her, and when she came back she didn't find her little ones. They were gone."

The elder's narrative trails off as she folds her hands in her lap. Motionless in the rocking chair, she allows her listeners a moment to consider the mother groundhog's plight.

"And that's how it is, that's human," she states, finally breaking the silence and beginning to rock slowly again. Her story speaks to parents who don't realize how much they oppress their children out of what they think is love but really is selfishness.

"These legends all have a meaning that shows how we are sometimes. A lot of human beings would like to keep their children, but the kids want to go away and have a home of their own, get married. You know, those kids always return anyway," she says, laughing at her advice for overbearing parents.

The groundhog story caps a morning of reminiscing and storytelling, and now it is lunchtime. My offer to help Abbie in the kitchen is spurned, so I step out her back door into the early April sunshine. Spotting an old car in the straggle of bush and trees beyond the clearing around the house, I walk toward it. The metal husk is almost hidden by the drab greys and browns of poplars, willows, and wild rose brambles yet to burst with green buds.

The car is uninteresting, but a flash of yellow and white catches my eye, drawing me farther into the bush. I make out lengths of cloth knotted around the trunks of two trees. I know inside each length of material is concealed a bit of tobacco, perhaps placed there by Abbie, who wanted her prayers to be lifted up by the wind to the Creator. She is a devout woman who makes no distinction between Indian spirituality and white-man's religion.

"I take both. I was raised in the Methodist Church, but I don't let my Indian religion go. They say you can't serve two Gods, but I just reject Satan and all his demons. I believe in God alone. Whatever a person does, that's their way. The sweatlodge — that's some people's way. Church — it's another way. All people have their own way of believing. No way is better or worse. We can pray anywhere, anytime.

"My heart is weak, my doctor said that, but he's not in control. God is. It's your heart you really need to think about," she said, impressing upon me that God, or life, will always say yes to me if I love and help others, and live humbly.

Back in the house, over tea and sandwiches, Abbie tells me she married into the Paul First Nation near Duffield in 1936. She had grown up milking cows and riding horses on the Samson Cree Nation to the south at Hobbema, but was introduced to the trapline when she married her second husband Peter Burnstick and came north.

"I loved to go with Peter. His trapline was around Lodgepole. We used to have a big log house there. He was a good hunter and we always had a big garden, so we fed everyone."

Abbie still lives in the house she and Peter raised their family in, on a rise at the north end of the reserve, surrounded by fields. Since her husband passed away and her daughter moved back to Hobbema, grandson Roddy has been staying with her.

"You know, I used to take my .22 around here, after supper, oh, just before it got dark, and I'd go out hunting. Maybe I'd get a [wild] chicken or a rabbit. I'd clean it, and, the next day I'd cook it and we'd really enjoy that. Now, you can't eat without money. Some people use their dollars really good, but other people buy the wrong things and they hurt themselves. You have to respect money."

Abbie asks if I ever wonder how the Indians met their needs for so long without money, depending only on what the Creator provided.

"Even medicine. Not everybody knew how to heal with plants, but the ones who could be depended upon had the knowledge handed down to them. Today, if you really want medicine, you have to pay for it, but not with money, really. You just have to give something you value. Then again, if you happen to come into a person's house when they're making it, they'll just give it to you and tell you what to do with it."

Abbie says her mother-in-law took her into the bush and told her the names of medicinal plants, when to pick them, and which parts to use.

"It's a big lesson. You have to learn which ones are mated together. Like ratroot [wild ginger], it goes with another plant to make a medicine. Sometimes, you need a whole bunch of things to put together to make one medicine." Old time medicine gatherings used to occur, she says, where people would come together and bring plants to mix together to make complex blends and everyone would take a bit of it home with them.

Other remedies are extremely simple. Abbie describes how her niece treated her husband Peter when he had cut himself with an axe. "Bella went to a poplar tree and skinned it from the south side. There's a certain way she knew to cut it, and she got to the inside bark. She chewed it and put that on him. Pretty soon, it healed, no swelling, no mark, nothing."

As we clear the kitchen table, Abbie mentions the time she served lunch to one of the Queen's representatives from the House of Lords in London, a man her son Edwin brought home from an Edmonton function several years ago.

"I roasted some moosemeat, and then I cooked some blueberries and fried some bannock. I baked potatoes so he could open them and put however much butter he wants on them. I made gravy and a few other little things, a good meal, anyway. When he finished he said, 'Oh, thank you, Mrs. Burnstick. This is a wholesome meal. I've been wanting to eat moosemeat. I've heard of this moosemeat in England.'

"Then he asked me how I made the frybread. He ate so much of it. I told him a long time ago, Europeans, when they first came here they knew how to make tea biscuits. 'This is the same thing, only you fry it,' I told him.

"I didn't treat him special. If they're high people or very low people, even if they're the Queen, I treat them all the same," Abbie interrupts herself, pausing for a moment to consider her English guest's rank, then continues, "Well, I guess he was the Queen's representative, he's as good as the Queen, isn't he?" The story illustrates Abbie's philosophy of treating all people equally, even outcasts shunned by others.

"A woman came to see me. She was drunk and I let her in. After, another woman said to me, 'I don't know why you're so good to the people. Didn't you smell that woman? She was smelly. You shook hands with her and gave her a meal.' I said, 'No, I gave her what I had to give.' I can't reject anybody."

Abbie's empathy stems from her understanding of people's shame. She believes drinking, stealing, and aimless living are symptoms of self-disrespect and she refuses to add to the shame those people already feel toward themselves. Instead, she tries to build them up so they can move beyond their vices and feel proud of themselves.

At powwows and other gatherings, she likes to talk one-on-one with people and let them know how special they are and help them on to the right track.

"Many times there are trials. That other one, the devil, can lead us to liquor, abuse, and killing. But we just have to follow the ways of a loving God to be free."

Once respect replaces abuse and a person begins taking care of himself or herself, a reconnection with spirit takes place and usually a person learns how, through that spirit, they are part of God, Abbie says.

"You know, even before the ministers came, the old people knew there was somebody higher than them. They had dreams and visions. They knew they weren't in control. Look at how they never got to today's bombs and war. God gives us our life but when it's time for us to die, we can't go around it. Same thing with the world, what will happen will happen. We're just like rags in the wind. I won't make prophecies like some people because there's somebody above who knows what's coming. I take life as it is. I don't worry what's going to happen tomorrow. I might not even live until then," Abbie says.

"There is a way to live your life. I'm not preaching, but you should look in the Bible and see how Jesus lived his life."

Like most elders, when Abbie prays she first expresses humility before "God of the universe, heaven, and earth," and thanks Him for all He has given humankind. Rather than asking God to "give us this and that," she believes humans were put on earth to carry out His laws and receive eternal joy in return.

In describing Abbie's spiritual philosophy, the words of medicine man Mad Bear, as quoted in Doug Boyd's book, *Mystics, Magicians and Medicine People* come to mind: "We are here to bring about, through our own wits and our own work, what the Great Spirit wants on this earth. What we are really seeking must be what the Great Spirit wants — that must be what is pulling on us." [1]

Abbie's God isn't the one of the church — punishing and exacting certain good behaviour for favours. To her, God is simply love. She silently offers herself to the Creator as His orator before speaking publicly, hoping to say the right words to touch people's hearts and help them appreciate all He has given them and all they are worth. Once, as rain threatened to soak dancers and onlookers at a powwow, Abbie surprised the crowd she was asked to bless by urging them to appreciate the rain instead of cursing it.

"I told them, even though it was raining all the time, we should keep up the powwow. I prayed, 'Thank you for this rain as we cannot survive without it, without water.' I never thought of that before. It just came to me that we should be thankful for the rain."

Puzzling aloud, Abbie wonders why she is often asked to officiate at gatherings and say prayers, "when I'm just a woman. There are lots of elders, lots of men, and they could do it. Maybe God wants me to do it. He works through me."

Abbie's recognition of the traditional woman's place in society "behind the man" belies the more liberal views she cherished as a young woman, considering she was one of the first women from her community to travel and wear pants in the 1930s. She also opted to become a working girl for a while after graduating from school, instead of marrying right away.

Although Abbie doesn't think it was right for the government, years ago, to threaten parents with jail if they didn't put their children in school, her early learning years were pleasant because she was allowed to come home after day school. But when she was nine, she had to leave her mother and live in Red Deer to attend industrial school.

"We only went home for a month in July. Many a time we had to cry, we were so lonely. We were taught how to do housework real good, but we didn't get much education. Young people are so lucky today with their schooling, but it seems to me they don't appreciate it — too many drop out. We signed treaty to have the right to education so young people should finish school. If they don't, they're breaking our treaty."

Abbie spent two-and-a-half hours a day studying and the rest working in the kitchen or sewing, as all her female classmates were expected to do, while the boys farmed. When the school closed, Abbie was only fifteen. While most of her fellow students returned to their reserves, she and a few others stayed behind to help clean the building. When the principal asked her if she was anxious to return home, she surprised him by saying no. She told him she didn't know enough and wanted to attend another school to gain further education. Once the principal realized Abbie's ambition, he arranged for her and seven classmates to attend a secondary school in Brandon, Manitoba. Abbie was delighted with her new placement.

"In my old school, they fenced us girls in like little prisoners. The boys were free to go most places — we couldn't go anywhere. But in Brandon, they gave us a chance to associate with the boys on Sunday or when we played games and things like that. It was much more sociable. On Sundays, we'd walk two miles into Brandon for church and then we had a good dinner after that."

After graduation in 1919, Abbie returned to Hobbema to look after the children of Reverend Roy Taylor, the local minister. After two years, the family rewarded her faithful service by taking her with them on a four-month road trip to see North America.

"Oh, the cars in those days. There were rugs on both sides and you could close them up, but there were no [glass] windows. We had luggage everywhere, and we had to sit on some of it. But it was comfortable for me. I wore knickers on the trip. I beat the other women all to pieces. I was the first one [from Hobbema] to go out and travel like that. We camped in Banff and Lake Louise and then we went to Vancouver. I loved the sea. . . I picked up lots of seashells. Then we went to Bellingham and Seattle and Portland, Oregon. In those years, the land was clean and the cities weren't that big. Even Los Angeles was nice."

From the western United States, the reverend drove eastward to New Mexico, returning home via Montana and Yellowstone Park to see Old Faithful, the famous natural geyser. When the whirlwind trip was over, Abbie found herself back home in Hobbema, with more than a few young men trying to catch her eye. She allowed Albert Lightning to court her, a worthy suitor who was considered one of the strongest men on the reserve and with whom she had corresponded while away in Manitoba.

"There were a lot who wanted me when I got back. I never acted smart, and, well, I suppose I wasn't bad looking," Abbie responds bashfully to my query as to the reason for her popularity. Albert succeeded in winning her hand, and the couple began ranching and raising a family, acquiring a frame house and property that had belonged to the reserve's farm instructor.

"Albert was a real good cowboy rider. He used to come and scare my horse and I would hang on, not knowing he was going to do that. That's how I learned to ride."

On a black-and-white horse named Babe, given to her by her husband, Abbie helped round up cattle until she became pregnant, but it wasn't long before she was back in the saddle again after giving birth.

"I can't even sit right in this chair now, but I used to be a good rider," Abbie jokes. "We used to ride to Buffalo Lake to fiddle dances to see our half-breed relations. It was about eighteen miles. We'd take horse blankets and things like that and go right around the country. There were no fences, nothing to cut across. We'd take bannock and something else to eat. We'd sleep out under the stars. We sure had our life!

"They had the most lovely dances at Buffalo Lake. The Métis girls were so pretty, they always had such nice complexions. And, talk about nice clothes — narrow waists and big wide skirts. Some used to put beads on them. When they danced, it was beautiful."

Abbie was related to her Buffalo Lake relatives through her grandmother, who was the child of a French trader and a Métis woman. Fair of complexion and curly-haired, "She looked just like a modern woman. But she was always busy. You know, I always tell children, 'Grandmother was the slave of the family. She knew how to make a living. Just look at her withered hands.'"

Abbie's grandmother helped raise her after her father Lazarus Twins died when she was only about a year old. "We moved in with my grandparents. I guess I was still in a mossbag because I've seen a picture of my dad holding me before he died." The little girl who had lost her father at such a young age stole the hearts of elders on the reserve. Among Abbie's earliest memories are those of old people picking her up, tears glistening in their eyes as they remembered her deceased father. She understands the reason for their sentiment now, but at the time it confused her.

"I never knew what they were crying for. I didn't understand. They were always hugging and kissing me. You know, I had lots of good things happen to me, just because I was an orphan girl."

Details of the big log home she grew up in are still clear. There was a fireplace made of clay and willow that extended through the ceiling and it, like the wooden floors, was kept spotlessly clean with her grandmother's constant scrubbing and home-made soap of rendered fat and lye.

On soap-making days, Abbie's mother or grandmother would drape a sack over four poles and place ashes from the fireplace in the middle of it. Hot water was strained through the ashes and collected in a container below. The brown liquid, or lye, was put in a kettle with fats and grease saved from cooking and butchering and then boiled for hours.

"After a while, they'd put a stick in the pot and if it felt thick they'd put it in cold water." The soft, jellylike, yellow mixture was allowed to harden, then it was cut into pieces and dried. "My goodness, that soap used to clean anything."

Abbie's grandfather was often away from home, accompanying traders as an interpreter on their return treks to eastern Canada, and for that reason he was called Kanatakasiw, which means Going East in Cree. He was chief of the Cree nation before adhesions to the 1876 Treaty established the initial Samson, Ermineskin, Muddy Bull, and Bobtail reserves.

Historically, Kanatakasiw's eastern relatives, the Woods and Swampy Cree, had long traded with the Hudson's Bay Company, and their move westward was accelerated by the demand for furs and robes by French traders, writes historian Hugh Dempsey,[2] but no one knows how long the Plains Cree had inhabited the prairies. As the eastern Cree pushed west, they exchanged furs for European goods and weapons and became strong enough to overpower poorer tribes and occupy much of Alberta. But by 1871, Dempsey writes, buffalo were becoming scarce and Plains Cree chiefs were approaching government for a treaty, because, as Chief Sweetgrass put it, "Our country is getting ruined of fur-bearing animals and we are poor and want help. . . our country is no longer able to support us. We invite you to come and see us and to speak with us."[3]

By 1880, Kanatakasiw's Samson Reserve at Hobbema had been designated by the province, but life was difficult. Rations were scant, and the government's early attempts to introduce agriculture on the reserve were unsuccessful. Conditions were bad enough to spur some Cree into joining the Riel Rebellion in 1885 at Batoche, Saskatchewan. "The Montana Band from around Cyprus Hills ran away from there when they had the rebellion," Abbie notes. "They stayed [in the United States] until it was over and then they came to Canada."

While Kanatakasiw was in eastern Canada, the Montana Band settled near Hobbema agency, bringing southern traditions to influence their northern relatives.

"My grandmother said she heard noise [from the Montana Band camp] and told her children to go see. Then she said, 'I'll take you there, but don't go near them.' She stood a long time on that hill, but she really couldn't see much because they had their wagons all around and they were covered with tents. She could tell they were dancing, but she'd never seen anything like it before."

Abbie thinks the Montana Band members must have been pow-wow dancing, although the movements her grandmother saw from the hill that day bear little resemblance to today's dances.

"The women danced on one side and the men on the other. They didn't jump around like they do now. It was something they really valued.

"Before the Montana Band came, we had only the Tea Dance. Every spring, my grandfather made that dance so the people could come and pray to the Great Spirit. When people heard the first thunder, that same night they would come to his place. They would pray and only dance where they were standing — it was no powwow. It was just like God spoke to them through the thunder and they respected all creation and things like that."

Abbie's grandparents lived next to the Methodist church on the reserve "and helped people, as long as I can remember." Kanatakasiw became good friends with the Methodist missionary John McDougall and raised cattle after being given one animal.

"Those who could take care of cattle, did. When my grandfather died, he left forty head for my grandmother to take care of. Us kids had to milk them. But they were nice and tame," Abbie recalls.

"Now, when I visit my friends' farm in St. Albert, I can't believe how the cows are. I see them marching into the barn to their stalls just like human beings. They get fed and something's plugged into them and their milk goes into a big tank — I think it supplies all of Edmonton," she jokes.

Abbie says she knows a bit about her grandfather's "buffalo days" and is convinced she wouldn't have wanted to live in those times.

"It was pitiful the way they suffered. One time, they were out hunting and their moccasins wore out, so they had to wrap their saddle blankets around them to protect their feet from the briars." But the physical hardships must have paled in the eyes of old timers who watched some of their people lose their self-esteem as the world changed around them.

"When my grandfather was alive, the land was clean. There was no relief and everyone worked and cared about each other. People had animals and gardens. Now, they just wait for relief to go to play bingo. I've never taken relief. I'm not interested in that."

The Creator gave each person a special talent, and if they are in touch with their spirit and know their special work on this earth they will flourish, Abbie believes. If people can keep doing what they are supposed to be doing, they can keep on living. People are supposed to support people so they can do what they are supposed to do — to carry out their identity, she says.

Though she hasn't said so, I assume Abbie feels her purpose in life is to speak about "the One above" and encourage people to follow God's laws and live a good life. She has found peace in her life by submitting to her Creator and wants others to know the same serenity. Though she likes one-to-one communication, she has also appeared in movies and instructional videos and on television to promote Native culture and improve community life.

In *The Red Dress*, a National Film Board movie, she played a wise grandmother who helps her son stop drinking and intervenes in quarrels between him and his daughter. She also appeared in instructional videos about water-resource development and health care. Her face is a familiar one to many Albertans, and sometimes that recognition overwhelms her.

One time, at a feast at the opening of the Ben Calfrobe School in Edmonton, some women recognized her and called her a "star."

"I'm no star or anything like that. The only thing is I tried to help play the grandmother in a movie. We're all equal, we human beings. No one outshines another."

1   Doug Boyd, *Mystics, Magicians and Medicine People* (New York, New York: Paragon House 1989), p. xv.

2   Hugh A. Dempsey, *Indian Tribes of Alberta* (Calgary, Alberta: Glenbow-Alberta Institute, 1979), p. 52.

3   Ibid., p. 53.

32

Jenny Salter

Stoney, Stoney Nakoda First Nation (Bearspaw Band)

Jenny Salter passed away on May 17, 1995.

With buffalo burgers on our plates — takeout food from the Aboriginal-owned Chief Chiniki Restaurant down the road, Jenny Salter, her daughter Rose Ann, and I begin eating our supper. At the foot of the Rocky Mountains, the elder's granddaughter's home is a stone's throw off the busy TransCanada Highway running between Calgary and Banff. You would never suspect the four-lane was so close to this quiet yard on the south side of the Stoney Nakoda First Nation. Past the pole fence and across the gravel road, the bush-covered hills rise to meet the slate-grey shoulders of the Rockies. The sky is cobalt blue, and the sun has hours to go before sliding behind the mountains.

Today's visit with Jenny is the result of a promise made several months before, when we first met at the Bighorn First Nation near the Kootenay Plains. She had travelled from Morley and was staying with her granddaughter, Vanessa Smalleyes, waiting to go to the Sundance. I couldn't speak Stoney, and Vanessa was uncomfortable translating her grandmother's language into English, but somehow we communicated.

To most of my questions, Jenny playfully responded with a joke and then laughed uproariously, sending Vanessa and me into fits of giggles. She kept up her barrage of one-word answers until I began to wonder how I would write a story about her if all we did was laugh all afternoon. If I asked her a question like, "What do you like doing best when you're at home in Morley?" she would answer, "Everything," in her stilted English, and then whoop and throw up her hands, scrunching her eyes until the tears came. But her demeanour changed when we finally got around to discussing the fate of mankind and the changes in the world she had noticed since she was a girl. She quietened and folded her hands, and now her repetitive, one-word answer was "Jesus, Jesus."

Before I left, we were laughing again and Jenny was a patient subject for my camera, wondering why I would want to take so many pictures of an "old, wrinkled woman." Her happiness was so infectious I knew I would travel to see her again.

Now, pulling into her granddaughter's front yard near Morleyville, I spot Jenny sitting in a lawn chair in the late afternoon sun. We hug and then giggle rather nervously together until Rose Ann arrives to interpret for us. When suppertime rolls around, I volunteer to get takeout food, and we are tucking into burgers when the front door flies open and Jenny's grandchildren burst through it, home from playing at the neighbour's house.

Although she has yet to taste her food, Jenny quietly excuses herself from the table and returns with a kitchen knife, neatly dividing her burger into four quarters and distributing the food amongst the children, who have already made short work of her French fries. She cuddles Brandon, one of her favourite great-grandchildren. Rose Ann says the two are always talking together, and Jenny even shares the dreams she has with him.

The elder pours herself strong tea and sips it as she tells me how special the mountains are to her, as they are to most older Stoney Nakoda people. As a girl, she travelled the long grown-over trails of her ancestors, climbing hills and descending into rocky passes on horseback.

"There are trails back up there only the Indians know about," Rose Ann says, pointing her thumb in a southerly direction toward the Highwood River. Most of the beautiful mountainous area she has indicated is included in a provincial government recreation area.

The late Goodstoney Chief John Snow wrote in his book *These Mountains Are Our Sacred Places* that the Stoneys prayed to Waka Taga, the Great Spirit, on the mountaintops and felt close to Him there. But, he adds, "It is not enough to say the mountains were our traditional place for prayer, because our life was not a fragmented one with a compartment for religion. Rather, our life was one in which religion (and reverence for nature, which revealed religious truth) was woven into all parts of the social structure and observed in conjunction with every activity."[1]

Before Jenny was born, writes Chief Snow, her ancestors had spent "the first three-quarters of the 19th century. . . little influenced by the white-man. . . hunting in the foothills and on the plains from the headwaters of the North Saskatchewan to the United States border. [They] hunted and lived in family groups, coming together in larger bands for special occasions and ceremonial purposes, and for wintering at Morleyville, the Kootenay Plains, or the Highwood River area."[2]

Many of Jenny's relatives live on the Eden Valley Reserve, established in the 1940s after officials finally gave in to Bearspaw people who insisted on living near the upper waters of the Highwood River. The reserve is Jenny's second home, and she used to hitch up her team and strike out for the small, isolated community, travelling in a southeasterly direction. Spending the summer living in a tent, Jenny worked on farms and ranches owned by white people in the foothills around what is now the town of Longview, returning in the late fall to put her children in school at Morleyville.

Jenny's ancestors were supposedly more warlike and proud than their relations in the neighbouring Chiniki and Goodstoney bands, also descendents of the Sioux and originating from the headwaters of the Mississippi River. Historians say they broke away in about 1640, aligning themselves with the Cree and settling north of Canada's Lake Superior, eventually drifting west. The three bands often camped and hunted together even before being forced to live in close proximity on the reserve near Morleyville after signing Treaty Seven in 1877.

Records indicate, as historian Hugh Dempsey writes, that Chief Bearspaw was the only leader who took an active role in treaty negotiations, the other Stoney chiefs being under the influence of Reverend John McDougall, who swayed officials to situate the reserve near his mission in Morleyville. He wanted the Indians close at hand so he could Christianize them.[3]

Bearspaw spoke out, saying, "Our hearts are not glad to see the Chief of the Great Mother and to receive flour and meat and anything you may give us." But in the end, he was pleased in general with the treaty — and the food and money that came with it.[4]

Born forty-one years after Treaty Seven was signed, Jenny is one of few Stoneys who did not attend Reverend McDougall's mission school. Instead, she stayed at home and helped her mother look after the family's cows, horses, pigs, and turkeys. She thinks education is good but implies that it also ruins humans, in a way. She believes the power of knowledge can influence people to lose their subservience to their Creator as they begin to please themselves instead of God.

Without having to learn English and mathematics in school, she enjoyed the freedom she had after her chores were done. As a little girl, she remembers playing in a miniature tipi her mother made for her out of old flour sacks.

"I had little dishes and dolls to take care of," she says. When she grew older, her mother taught her to cook, sew, make dry meat, and tan hides. By the time she was sixteen, she was already an excellent horsewoman, riding "wild ones" in races at Black Diamond, a southern Alberta town still popular for its rodeos. "I won other contests, too. I used to saw big logs. I could drink a bottle of pop faster than anyone," she laughs.

Daughter Rose Ann says her mom liked nothing better than to compete in friendly competitions and, "Even today, whenever there's a volleyball or baseball game around here, she always goes and watches."

Healthy and active all her life, Jenny worked hard to support the five children she had. Raising her family herself, she shot a good number of deer and snared squirrels and rabbits to feed hungry mouths.

Says Rose Ann, "My mom is a tough woman. I remember her in the winter hitching up the wagon and going way back up into the hills for wood. She worked like a man. She's in better shape than I am. She has never been sick a day except when her asthma bothers her."

Jenny says, if she could, she would "teach people to live well again. I'd teach [them] how to cook and make dry meat. We would live in the old ways. I don't like the white-man's ways. There's too much drinking and smoking now. Me, I just drink water. When I was little, I had a toothache once and my brothers tried to give me whiskey. They tried to pour it down my throat. I've never touched that stuff. It really hurts me to see people get hurt from alcohol. I'm always so sad whenever anybody dies."

Jenny sometimes indulges in her only bad habit, chewing tobacco. "When I get lonely or unhappy, I chew a little bit. I'm addicted to it," she confides.

The elder says it has been difficult to live on the reserve amidst the fighting that has gone on between the three bands. The reserve was made rich by natural gas royalties in the early 1970s, and conflict about the way the money was spent was well publicized by the media. She disdains money and "rich things" and observes that greed for these commodities seems to make people want to fight one another and neglect their responsibilities.

"I don't know why everybody wants to go to bingo," she says, furrowing her eyebrows in disgust for the priorities some parents place above staying at home with their children. "I don't go there. I just think about God all the time." Granddaughter-in-law Glenna Two-youngmen says Jenny loves music and western dancing. "Some of her grandchildren have a band, and when they go out to play they take her to watch. She even brings her own chair to sit on." She takes in as many powwows as she can, too, and especially enjoys the Owl Dance Special, the only one performed by male and female partners.

"When I was young I used to have lots of boyfriends to dance with," she says, muffling giggles with her hands.

Jenny is a member of the Full Gospel Church but also holds on to her Aboriginal spirituality, fasting every year at the Sundance and helping band members who seek her support.

"Everyone knows me. Even the dogs all know me," she jokes. "I love the land. I even like the winter because the Creator gave it to us." When I ask how people can prepare for the future, she folds her hands. "There's nothing we can do except pray and be good to each other."

As I think about Jenny, I am reminded of something American powwow dancer and teacher Boye Ladd once said at a cross-cultural workshop: There are only a handful of real elders in North America — the ones who stay at home, in the background, sometimes not eating, and spending all of their time praying for others, praying for the earth and all creatures on it. Jenny must be included in that handful.

1   John Snow, *These Mountains Are Our Sacred Places* (Toronto, Ontario: Samuel-Stevens, Publishers, 1977), p. 2.
2   Ibid., p. 18.
3   Hugh A. Dempsey, *Indian Tribes of Alberta* (Calgary, Alberta: Glenbow-Alberta Institute, 1979), pp. 44–45.
4   Ibid., p. 45.

33

Catherine Yatsallie

Dene Tha', Meander River (Dene Tha' First Nation)

"My mother was a very quiet lady," says Elizabeth Yatsallie. "I can still see her sitting in a corner beading a pair of mukluks or slippers. After my nephew committed suicide and my sister Virginia died, my mom withdrew into her beadwork. I think she focused on the colour and the stitch and it helped to keep her strong in her mind. I think she was praying as she sewed and it helped her to feel better even though she was so sad.

"My dad built a beautiful log house for her in Meander River and she lived in it for a long time. Then, around 1971, the band built a new house for her that was bigger — it had an upstairs. In the new place we noticed she kept her jacket on and she wouldn't take off her rubbers. Finally, one day when she was away in High Level shopping, we took all of her stuff back to her old log house. Oh, she was happy to be back in that old house. She took off her coat and boots and sat on the floor just smiling.

"We used to live in a trappers' tent in Steen River, north of Meander River. I loved it there. We had an airtight stove and a bus would come along and take us to school. We used to walk a mile to the south and go fishing in the creek. One time my mom caught a big jackfish and my sister was just laughing at her struggling to catch that fish. Then, my sister got a great big fish on her line and, oh, did my mother ever laugh right back at her moving all over trying to catch that fish. My mom would cook the fish right there over the fire and we'd enjoy our little picnic so much. We used to walk three miles to find Saskatoon bushes for berry picking.

"My mom was strong right until she turned seventy, but after that she started to get weaker," comments Elizabeth.

Catherine passed away in March of 1996. She had ten children — seven girls and three boys.

THE WINTER OF 1891

As the hunters catch a glimpse of their Dene camp, they urge their tired dogs into a run. Ahead on the trail, a woman walks toward them, her face set in grim lines. She has unsettling news for one of the men, the husband of a pregnant woman.

In a tent pitched well apart from the others, the hunter's grandmother watches a battle for life play out before her. She looks compassionately into the glassy and unseeing eyes of the sweating woman struggling so hard to bring new life into the world. Her daughter-in-law has given birth to sixteen babies in the past, but she's too old to be having children now, Old Lady Hooka-Nooza mutters to herself. The labour has been long and difficult.

Suddenly, the moans subside. Old Lady checks the shallow breathing and notices the woman's lack of response to her urgent commands to "push, push, push." Old Lady fears the worst. She realizes the child's spirit has already departed, but now the mother is in danger because she has no strength left to expel the lifeless child within her.

Old Lady motions for her assistant to lay the woman down. With gnarled, wrinkled hands, she reaches for a birch bark water container and sets it beside the bed of new spruce boughs and soft rabbitskin blankets. Whispering a prayer over the water — a plea to her spirits to help the dying woman — and blowing on it, Old Lady lifts her daughter-in-law's head and pours a little between her lips. Laying her down and cradling her head, the elder waits for the baby to come. Not many minutes pass before it does.

THE WINTER OF 1990

"If there were problems during childbirth, my mother would give the woman some water and blow on it. She would say a few words and the baby would just come," explains Catherine Yatsallie, a seventy-three-year-old Dene Tha' grandmother.

She tells of men who received supernatural powers from animals after spending days alone in the bush. "These people who have a power through animals could help people. They could cure all kinds of sickness," she says, giving some clue as to methods of doctoring so prevalent before modern medicine.

Traditional Dene elders like Catherine have spent their lives in the bush and know the powers inherent in nature. They recognize that animals, for instance, have specialized natural abilities for survival and sometimes give them away. Animals are drawn to people who are pitiful — sitting alone in the bush without provisions — and are sometimes willing to share a bit of their power with the less fortunate, just as some rich people will sometimes share their wealth with the poor.

As one Dene Tha' elder put it, "People may think that they know about animals, but it isn't true; a human's powers are insignificant. We are people; we know only a little about animals and their ways. Animals have special abilities, which they depend upon to live, giving us only the powers that they no longer need. They hold fast to their secrets until they are used up, and then they throw them away. An animal chooses someone to receive these leftover powers, a person who has treated the animals with respect. My father talked to me. He taught me in many ways, and that is how I have learned these things." [1]

Some Dene carried a bundled frog in their clothing to help them to shoot straight, because they considered the reptile to "be a powerful animal which can project itself straight up through the frozen ground in the middle of winter." [2] Animal people were also thought to be able to send visions to individuals who are seeking to, as the Dene say, "know something," or to have medicine. These individuals go to the bush alone to seek their vision.

Many spiritually gifted healers and visionaries sprang from these beliefs and traditions. Perhaps the most well known was Nógha (pronounced No-ah), who received his visionary power from the wolverine (Nógha means Wolverine in Slavey). Though it has been about sixty years since his death, today even the youngest Dene Tha' can repeat stories about Nógha and his foretelling of changes to come, ending traditional Dene life forever.

"I saw Nógha a long time ago. He used to travel around on a horse. Everywhere he went, there was always a big Tea Dance," Catherine recalls, adding that Nógha used to speak of his predictions and urge people to care for each other and pray to the Creator to help them through the hard times ahead. He foresaw a black cloud over a large hill, where the people would crowd together in the future and harm one another. In fact, the Assumption Reserve, where about a thousand Dene Tha' live today, is located next to the hill which runs along the valley containing Hay and Zama Lakes.

The prophet inspired people to develop themselves spiritually with prayer by holding Tea-Dance ceremonies and living good lives. He urged them to be strong and avoid temptations like drinking alcohol and gambling because those habits would throw them off the trail to heaven. Sometimes, his prophecies were full of despair but he was not a solemn man, affirms Catherine, describing him as a humorous fellow who loved to tease people. "One time, he pulled the blankets off my grandmother and told her she should get up. Then she got really mad at him but she was only pretending."

When Catherine speaks about the old, powerful people she knew as a young woman, her voice is hushed. Her grandchildren Stephen and Arnold drift into the living room to hear her talk about Nógha and add their own impressions of Dene heroes and culture.

"Other tribes like the Cree have medicine circles and different animals for the different directions. They have ceremonies. We don't have anything like that. Our religion is simple. We have the Tea Dance and the drum," Arnold, eighteen, explains. The hand drum is the symbol of Dene Tha' identity, a spiritual instrument used to sing prayers or communicate with the Creator and honour elders, mothers, children, and nature, for example. The Tea Dance is a spiritual celebration of thanksgiving, involving prayer, dancing, feasting, socializing, and elders' speeches.

As the conversation swings back to Catherine's life, she shyly explains she was born on a trapline about five miles from where her house stands in what is now the Meander River townsite. But, as a young girl and woman, the whole of northern Alberta was her home when she travelled with her family following animals for food and fur.

"In the wintertime, when we were kids, we used to go all the way to Wood Buffalo Park by dog team. My father was still alive then. When we got there, we shovelled snow and lived there in a tipi. We went that far to trap and to hunt moose."

Thousands of miles of ribboned tracks have been left in the snow by her family's dog sled during winter travels. In the summer, her canoe cut the waters of the Hay River as it carried her to seasonal hunting and fishing areas and to the camps of friends enjoying a more relaxed pace of life in the warm days of summer. The winding Hay River bends to the north only a few yards beyond Catherine's door, its waters a constant reminder of days when she roamed freely. "Whenever I think about that river, I get lonely to go up it. We were always on the river with a boat. In the summertime, we'd go up past Indian Cabins, sometimes all the way to Hay River."

Catherine vividly recalls following her mother as they walked the miles between seasonal camps. "Women were always packing babies in a packsack. They covered their heads from the cold. When we made camp, they just set the mossbag in the snow until it was ready. But the baby was so snuggled up in there it didn't get cold or sick.

"I remember coming out of Alexandra Falls in the springtime.

It must have been March or April. There was a lot of water, creeks running everywhere. We were walking back with our moccasins. When we got to those creeks, you just had to do it, you had to cross. At night, we hung our socks and moccasins up to dry. We slept on spruce boughs with rabbitskin blankets. Sometimes, it was very cold and we lived in this kind of tent. Some are made of moosehide, they were warm, and some were made out of canvas. In the morning, it was freezing but my mom put blankets around the tent to keep warm. In the winter, we had to pile spruce branches on the floor to keep the cold out and the snow from turning to ice."

When families moved, toddlers were tied into a toboggan amidst a small mountain of blankets and cooking utensils. Catherine enjoyed her day riding behind dog teams, but all too soon she was given a pair of old snowshoes and made to walk.

"We used to travel by snowshoes. My brothers used to make nice, fancy shoes, but mine were never as nice, so I used to throw them away. I didn't like them." But she was always made to retrieve them and subsequently spent a lot of her childhood with snowshoes fastened to her feet.

"We used to walk and walk. Not too many people had horses. It was really cold. In the summer there were mosquitoes. My mother would make a smudge in a lard pail, and we carried that to keep the mosquitoes away. I don't know how I survived. I must have been very tough."

Catherine says no one looked forward to winter's cold winds and drifting snow. Trips from Meander River by dog team to get supplies in Fort Vermilion took a month. "On the way back, the dogs would be played out and the sled was always getting stuck. The men would have to use a stick with padding, with the padded end against their stomach and the other against the end of the sled, to push it out."

The hardships of living in a subarctic climate were many, but the challenges were ably met by the adaptable Dene. Extreme cold and bugs could be warded off. Starvation during winters when fish and animals were scarce was always a grim threat. But as Catherine puts it, the sanity-sapping loneliness of long winters spent in near isolation was almost more than she could stand.

"People in those days were not always together. We lived apart as separate families. If someone died, we sometimes didn't know for two or three years after it happened. Many times, you saw other people only if you ran into them when you were moving." The old people always made time for each other, and if two trappers or families met on the trail it was unthinkable not to stop and visit. A fire was quickly made and a pail of tea shared, no matter how cold it was.

When she was barely in her teens, a young man made it clear he wanted to keep Catherine company for the rest of her life. He began courting her with a steady stream of visits to the home she lived in with Old Lady Hooka-Nooza, the woman who raised her after her parents died. But while he was trying to prove to the old folks how capable he was of taking care of Catherine, she wanted nothing to do with him.

"This guy started coming around and bringing food for me. I never did touch that stuff. I just gave it away. Finally, the old people said, 'You better make a life with this man. He's going to support you.' I started to cry, but the old man told me to go. At that time, you didn't marry the one you loved. Your mother usually decided. But first, the man has to work for three years for your father before he could take you."

Unprepared for marriage, Catherine admits she didn't enjoy her first year of marriage. Her new husband took her away to live at Bistcho Lake, and she missed the people she had grown up with. "The next spring we went north on the river as far as Indian Cabins and we lived there for a while. I was still playing around like a little girl," Catherine laughs.

Though the young couple were uncomfortable with each other at first, Catherine says she couldn't help but gradually grow closer to the man who helped her survive and shared the unfamiliar experiences of raising a family. Today's married couples still make ceremonial vows to support each other through good and bad times, but modern-day challenges pale in intensity against the young Yatsallie's experiences in the isolated north. When Catherine went into labour with her first child, she and her husband were alone in the bush.

"I was scared to look after my baby. I didn't know what to do with the cord. But my husband helped me. It took me about two years to fall in love with him. Before that I didn't know what love was with a man. The only boys I saw when I was young were my brothers. We hardly ever saw any young men.

"My husband was very tough. If a horse was loaded with supplies and we were crossing a stream and it fell, my husband would just grab that horse and shove it on to the shore. I remember once I was putting medicine on his back. He'd been shot twice in the back, and I can still remember today what it felt like. His back was just like a rock."

1   Pat Moore, Angela Wheelock, and the Dene Wodih Society, *Wolverine Myths and Visions — Dene Traditions from Northern Alberta* (Edmonton, Alberta: The University of Alberta Press, 1990), p. 7.
2   Ibid., p. 7.
3   Ibid., p. 84.

34

Tommy Wanyandie

Cree, Wanyandie Flats

As soon as Tommy Wanyandie saw the bear cub in a tree, he felt dread. The sick feeling in his stomach told him his evening search for moose antlers was about to turn ugly.

His son James saw it first, and wordlessly pointed at it. Seeing the baby, Tommy knew the mother must be around somewhere. They had to get out of there.

"But before I could even move, I heard branches snapping and a mother grizzly was heading right for us," Tommy says in Cree, translated by his daughter Emily. James, thirty-nine at the time, tried to shoot her with his rifle but his gun misfired. The father watched in horror as the animal pinned his son to the ground, clamped her huge jaws on his arm, and snapped the bone in half.

That's when Tommy "thought about God and that He would protect us." With his son's life at stake, and with the confidence that comes from years of living in the backcountry and facing the unpredictable, he took on the wild animal.

"With God in my head, I went after that bear. I waved my arms and yelled every Cree swearword I knew," he recalls. He brandished his walking stick and finally managed to ram it down the bear's throat. The sow left James alone and angrily turned her attention to Tommy, smashing off his glasses — leaving him almost blind — and breaking his hand as she bit into it.

Now James defended his father as best he could with a broken arm. He tried using his gun again — it jammed — and so he used it to poke the bear until she attacked him, dragging him by the legs. Seeing this, Tommy rallied his strength and repeatedly hit her head and nose with his stick. After what seemed like hours, she finally ended her attack and walked away.

Shaken, Tommy and James struggled about six hundred yards up an incline to their vehicle, continually looking behind them, half-expecting the bear to reappear. They made it to their truck, and James drove with one arm, wincing each time he hit a bump, until he reached the highway. When his cell phone reception kicked in, he called his wife Carol and told her to call emergency. The response team met father and son on the road and sped them off to Grande Cache Hospital where Tommy was treated for his hand and released. James was transported to a bigger hospital in Grande Prairie for treatment of his broken arm and deep gashes in his leg.

As he recovered, the younger Wanyandie was interviewed on television from his hospital bed while his father became the subject of newspaper and internet headlines like "Feisty Senior Sticks it to Grizzly," and "Even if You're a Grizzly, Don't Mess With Old Men or You'll Get Your Butt Kicked." Around the world, images of a tottering, cotton-haired pensioner waving his cane around were evoked.

Tommy Wanyandie is far from that. At eighty, he's straight-backed, wiry and loose-limbed, rising up out of his chair like someone half his age. Still riding regularly into the Rocky Mountains west of Grande Cache, especially during hunting season as a guide, he likes to keep busy cutting and selling wood to the Grande Cache Coal Company, acting as an advisor to the Aseniwuche Winewak Nation of Canada, and carving pack saddles.

Today, sitting in his little house on Wanyandie Flats about twenty kilometres northeast of Grande Cache, two years after the grizzly attack, Tommy rubs his hand and says it hurt for a long time before it healed. Less fleeting is the pain of losing the son he fought so hard to save from being killed by a bear. James wore a pacemaker, and on April 9, 2011 his weak heart gave out and he died.

James had been a light in Tommy's life. So much like his father, he was a mountain man, revelling in the hunt and helping to lead groups into the backcountry for big game. He played the hand drum and led a group of singers who called themselves "The James Gang." A sure shot with weapons besides his rifle, he competed in archery competitions at the Alberta Summer Games, and in his spare time he carved antlers into furniture and showpieces.

My friend Francis and I bumped into Tommy at a round dance in Jasper a month before today's visit. He told us right away about the loss of James and I sat on the sidelines with him all night because he was in mourning and didn't dance. I was heartened, though, that he wasn't too morose; he mischievously nudged me and pointed at Francis as he got up to dance and each time positioned himself in the circle between the same two pretty girls.

We said our goodbyes later that night, but the next day we caught up with him at yet another function — the Lac Ste. Anne Pilgrimage. It is an annual July event that draws thousands of Aboriginal people to a lake west of Edmonton, originally called Manito Sakahigan by the Cree. After wintering in small camps the people used to gather in summer by the lake for the buffalo hunt and since it was a natural gathering place, the first missionaries ministered to the people there. Later, the priests built a shrine to St. Anne near the water and held the first pilgrimage in 1889.

Though I didn't think Tommy had Christian beliefs, I find out he's been going to the pilgrimage since he was a child.

"It took us about two months to travel to the pilgrimage and back," he recalls, naming Garfish Lake as one of the many places where his family would stop and camp along the way with their horses and wagons. The trip wasn't a hardship for the Wanyandie's. Like most Aboriginal families of early Alberta, they moved with the seasons and covered miles and miles of territory as they hunted and trapped to make a living.

In a Grande Cache history book I read in Tommy's living room while he cooked sausages and fried eggs for supper, I learned that he traces his roots back to the Iroquois who came west with the Northwest Company — a fur trading enterprise — around 1804. His great-great-grandfather was known as Ignace Nawanionthe, but the priests recorded his name as Wanyandie. He was from Kanawake, near Montreal, and was likely an expert river man, able to guide a loaded canoe through tortuous rapids. Early European explorers were eager to open up new fur harvesting area in western Canada, and so Ignace signed up to guide them to Jasper. He was one of the few who decided to stay here when his contract expired. Ignace married Marie Sekanaise, of the Sekani people who lived in the mountains, and the couple gave birth to Jean Baptiste, Tommy's great-grandfather, in 1820. Ignace died in 1836.

Tommy's grandfather, Vincent Wanyandie, was born near Jasper around 1858. Much is written about him, including the fact he married Isabelle Kwarakwante — who was ten years his senior — in 1890, the same year they started their family with the birth of Tommy's father, Daniel. The couple started their married life in a tipi at Mile 119, known as Wanyandie Flats East, but they worked hard to build a big house at Graveyard Lake, north of Hinton. After Isabelle died in 1910, Vincent fell on hard times and moved to McDonald Flats, where he died and is buried.

In the prime of his life, Vincent was almost infallible. He knew the mountains like the back of his hand, never failing to provide fur traders with food and animal pelts. He was too young to witness it, but his father told him stories of how he used to join others in obtaining large amounts of meat required by the Hudson's Bay Company at Jasper. As late as the 1860s, they would drive buffalo and moose over cliffs near Eagle's Nest Pass, using a Great Plains buffalo jump hunting technique. Tall, gregarious and honest, Vincent was also big-hearted, as evidenced by the trade he made with a hungry work crew he encountered one day. Taking pity on them, Vincent exchanged an entire moose for only half a bag of flour.

An oft-told story about Vincent occurred when he was over sixty years old. After shooting a sheep in the fall hunt he was returning to the kill site to retrieve a knife he'd left behind when his horse slipped on a rock and dumped him. When the animal showed up at camp riderless, his daughter went looking for him and found him, quickly fashioning a splint for his broken leg. She eventually got her father home and he recovered quickly.

Tommy's father Daniel, who is as celebrated a mountain man as his father Vincent, was born at Brule, just outside of Hinton, in 1890. He was a guide, outfitter, hunter, trapper and packer, having hauled groceries for the store at Sheep Creek before World War I. He worked for wages on a surveying crew for a logging company for Imperial Oil on the Muskeg River at one point in his life, but was listed as a trapper in the 1930s. At that time, and up until 1941, he could trap anywhere he wanted for a $2.50 fee, but after that he paid ten dollars and had a trapline near Wanyandie Flats. He traded wolf, coyote, fox, lynx, marten, squirrel, and weasel pelts for the supplies he needed, and walked the trapline in his snowshoes in the winter with his pack dogs.

Daniel married Louise McDonald and the couple had three boys: Daniel, Harold, and Tommy.

"A midwife delivered me at home in 1931," Tommy says. "My dad moved to McDonald Flats to be with his father, Vincent, for a while, but then he moved back here to Wanyandie Flats West." Louise died in 1952.

Tommy lives in a small house close to the site of the big log house and sheds his father built decades ago with trees located on the west side of what would eventually be a coal mine. Daniel floated the logs down the river and used horses to skid them to his building site.

"My dad had a big garden. He grew turnips and potatoes — the white and red kind. After about 1987, we grew our own garden and we had so many potatoes we sold bags of them to the Super A grocery store," Tommy says. Until the 1950s, the Wanyandie family had numerous cattle and horses, too, but then the pasture failed.

Daniel upheld the hardiness of his ancestors and enjoyed wonderful health right up until he passed away in 1984, Tommy remembers. "When he was ninety-three, he disappeared one day on his snowshoes to check his traps just north of the flats and he came back with a frozen wolf."

Just outside of the fence that surrounds Tommy's yard is a patch of grass surrounding a lamppost where his father's garden once grew. Tommy was never as much of a gardener as his father, but like him he roamed the mountains and Kakwa River area south of Grande Prairie and knows it intimately.

"We had hunting cabins all over in different places. As far back as I can remember I was travelling these trails with my parents. I know all those ancient grave sites and I take people around to look at them," Tommy explains. He refers to the work he does for the Aseniwuche Winewak Nation, the organization formed to represent Aboriginal people's interests and rights in the Grande Cache and Willmore Wilderness areas.

"We do own a lot of land," he jokes. It's ironic that his great-great-grandfather Ignace settled and made his livelihood in the Jasper valley, but he and other Aboriginal ancestors, including many Métis families, were ousted when their homeland was made into a national park in 1910. Tourists now play where Tommy's family once hunted and trapped.

"We were promised no one would ever bother us again," Tommy says, another ironic statement since the Grande Cache Coal Mine looms over Wanyandie Flats today. In fact, to reach the Flats, you must enter mine property and cross the Smoky River to reach Tommy's house by traversing the company's bridge.

As we talk, Tommy often disappears from his living room to get old pictures of himself in the mountains with hunters he's guided through the years. These, and the many photographs that decorate his living room, invariably show him beside a smiling American or European hunter propping up the head of a freshly killed sheep, elk, or moose. There are visitors who return year after year to ride into the mountains with the Cree guide who's become their friend.

"My poppa's kind of a jokester," says Chehala Leonard, Tommy's youngest daughter. "He'll pick a guy in the group of hunters and he'll just keep teasing him. His laughter gets us all going."

"His stories around the fire at night are amazing when you get him started. He has experienced things in the backcountry that few people will ever see. He'll point at a mountain and say, 'A sasquatch lives there,' because he's seen it or he's seen its tracks. He'll mention that we probably shouldn't camp in the vicinity and so we move on."

In his younger days, after sweatlodge feasts, Tommy used to climb trees and leave containers of food — offerings taken from each dish shared by participants after the ceremony — high in the branches.

"He's told me many times he's checked the next day and the food is gone," says his friend Francis. "And he says around his yard at Wanyandie Flats he'll hear them in the night 'hollering' to each other. They've even come to check him out and left footprints in the yard. Tommy is blessed like that by those beings."

Francis also approaches Tommy for medicinal plants that grow nowhere else but in the mountain backcountry. "He can dream of the medicine he needs and then he goes and gets it," Francis says. Tommy agrees he knows where to get some plants sought after for healing but they may not be as powerful as they once were.

"Medicine used to be so powerful it would break down the bag you put it in. You'd come to get it out of the bag and it would be lying all over. You had to be careful where you kept it," Tommy explains.

Rachelle McDonald, Executive Director of the Aseniwuche Wine-wak Nation of Canada, has hired Tommy numerous times for his traditional knowledge of the mountains rather than his hunting skills. With his years of travelling in the areas around Grande Cache, Hinton, and in the Willmore Wilderness backcountry, Tommy has intimate knowledge of traditional land use that requires protection from industrial development. "He can point out graves and old camps of the people. Even if a stick house (or wikiup) has deteriorated beyond recognition, Tommy remembers where it used to stand," Rachelle says. Elders like him know things like which streams hold spawning bull trout that shouldn't be disturbed, or if certain populations of big game seem to be up or down, she adds.

A testament to Tommy's travels in the Willmore Wilderness area are the blazes he's left on countless trees with his axe. "If you're riding or hiking those trails, just watch for the initials 'T.W.' because they're everywhere," says Rachelle. In his lifetime, he's cleared a lot of trails with an axe or chainsaw, and after he worked hard to cut and haul logs off it and clear the path of brush he'd yell, "I'm gonna make this trail live again!"

When I ask Tommy what he likes to do to relax, he jumps up from his seat yet again and disappears into a back room. When he returns he's holding two small, carved lengths of wood I'm told are the side panels for a pack saddle frame.

"Modern saddle makers don't make pack saddles like this," he says. In his life, he figures he's made over a thousand of these carriers that fit over a horse's back; the one he shows me was carved last winter.

"I can sell it for about one hundred dollars," he says, disappearing again. This time he emerges from his bedroom with an ancient hand planer he's owned for more than fifty years, the handle worn smooth and the metal rusted to a dark brown. This is the tool required to carve the shaped panels of the saddle from plain, wooden planks.

"I won it playing poker," he explains. "I used to go around gambling like that. Long time ago, we would play for days and people would throw anything in the pot: tools, belts, dogs, horses. . . our shirts," he says, grinning. The earliest "saganapi" poker games would often last for a week or more, played on cabin floors with no money or alcohol involved. People played until they had to sleep, and while they snoozed another player woke up and took their place.

About the time of the marathon poker games, in the 1940s, Tommy was also an up-and-coming bull rider. He used to love competing in the rodeo competitions at Victor Lake, just south of Grande Cache. "I was always athletic. I wasn't afraid of anything in this world, especially if it had anything to do with riding horses or bulls," he says.

Arnold Steinhauer, who met Tommy fifteen years ago, has come to camp at Wanyandie Flats with his family for two weeks every year since then. As Francis and I leave Tommy's house to head south back to Edmonton, we stop and talk to him.

"This morning, we almost got an elk. I love going out with Tommy. It's good to listen to his stories about all the places he's travelled in these mountains. He was showing me yesterday where the grizzly attacked him. He's got a sixth sense for animals and it's no wonder that bear didn't get anything up on him," Arnold says.

The comment reminds Francis of a story about a fight between a bear and a moose that's been passed amongst Willmore Wilderness outfitters for years. Late one evening a wrangler heard a terrible commotion, so he tied up his horses and hiked up over a hill that looked down along a creek bed. There, he saw a bull moose and a grizzly fighting. They must have been fighting for a long time because they'd torn up a good half-acre of ground. He watched them for about thirty or forty minutes: the bear would charge the moose and jump up on its antlers. The moose would put his head down and ram the bear into the ground and toss him like a child throwing a ball. Sometimes the competition looked pretty even, but then the bear would gouge the moose's shoulders and bite him. Then they'd turn around and charge each other again. In the end, the bear was badly gored in his stomach area, but the moose died from losing so much blood from his cuts. The bear crawled about a hundred yards from where the moose died and fell dead in his tracks.

It's usually so peaceful in the mountains I can't imagine a horrific fight to the death happening there. But if animals have something to protect, they will fight, Tommy says, referring to his near-death experience with the female grizzly.

Chehala once mentioned to me her dad's favourite place in the world is at Jackpine cabin, a sixteen-hour horseback ride from the Sulphur Gates staging area northwest of Grande Cache.

"It's so secluded back there," Chehala says, describing the lush plant life and moss that grow at Jackpine. "We get our water from a little creek that flows right by the cabin and there's bush trails you can follow all over the place."

Chehala grew up with her mother apart from Tommy, and so she doesn't speak Cree fluently, yet she has a special childhood memory of being with him that goes beyond language.

"We were out in the backcountry and he motioned for me to come with him to check his snares. After we bushwhacked for a while he stopped to pick up a stick and I wondered why. As soon as we got to where he'd set a snare I saw he'd gotten a gopher. I guess he could see the bushes moving from a ways back so he knew he'd caught something and would need something to kill it with.

"He made a little fire and sat down on a fallen tree. He singed the hair off and gutted it and then cooked it on a stick over the fire. The smell of roasting gopher is strong but he gave me some. People don't think you can eat gopher but it's different in the mountains because they eat differently and they're clean. It was only gopher, but I still remember our little campfire together. He's shown me so much and I've learned so much. We've never had to talk a lot."

35

Christine Horseman

Cree, Horse Lake First Nation

"My mom loved people. When she was in her late thirties and up into her sixties, she was always travelling to visit her friends," says Eileen Horseman, daughter of the late Christine Horseman, who passed away on November 3, 1997. "She knew people from Grande Prairie, Beaverlodge, Hythe, Chetwynd and Peace River — from all over the north. She loved sharing and giving. You couldn't sit in her kitchen for more than a minute before she had something for you to eat and a cup of tea."

Eileen says her mom experienced "hell on earth" as a child in the residential school she attended in Joussard, Alberta, and so she followed the way of the pipe as an adult to help herself heal and return to her birthright. "One of her nephews, Andy Peterson, is a pipeholder and he's travelled around the world visiting spiritual people."

Pure bliss was being on Saskatoon Island on a summer's day when the berries were ripe. As seventy-year-old Christine Horseman describes the experience, you can almost hear the wagons creaking, harnesses jingling, and people calling in Cree to each other as they set up their camps for three weeks of berry picking and visiting.

"We used to go there every year in about July. We'd all pick and then dry the berries in the sun. There'd be sacks and sacks of them. Enough to last all winter long and even through the next summer." From the number of arrowheads found on Saskatoon Island, Christine says it is probably safe to say the spot was a traditional gathering place.

"It was a big island, but now there's only water around two sides. When there was a big fire a long time ago, everyone ran to that island to be safe," she says, implying the area may have been considered sacred to her ancestors of long ago. Today, Saskatoon Island, on Little Lake, a short drive west of Grande Prairie, has manicured grass, cement walkways and visitor signs. The distant flame of an oil stack glows from a hill at the west end of the water.

"In about 1975, they were starting to close the area off to make it into a park, but there was a place where you could still drive into our old area," Catherine recalls. "My mom came with us to get berries that time, and she made a fire. Well, here comes a park ranger. He tells her, 'You're not supposed to be making fires here, don't you know that?' And my mom was so funny, she answered him in her broken English, 'And why not? I can make a fire anytime.' The ranger told her, 'No, you can't make a fire anytime,' and then my mom said she'd been making a fire here since she was a little kid. She told him, 'I've never started a forest fire yet, and I'm not going to start now. And I'll pick berries as long as I want.'"

The flustered young ranger ordered everybody to leave. "We told him he'd have to take us out one by one. We told him our ancestors had been coming there for maybe thousands of years to pick berries, and now you're going to kick us out?"

The ranger's supervisor arrived on the scene, and after threatening to issue fines he relented and let them stay, specifying that they close and lock the gate behind them when they left. "He told us we should have come to the office and asked him to open it. We thought that seemed so funny since it was our ancestral land."

The clash of cultures put an end to the family berry-picking era, and Christine still wonders how many saskatoons drop off the bush, wasted because the spot is closed off now and it's a long walk to get to it.

"Those berries. . . in the trapping days it always got hard around January. But we didn't starve, there were always those sacks and sacks of saskatoons." As the oldest of eleven children, Christine had to worry about food supplies early in life. "By the time I was fourteen, I was looking after my brothers and sisters when my mom and dad went trapping. They had to make a living, right? But they were gone for maybe one or two weeks. So really, I was the one stuck at home. I was like a mother right away. I wasn't really much for motherly things when I was a kid. I'd rather be out getting wood and loading it on the sled than sewing."

Despite her "boyish" interests, she learned a lot about cooking and still loves working in her kitchen. From her mother Eliza Horseman and her grandmother Caroline Bessont, she learned to sew and cook meat — especially moose — in a variety of ways, with nothing wasted, not even the hooves.

"Moose nose. . . I put it in the fire and take all the hair off and scrape it real good. Then I wash it and boil it. If it's a young moose, then I might roast it or put it in the oven for a different taste. Once you get used to it, you love it. We've had some [Blackfoot] people from the south come here to put on sweatlodge ceremonies, and I always laugh at them. Down there, everybody eats beef. I guess they're more surrounded by cities and that and there's nothing left to hunt. But up here, there's lots of moose, especially a little to the south of here.

"Hooves? Hmmmmm. I haven't eaten those since my grandmother died. She used to put them right by the fire and kept turning them. Eventually, they'd cook and she used something sharp to pull the hard part of the hoof off and ate what was inside. If you're going to turn your nose up at hooves or nose — then I wonder about people who eat wieners or hamburger. Do they know exactly what's in that?"

Christine's favourite moose delicacy is the head. "It doesn't matter what time of the year you kill a moose, the brain will always be fat. It's very rich." She also makes headcheese from the eyes, ears, tongue, and nose of a moose and is quick to point out she never adds spices to the meat because its natural taste stands alone.

"The ribs are good. Oh, and then there's the stomach. Well, not really the stomach. When you first slice into a moose there's a layer of meat, and then the guts are in a pouch. You just take that covering right off. It looks kind of like a web of fat that holds the guts in. It's really thin, and you can see through it. Just roast that by the fire, and it gets nice and crunchy. It's good. The horns we ate only in the springtime, when they were soft. You put them by the fire to burn all the hair off and then lay them beside it to cook." The only parts of a moose she does not use today are the thick leg tendons, not because they taste bad but because they were eaten only as "starvation food" in her younger days.

"The sinews used to be taken off and dried. When people ran really short in the wintertime, say in the middle of winter or right after New Year's, when they ran out of everything and it's hard to get a moose, then they soaked it for a day or two and made soup. They did the same thing with a piece of hide."

Christine remembers her grandfather Albert Horseman also supplementing the family's meat diet with "a cellar full of vegetables" from his garden.

"People still get together for feasts these days, but in my time they even got together to go get the food. We'd all take our wagons and teams and head for the bush. A few people would get moose, and we'd make dry meat together. That was fun. When somebody killed a moose, everybody heard about it and everybody got their share. I thought it would go on forever. But in the '70s, people started taking their vehicles into the bush to hunt. They'd kill a moose and come right back home. And gradually. . . nothing. Some don't even step into the bush now.

"I still like to go, but it's pretty hard for us. You need money for gas, and everyone is so busy now. You can only make it out on the weekends. It's not the same."

36

Maggie Black Kettle

Siksika, Siksika First Nation

After being honoured at the Calgary Stampede Indian Village closing ceremonies in July 2011, Niinayiiniimakii, "Chief Capturing Woman," would never again pitch her tipi on the fair grounds. She passed away in hospital two months later on September 14, at the age of ninety-four.

"We'll still pitch a tipi at the Stampede in her name and in a couple of years the tipi will have her hugging bear design that she gave us," says Kelly Good Eagle, the husband of Maggie's daughter Daphne, whom Maggie treated as a son.

Maggie gave her Old Woman's Society and Horn Society bundles, as well as her stand-up headdress, to Kelly and Daphne's oldest daughter, and the Good Eagle family retains her tipi designs. Kelly says the matriarch of the Siksika First Nation shared immense amounts of traditional Blackfoot knowledge with him, and took him with her on the powwow trail when he married into her family in 1980. He and fourteen other members of her family cut their braids when she died.

"She told us that our hair is a part of our soul. If we give that part of our soul away it will alleviate our pain when we lose someone. She said we could go to the sad part of mourning and shut out life after she passed away, or we could live our lives joyfully in her memory."

People from as far away as Ontario, Nova Scotia, California and Florida attended Maggie's funeral.

"After the funeral was over, flowers continued to arrive from well-wishers who knew Maggie from the powwow trail and Sundance ceremonies," says Daphne. "The funeral was a fine tribute to her spirit. She lay in her coffin in a tipi under the arbour of the Yellowfly family. She always said she was born in a tipi and so we also laid her to rest in a tipi."

Maggie taught generations to speak Blackfoot, along with traditional arts and dancing, and was recognized with the YWCA's Woman of Distinction award for culture in 1994. She was an ambassador both in and out of her community, called upon to receive Prince Charles in 1977 and, later, to name a white bison calf at the Calgary Zoo Natoyiini, "Holy Buffalo."

Though she chastised me for putting her image on the cover of the first edition of Those Who Know, it may have helped her win roles in movies such as Wild America, Medicine River, and in the popular television series North of 60.

"Mom taught our family the power of prayer and to love each other," says Daphne. "She had so many adopted grandchildren from the powwow circuit. Adam Beach, the movie star, called her "grandma" ever since they were in a film together.

"She devoted her life to renewing Blackfoot traditions."

Nine children, twenty-four grandchildren, fifty-seven great-grandchildren, and two great-great-grandchildren survive Maggie.

In the grand entry at Ermineskin First Nation's 1991 powwow, Maggie Black Kettle is the peaceful eye of a whirling, pounding storm of dancers. Bending at the knees, her rhythmic, measured traditional dance is so fluid and controlled it warrants a closer look. The colourful flash of the fancy dancers can't touch her.

She is wearing green tonight, row upon row of lime, yellow, and blue beads painstakingly sewn on to the shoulders of her long, white deerskin dress. Raising her eagle-feather fan, she shifts her eyes upward as though shielding her gaze from the sun's intense light, searching the sky for rain-filled clouds or an eagle's flight. Turning to the right and crooking her elbow, the fan comes to rest at her side.

Something about her bronzed complexion speaks of time worn, wind-etched plains, or sun-baked desert. A face like that should be photographed only in the diffused light of a prairie sunset with the tarnished sky for a background. Proud Blackfoot face.

Maggie, seventy-one, sits on the sidelines of the dance ring with twelve-year-old granddaughter JoAnne Goodeagle, whom she taught to dance at three. JoAnne told me, at Stoney Nakoda First Nation's 1988 Olympic powwow in Morley, that her grandmother had instructed her to pay close attention to the way she held her upper body when she danced. As soon as she started to move her head the way she had been taught, competition winnings started rolling in. It was good advice from one of the most well-known and long-time dancers on the circuit. Maggie still attends as many powwows as she can, regardless of the time of the year, to "get some exercise and meet friends."

Tonight, many stop to shake her hand. She jokes about being the only Blackfoot dancer in the midst of long-ago adversaries, the Cree. "But that was a long time ago — the times when we fought the Cree and the Crows. It's all over, all in the past. I come to powwows to make friends and have a good time."

She enjoys hearing elders offer opening prayers at the powwow, asking the Creator to bless the gathering and help people make friends, enjoy themselves without alcohol, and arrive back home safely.

"But you know, it's the elders that like to make friends. The young people, sometimes, think about the past too much." A few skirmishes, sparked by historic rivalry, have erupted between students of different nations at the Plains Indian Cultural Survival School in Calgary, where Maggie teaches. "Maybe their grandfathers or grandmothers told them stories [about old battles], and that's what they're thinking about. But at Gleichen and at school we tell them, 'Don't look back. Just keep on going the way you're going. The past is gone, just leave everything back there.'"

Maggie invites me to visit her at the school. I arrive on a day when she is teaching students to make bustles (feathered regalia) for fancy dancing. Later, in the staff coffee room, she describes how she arrived at the cultural survival school after resigning herself to the fact that no one would hire her.

"I went to mission school at Cluny, but I couldn't speak English very well; they spoke French to us there. In about 1962 or '63, I started cooking meals at the Crowfoot school in Gleichen, but then it closed down. I couldn't get a good job because I had no education, no papers to show I could do anything."

After moving to Calgary in 1966 and working at the downtown Greyhound bus-station coffee shop, Maggie's granddaughter mentioned that instructors at her school were looking for someone to instruct beadwork. "I thought, 'Well, I don't think they'll hire me because I don't even write or have a good education.' At that time, I couldn't even talk to people. I pronounced [English] words funny-like. I was scared to go and see."

She needn't have worried about her qualifications — she was hired during the job interview and was teaching beadwork and the Blackfoot language at the school a few days later and has been doing so for the last eleven years.

At the alternative school, Maggie was surprised to learn that the skills her grandmother and aunties had taught her were valued over those of the mission-school nuns. Suddenly, the Blackfoot part of her was validated by mainstream society. Most importantly, she emerged from the shell she had begun retreating into during her mission-school years. Painfully shy as a child and young woman, Maggie has become used to talking to large crowds as a teacher, but she has retained her unassuming, soft-spoken demeanour. Her voice is raspy and sometimes dips so low it sounds as if she is whispering as she explains she was "born on August 20 in 1917, in a tipi somewhere out in the hills of Gleichen," and is the daughter of traditional Chief

Sitting Eagle. She has fond recollections of a carefree childhood, spent within the nurturing circle of her extended family. She played with spruce-cone dolls with painted black dots for eyes and cut gopher-skin rugs for their playhouses.

The almost-forgotten memory of those childhood playthings came to Maggie as she touched a small, tightly closed spruce cone on an evergreen tree in a Calgary park. We had gone there to take a walk after she had finished at the school. She had spoken of how fragrant spruce boughs and sage on a tipi floor smell. "We used to put pine cones in the fire. Oh, what a nice smell they made. The Creator has given us all things wonderful and beautiful."

At the age of seven, Maggie entered the convent, where cultivation of a meek personality helped her survive. "We were punished if we even looked at boys. The nuns said, 'You'll have a baby if you talk to them.' At that time, they used horsewhips to strap us. I never did anything wrong to make them mad, but one time I was really scared. I saw this girl getting punished. She thought the sister was going to smack her, so she put her hand up across her face and she accidently hit [the nun].

"Well, sister just ran to the priest in charge and told him this girl hit her in the face. Then they made us sit all around the room. We knelt on the floor. The nun had a big strap, and she started using it on that poor girl. We'd all be trying not to look but the sisters started getting mad. 'Look at her!' they said. That's why I get scared easy and if anybody gets hurt I get a really cold feeling in my stomach. I don't like to see anybody get hurt or somebody to be hitting another person."

Maggie may be soft-spoken, but her sense of justice and compassion overpowers her timidity, even as it did in her mid-teens after she had graduated from school and returned there to work.

"In the kitchen, there were always three women working. We had to make the food for three hundred children, besides the fathers, sisters, and staff. We had to cook great big meals on a huge stove. This sister was working with us, and she was getting after this other lady. She wouldn't talk to her, and she ignored her. Let's say, if I was mad at you, I wouldn't have anything to do with you — that's how she was acting. It was getting on my nerves. When the sister was going up to the chapel, I ran after her and called her. I said, 'Sister, why are you doing this to us? You don't want to talk to us. We're not children anymore. We're full-grown women, having our own kids now. You always say you're married to God, helping the poor. . . the poor children. You're supposed to be doing all these things. Why are you doing this to us?' She didn't say anything. But when she came back, she changed."

Just behind the convent, the Blackfoot held their annual Sundance in the sand hills. From the top floor of the school, Maggie and her classmates could see the tops of tipis pitched in a circle, but "The nuns came and got us and scolded us for looking at the 'pagan rituals,'" Maggie is quoted as saying in a *Windspeaker* newspaper article.[1]

Life wasn't all bad at the school. Maggie has fond memories of being favoured by the Mother Superior. "We were always baking bread. The big boys would knead the dough, and we little girls would just put it in the pans. Mother Superior would always call me. She'd make me a special little bread. I don't know what all she put in it, maybe sugar and butter. It tasted so good. I was always hanging around her."

Maggie's father died when she was a little girl, and her mother passed away when she was fourteen. She had only been allowed to see her mother and stepfather for two hours each week during her nine years in the convent. After graduating at sixteen, Maggie was told she'd been offered to Nickolas Black Kettle in an arranged marriage. After both of her parents passed away, an uncle assumed responsibility for her and made the proposal.

"It was really frightening," she explained in *Windspeaker*. "When my uncle asked Nickolas if he would accept me as his bride, I was afraid he'd say no."

But Nickolas said "yes" and the Black Kettles were married and lived with the groom's parents for a while. The young couple were so poor, they worked side-by-side in farmers' fields and Maggie did a man's work — even as she had her babies — for ten years, helping to clear land, drive horses, mend fences, and plough fields. Eventually, they assumed their own home. Maggie gave birth to seven children, but two of them died.

"When I was pregnant, my mother-in-law told me everything, what to do, what not to do. She said the leg bone [meat] of a cow would give you cramps if you ate it. If I opened a door, I was told not to just put my head out and then come back in. They [the old people] always told us if you want to look out the door, open it, go out, and then come back in. They say if you just stick your head out your baby will be born feet first."

Pregnant women were advised not to stare at individuals who were crippled or had other visible infirmities. "If you stare, then your baby will be born crippled or with something else wrong. If the stomach of a pregnant woman is flat, she's going to have a girl. If it's very rounded, then it's a boy."

Maggie's mother-in-law also taught her to bead and mentioned the ceremonial lifestyle she would assume if she was to carry a sacred bundle. Members of the Buffalo Women's Society soon approached her.

"The different societies. . . when they want to have somebody for their group, they come around [the camp] for people during the Sundance. I was sitting in the car, and suddenly all them ladies started coming this way. They started walking around the car, and I was just watching them. At that time, I didn't know much about Indian spiritual things. When I was little, I remember smelling sweetgrass around my grandmother and thinking, 'That's how an Indian smells.'"

Maggie worried about her membership. Was she ready to uphold the society's strict vows and responsibilities and submit to personal sacrifice? Her brother, who belonged to the Horn Society, the highest spiritual order, counselled her to turn the women down. But saying no was not that easy and Maggie went to Cluny to see her oldest sister for advice. She suggested Maggie request preparation time and promise to join the society the following year. Maggie's proposal was accepted.

"You have to look after the people when you join," Maggie says. Members fast, sacrifice, and pray for others. "Then, after, you can put up the Sundance. You have to be pure and not have anything bad on you."

The Women's Society consists of women who have displayed flawless behaviour and who take a leading role in the Blackfoot Sundance, along with the Horn Society. The main lodge, built for the pledgers to fast and dance in, is erected only after the women have raised their own lodge to pray and dance inside, wearing ancient headdresses that must be handled with infinite care. When they are finished their ceremonies, the lodge is dismantled.

Maggie became further involved with Blackfoot ceremonial life after her husband died of cancer, often travelling to the United States to be with elders. She participated in Sundances, powwows, and other gatherings, including Shaking Tent ceremonies in which diviners request the help of spirits who sometimes announce their presence by moving the tent or sounding a bell or whistle. She was deeply moved by the people she met.

"Somebody was always behind them," she says, speaking of individuals who were in spiritual contact as they led ceremonies or helped others. "We were told never to walk around them or in front of them. That's why so many elders don't like it when children are running around them. An elder could go blind if someone walks in front of him while he's smoking the pipe."

Maggie has heard elders speak of the Happy Sand Hills, the place good people go when they die. She says spirits have told elders what to expect upon death.

"Everything we suffer here on earth, in the Happy Sand Hills, we don't have it anymore. . . no sickness, no worries about our children. When my kids were all young, they missed their dad so much after he died. My oldest daughter and my second oldest. . . at night when they slept they dreamt about their dad. He was taking them up a hill, and he told them to look down. They looked down, and there were all these tipis. It was so beautiful. . . green grass and flowers. He told them, 'Don't miss me. I'm happy here. Look around. We have nothing to worry about. This is where we all live our life.' The two girls had the same dream, and ever since then we never talk about him."

Besides the elders Maggie met on her travels, another of her spiritual mentors was her uncle, the late Ben Calfrobe, after whom an Edmonton school and a Calgary bridge are named. "He came to stay with us in the city after he separated from his wife. He was working with people. Someone would come and pick him up, and he'd go talk to them about the old ways. I remember whenever we sat around at home, he'd start talking about spirituality."

While she attended a conference in Denver, Colorado, with her uncle years ago, Maggie found herself sitting on a stage and expected to address three thousand students in a huge gymnasium. "I was still shy. I never knew what to say. I was kind of listening to my uncle, to hear how he spoke," Maggie recalls. Though she shook like a leaf as she began her speech about "the old days and how the Indians survived," the experience paved the way for future public-speaking engagements.

Maggie continues to work hard at keeping the old ways alive but worries that Blackfoot heritage will die because young people aren't interested in traditional pursuits. When she is gone, she doesn't know who will teach children the long syllables of the Blackfoot language. "It's what I think about. What's going to happen to them in twenty years? They won't be able to do anything without education, so I tell them how important that is."

Maggie explained in a 1988 *Calgary Herald* newspaper article that most of what survived of traditional ethics was annihilated on her reserve in the mid-sixties by alcohol. Two years after liquor was legalized in Gleichen, she left to live in Calgary.

But it is a return to traditional values that will save young people, she insists. Families used to bond both physically and spiritually, and people shared what they had. Now, alcohol and political cliques stop people from visiting each other on the reserves. Maggie says she prays constantly for young people distanced from their heritage and caught up in the dominant society. Her grey braids swing as she shakes her head in concern, but in the next moment she finds something to laugh about.

"When the old people used to work for white people, they never asked how much money they were going to get in wages. All they wanted to know is, 'Are we going to get a good meal?'" she chuckles.

"And then we started learning about money. People kill for that. A lot of Indians spend money the day they get it, instead of putting it in the bank, because it makes us do things we're not supposed to do. I always say, 'Indians were not born with money. We were born with animals.'"

1   Lesley Crossingham, "Powwow Lifts Spirits and Mends Scars from the Past" (*Windspeaker*, 11 June 1987), p. 13.
2   Ibid.

37

Mary Mae Strawberry

Cree and Stoney, O'Chiese First Nation

Mary Mae Strawberry passed away on January 30, 2008.

Head wrapped tightly in a cotton scarf, wiry strands of grey moose hair clinging to her sweater, this sunny autumn morning finds Mary Mae doing what she almost always does, tanning hides. She is working behind her house, which sits in a lonely spot miles away from the busy O'Chiese First Nation Band Office, and her yard is a jumble of spruce-pole frames, smokehouses, fire rings, and old cars.

"When I was ten years old, I started making hides," Mary Mae tells me in Cree, closing the flap of her tipi-pole smokehouse. "I was given deer hides at first. When we were pulling and stretching the hide, I fell over and started crying. My mom came over and kicked me, so I kept quiet and started to pull the hide again."

These days, Mary Mae, sixty-seven, is one of few women left on her reserve who still tackles the muscle-aching job of tanning hides.

She is left pretty much alone to her work except for visits from her children and individuals seeking her traditional knowledge and spiritual advice. If there is a death on the reserve, Mary Mae is called to prepare the body. She doesn't stray far from her home, except to go to Sundances in the summer and to speak periodically at alcohol abuse prevention meetings and other conferences in Spruce Grove and Edmonton and in British Columbia.

Inside her bare, drafty house, Mary Mae places a cookie tin full of pictures on the table and sifts through them. There are dog-eared photographs of children taken at Christmas, sons' and daughters' birthday parties, and a few of Mary Mae standing beside hanging fox pelts and, of course, scraping and smoking hides. Widowed early in life, she worked hard trapping, hunting, and tanning hides — swapping the latter for things she needed to raise her five children. She continues to tan hides and says she works on them at night when she can't sleep from worrying about her children and grandchildren so much.

"They live in Red Deer, and so much smoking and drinking goes on there," she frets.

As Mary Mae gazes at a photograph of a man sitting with his back to the camera and gazing out over a field, her eyes become watery. Taken just after the death of one of the couple's sons, the picture is of Jim Strawberry, Mary Mae's late husband. "He just sat there for days, staring out toward the trees," Mary Mae says. Tears come when she explains her husband's death was alcohol-related. She feels obligated to speak out publicly against the poison responsible for the deaths of so many of her loved ones.

"I promised the devil I would never drink. It brings too much pain," she says, mentioning that she sometimes puts off going places with people in their cars, fearing that alcohol might prohibit the driver from getting her back home when she wants to return.

Without words, Mary Mae answers my questions about how she copes with the painful blows life has dealt her. She removes a small cast iron frying pan with a half-burned braid of sweetgrass in it from a shelf and hands it to me. Her daughter Sharon tells me that every morning her mother prays to the Creator for strength, smudging and purifying herself with the sacred, purple-rooted incense that grows amongst other grasses.

"Her spiritual faith is strong. She goes to the bush lots too, to clear her head," Sharon explains.

Mary Mae mentions that she was a teenager when she danced in her first Sundance and has danced every year since. When her oldest son was ten, she wanted to attend the Paul Band Sundance in Duffield, north of Edmonton, where many of her relatives live. She had no transportation and left her house determined to walk three hundred or so kilometres to the religious ceremony.

"I had not a penny and Percy had about two dollars, but we started walking at four in the morning. We were lucky to get a ride from Drayton Valley to the store in Highvale. I wasn't eating. I walked just to go to the Sundance."

She found herself walking to the Sundance another year and again was offered a ride, this time by a white man who drove her all the way to Duffield when he learned why she wanted to get to the reserve. Carrying lengths of cloth (her Sundance offering) and arriving late in the day, Mary Mae was met by an old man who told her "those cloths and your strong heart took you a long way."

Born at Buck Lake, southeast of Drayton Valley, Mary Mae spent her early years tanning hides and working in the Rimbey and Caroline areas, taking odd jobs and working on white-people's farms. In 1947, the Saulteaux and Cree families in the Rocky Mountain House area accepted treaty and the Sunchild/O'Chiese Reserve was created not long after. She moved to the reserve after marrying her husband, making hides and dry meat while he hunted and trapped in the winter. She learned to speak Saultcaux on top of her Cree and Stoney languages.

Mary Mae still traps, and in 1990 she made $330 before Christmas, selling marten furs and a tanned moosehide. "I gave all the money to my kids. I just can't say no to them," she laughs.

"That's the extraordinary thing about her. She'd give away her last tea bag," says Alexander First Nation's Ella Paul, who translates the elder's traditional teachings at conferences and workshops. "You'd think she was poor, looking at that old house she lives in. She could be living in a brand new trailer, but she gave it away. Besides, she likes that old basement in her house for doing her hides. It's cold — good for storing furs. She probably wouldn't have any furniture if a worker at the Yellowhead Tribal Council hadn't given her some."

Ella describes Mary Mae as a self-sacrificing woman who has travelled so far along the spiritual path she no longer takes heed of the physical world's trappings. Mary Mae believes that her Creator gives her things so she can pass them on to the needy, says Ella. "Giving away her things to others who need them makes her feel rich. We think she's poor, but, to herself, she's rich beyond this earth."

Ella learned a little bit about Mary Mae's spiritual philosophy after spending time with her in the bush. Filled with sorrow after her mother's death, she went to stay with Mary Mae on the O'Chiese First Nation to grieve and heal her pain. Mary Mae suggested they go for a walk, and once they had gotten into the bush the elder started making a fire. When Ella asked if they were going to stay the night, Mary Mae replied, "Yes, I brought you a bedroll."

Ella was apprehensive about camping in the bush and became even more agitated when she spotted a bear track in the dirt. Mary Mae calmed her and said, "Don't worry. We're in the hands of the Creator. Whatever happens will happen." Ella tried to settle in for the night, but the sound of wolves howling unnerved her. Again, Mary Mae soothed her fears by repeating that the Creator balances all things in His hands and would watch over them.

In the morning, as the two women were emerging from the bush on to the gravel road back to Mary Mae's home, they caught sight of a fresh bear carcass.

Says Ella, "I realized then about the balance Mary Mae talked about. That bear had come into our little circle to distract the wolves so they wouldn't bother us. Even though I was scared of the bear, he was really our helper because the wolves eventually fed on him. He balanced off the circle. If I'd have been scared, maybe I would have upset the balance. I needed to act naturally and have the faith that Mary Mae has. She told me, 'We're just like animals so we blend in. Don't be worried.' She was right all along."

Ella laughs about the first time she took Mary Mae into Edmonton to attend a workshop in one of the city's glass-and-steel office towers. They passed by water fountains and escalators in the lobby, finally riding in an elevator to reach their floor. "When Mary Mae got up to speak, she said in Cree, 'Well, I'm not so sure how I got here. Now, I'm up in the sky, and I came here in a big box. I passed by some water that was jumping all over the place and got on some stairs that moved. When I got to the end of those stairs, I didn't know whether I should try to jump off or what!'

"Everyone started laughing. I just didn't realize she might not be used to these things. Maybe some elders would have been mad about it, but Mary Mae just laughed," says Ella, chuckling at the memory of the first time her beloved elder tracked new territory in the big city.

Mary Mae

i have watched her wind-roughened, lye-toughened leather
hands, with their bear-trap strength, lashing rawhide to spruce-
pole frame. dried-berry face on a young willow spine

old yellow legbone, worn to her grip, she keeps that mihkehkwun
in a deerskin pouch like some precious thing. sharp, notched
tooth-edge shears sticky flesh from hide and the gristle drops
off for the dogs and the flies

arm muscles bunch as her scraper strikes down, chopping stroke
memorized in her marrow. moosehair softly rains into mounds of
curled wire, grey and white snowdrift blown away by the breeze

knotted finger taps, drumming stretched skin, her sensitive ear
tuned to the sound, high or low. thick places die quick, she
knows where to scrape and the skin is made smooth with her sweat

hot kindled fire, boils bones, brains, and soap. with a circular
motion she polishes and soaks 'til the soup sucks the stiffness
and fibres go limp. industrial machine, she washes and wrings,
says timing is now all that matters

her cloth must be coaxed by the wind and by fire to dry slow lest
the stiffness creep in. stretching, flapping, waving white flag,
are you really worth all the bother?

rough metal edge gnaws hardness away, obstinate rawhide comes
soft as a lamb. well-rotted wood makes the fire breathe smoke and
the snowy white cloth turns to gold

i touch the moosehide so soft and i smell the woodsmoke so wild.
i hear my grandmother say everyone has to depend on what they
make. how to use your hands needs to be taught again

By Dianne Meili

38

Joe & Josephine Crowshoe

Piikani (North Peigan), Peigan First Nation

Joe Crowshoe passed away on October 28, 1999. Josephine passed away on January 31, 2002. The late Joe Crowshoe repeatedly told his son Reggie, "If the white-man can understand us like we understand the white-man, then we'll have a good life." To help this happen, he was known for his openness about Black-foot ceremony. At one of his bundle-opening ceremonies, a group of journalists entered his tipi and many thought he would ask them to leave. Instead, he told them to stay and take notes if they wanted. He encouraged the dominant society to understand ceremony — to value the practicality of it to address such circumstances and conditions as healing, mediation and conflict resolution.

Reggie, who has acted as Peigan chief and has an honourary Doctorate of Laws from the University of Calgary, follows in his father's footsteps and teaches Akak'stiman, which means "law-making" in Blackfoot. He's written a book about it and maintains that a model based upon the Blackfoot Circle structure used in ceremony is more appropriate than mainstream process for making policies and decisions in such areas as justice, education, health and child protection for Peigan people.

Reggie believes Indigenous people are victims of romanticism, and long-standing spiritual processes are often dismissed as exotic flights of fancy. But as a ceremonial technician, and as someone who has studied Blackfoot culture, he sees the Sundance, the caring for and opening of sacred bundles, and smoking of the pipe as valid processes that can be used for numerous modern day situations.

Reggie also purports that, in many ways, people are just playing with ceremony right now. But as they begin to see how the future must be spiritual instead of materialistic, the ceremonies will find their rightful place in society. Working with the spirits in all of life will be necessary when man finally realizes he cannot dominate creation, but, instead, must work with it.

"I used to hate the time on this reserve when people were starting to have Sioux, Cree and Ojibway sweats. They were mixing things up. My dad explained to me that in the old days children were encouraged to play with ceremonial things. Some parents might even make their 'minipoka' (favoured child) a painted tipi and little medicine pipe bundle to hang up in the tipi. You could play with ceremony and even mishandle animals as a child, but when you got to be an adult, you'd best get serious. After becoming an adult, you'd better know what you're doing. For example, now when I see motor homes in the Sundance circle and powwows for money, I can accept the amalgamation of the old and the new, but once we get through this playing around, we are going to have to come back to the way things were originally laid out for us. When we get to the point where we have to rely on ceremony once again and be totally real, we will return to our powerful Peigan ways."

Reggie recalls many philosophical conversations he had with his father before he passed away in 1999. One night, Joe was sitting outside, smoking. He sat back in his chair, looked up at the stars and said, "My Indian name is Weasel Tail. I have lived more than one hundred years. I can think of times when I was in ceremony as a young man, when I sat and drummed for the powerful old people. I looked across at the old man leading the ceremony, an old person like Eagle-speaker whom I once knew, and I watched him handle rocks that had been heated up, in the fire, until they were red hot. I would watch as he picked one up in his hands and licked it with his tongue. I can say that I even saw the mark where he ran his tongue along it. Another old man. . . he would strike two hot rocks together and out would come butterflies. My son, where has the magic gone?"

Reggie interprets what the old man was asking and has an answer for his question. "The magic came at the moment everyone in that tipi understood our Piikani practice, a way of life. We need to come back to that time of understanding and then the magic will return."

It is early afternoon on September 7, 1990. As the wind flattens the brown grass outside the Crowshoe residence on the Peigan First Nation, the atmosphere inside the house is still and heavy.

Joe Crowshoe, eighty-one, smokes cigarettes while he and his wife Josephine debate the consequences of visiting the Peigan Lonefighters Society camp. The group is making a well-publicized effort to divert the Oldman River with an earth-mover to restore it to its original flow and render useless a $355 million dam ten miles upstream from the Peigan community. The activists charge the project will cause environmental damage and flood sacred burial grounds.

The Crowshoes' friend Buff Parry, who fasted for twenty-one days several years ago to protest the dam, suggests the couple visit the Lonefighters' camp today and help pacify the group's leader Milton Born-With-A-Tooth. Radio news reports say the RCMP want Milton's arrest because he fired gunshots into the air around advancing officers earlier in the day. But Joe wants nothing to do with the group, even though his wife thinks their appearance at the camp might ward off violence. She is especially worried about the welfare of women and children at the camp, her own daughter being one of them. Disheartened, Joe rubs his furrowed forehead and hunches over the table.

"It's bad. I don't want to be involved with violence. I told them I would come if they would take away all the guns, but they haven't. They didn't listen to the chief, they won't listen to me." Earlier that week, Chief Leonard Bastien and his councillors had visited the Lonefighters' camp and subsequently divorced themselves from supporting the group.

Josephine argues Milton might respond better to traditionalists such as they. The couple is respected and each takes a lead role in the

Pekuni Sundance. As a Medicine Pipe Bundle-holder, Joe maintains the vows he made to live a moral life when he took ownership of it in 1930, and Josephine is a Holy Woman, expected to lead a pure life and to show kindness toward all.

A debate follows, and the couple fall into an uneasy silence. Finally, Joe turns to look at his wife, speaking quietly in Blackfoot. She replies and nods her head, reaching down to put on her shoes. Joe follows her lead and excuses himself to dress for the visit in a white western shirt and cowboy hat.

"We decided we may as well try," Josephine says, sounding relieved a decision has finally been made. "Then, if something happens, at least we know we tried to help Milton."

Down at the camp by the river, the elders are welcomed into the circle of Lonefighters sitting beneath a poplar-tree arbour covered with sheets of plastic. Half an hour later, whoops of victory rent the air as the RCMP retreat from their posts across the river. Milton emerges from his hiding place, and a meeting convenes. Joe is first to speak. He maintains his stance against violence and asks the Lonefighters to go slow, attempting to calm their excited bursts of bravado.

"Go the peaceful way. Work from your treaties, then you can bring about what you want," he implores, stressing the futility of violence. The Lonefighters listen politely to his words, but it is obvious they are not about to heed the restraining advice. One by one, they deliver their own speeches about bravery and a willingness to die for Napi's River, the Old Man's River. Days later, their leader is arrested in Calgary and diversion tactics are foiled by the Alberta government.

Back at home after the visit, Joe reflects on the day's events. He mentions that the Great Spirit gives him the strength to stand up for non-violence and he isn't offended if his pacifist's approach is considered wishy-washy. Both he and Josephine have taken a passive stance in their opposition to the dam, believing the situation is in the hands of the Creator and the structure will come crashing down of its own accord if it is not supposed to be there.

When the Crowshoes talk about divine forces, it is obvious they have total faith in the Creator. They teach others about the Great Spirit's willingness to lead everyone if they live according to the four words their elders speak of: love, unity, sharing, and peace. They are simple, traditional, and compassionate people. As Joe paints buffalo skulls with sacred red paint and Josephine speaks of sweetgrass and the pipe, time stops and you sense the hand of an unseen benefactor who set you at their kitchen table to learn something.

Serious teachers, they balance complicated spiritual discussions with humour. The first time I met Josephine, she told a joke about Cree people being known for having lice in the old days, and when I mentioned I was Cree she laughed and told me, "Well, don't feel bad, we Blackfoot all have big noses." Josephine is younger than her husband, who has grown a little hard of hearing. She translates questions from English into Blackfoot for him, and he responds slowly in English. Always on the road, they travel throughout southern Alberta and the northern United States in their truck, speaking to young people and attending Sundances like the one in southern Dakota they had just returned from.

Service, people, and travel are Joe's interests. Abandoning his childhood dream to become a lawyer after learning he could advance no further than grade eight in mission school, he managed to serve in other ways. He has been a band councillor and studied to be a minister, but when he was told to go home and burn his bundles, pipes and ceremonial things, he left the clergy.

"I'm going to tell you priests today, each of you priests take some kerosene and pour it around the church and burn it," Joe is quoted as saying to the clergy who tried to ordain him, in *Weasel Tail*, a book about his life. "After it burns to the ground, then I will go home and take my ceremonial stuff and burn it also. . . if I burn my things it will be just like burning all of my elders of the past and today." [1]

"I told them, 'No, I have my own responsibilities. My own people need me more than they need me in India,'" he says.

Cultural exchange projects have taken him to the South Pacific for a series of meetings with Australia's Aboriginals and the Maori of New Zealand, and he is an advisor to staff at the massive Head-Smashed-In Buffalo Jump Interpretive Centre near his reserve.

Returning from China in 1988, after presenting the Khazak people of the Gobi Desert with a painted tipi, Joe remarked how similar he had found Asian herbalists and Blackfoot healers to be. He was amazed at the number of bicyclists he saw in the big cities and joked about Chinese insect life. "They sure have big 'buffalo' there," he said, referring to the cockroaches that "rambled" over his bed in the desert night.

Together, the Crowshoes have eleven children and have adopted some of their regular visitors as their own — Native and non-Native alike. Attracted by the couple's warmth and hospitality, they come seeking advice or just to hear Joe sing ancient songs and laugh at Josephine's hilarious stories about the antics of Napi, the "holy man from God" and prophet/trickster/hero of the Blackfoot. The couple are generous with their time, and it is hard to find them alone or not on their way out the door. Joe says he has gotten up from his bed many a time to find someone waiting in the kitchen to see him, and sometimes he doesn't finish with them until late at night.

"Some tribes say they don't want white people or they don't want young people [at ceremonies]. Well, that's not sharing or communicating," says Joe. The world is changing and now is the time to reveal much of what was once considered secret, he believes.

The second time I met the Crowshoes, Joe was officiating at a spring ceremony. He had heard the first thunder of the year, signalling that it was time to open his sacred bundle. In his backyard, two tipis had been joined and the Alberta Minister of Culture John Oldring had been invited to sit in the inner tipi. Toward the end of the ceremony, held to give thanks to the Creator for blessings over the cold winter and to request providence in the coming season, Joe painted the faces of the Oldring family and other band members with sacred red paint.

Some of Joe's ceremonies have been photographed and the pictures published. He has used the white-man's tape recorder to record the songs of elders before they passed away and has allowed spiritual legends to be written down. The Crowshoes share with people sincerely interested in learning about their culture, and Joe stresses the decision to open up was made only after deep meditation and consultation with others.

In a 1988 newspaper article about his openness regarding Blackfoot religion, Joe is quoted as saying, "My teachers told me they [opponents] are going to say bad things, but just keep going on because you are doing the right thing."[2] His teachers were right; his candor has brought criticism.

"A lot of fingers have been pointed. But I like it. It keeps me strong to work even though I have critics. I want to be beneath people's feet," he says, treating criticism as a humbling mechanism. Joe doesn't seek publicity regarding his teaching, "because the old people always told me never to pride myself about anything. I don't want to be important. We're all walking the same way, anyway. It's our Indian way to sacrifice and humble ourselves to work with all people. The greatest meaning you can take from our way is we want to sacrifice. When you do that your purpose in life is known. But if you start to take pride in your sacrificing and put yourself above others who don't suffer like you, there's something wrong working there."

Above all, teaching and healing must be a selfless act that does not glorify the teacher — only the Great Spirit, Joe stresses.

"When you hear someone talking about hanging themselves or shooting themselves, what do you tell them? You feel so helpless to tell them anything because they're in such pain. But, if I burn my smudge and pray, then I know what to tell them. A boy who almost shot himself came back to tell me he owed his life to me. I told him, 'No, it's the One above you should thank. He gave me His message to give to you."

Joe says he is glad if his words can help someone but stresses that listening and reading about the proper way to live are not enough.

"I wish our young people could go through the Sundance ceremony.

They might not understand what they're undertaking, but in the end they will know something."

Josephine claims the wisdom she took away from her first Sundance ceremony completely changed her way of looking at life. "An old woman helped me through. When it was all over, she told me to look at everyone there and said, 'All those people are your children now. You must help, you must pray for them. They are your sons and daughters.' I took what the old lady said and now it's what I go by." Divisive feelings like jealousy and competitiveness melted within her.

On the spiritual path, "Things don't come all at once. You have to wait and be patient," Joe cautions, but at the same time Josephine warns of the perils of waiting too long to seek the truth. "With that old lady who helped me, I wanted to go back and talk to her but then she died. If you want to learn something, do it now. Don't think you have lots of time, because you don't. You do have to ask questions to find out things."

Until she finally queried an elder, Josephine didn't know why the Piikani wore the sacred red paint made of mineralised earth. Ancient graves of Circumpolar Red Paint People who traded with Europeans long before Columbus "discovered" America had been dug up, revealing funerary offerings coloured with red paint and indicating historical reverence for the practice, yet the significance of its local use evaded Josephine.

"I asked the old lady why we wear the red paint. 'For the Great Spirit to recognize His people, so He will see the ones who still carry on with the things He taught them,' she told me. So when the missionaries came and told us to put it away — I heard them with my own ears say what my grandfather and grandmother were doing was heathen and not to use it anymore — I felt bad because I was raised to believe in it. It got me confused. It got us all confused, but some people stayed with it. Others were led away."

Like many elders, the Crowshoes lament teachings lost with ancestors who have passed on and sacred objects sold or traded to museums and collectors. Though nothing was written down and it is hard to teach people "like you can with the Bible," Joe points out that "There's a spiritual contact about these ceremonies and prayers," where people are shown how to proceed in religious, healing, or counselling matters through information received in visions, dreams, from animals, inner voices, and signs in nature. Constant keepers of tradition themselves, the Crowshoes strictly adhere to wisdom passed to them by their own elders. "The old people said not to argue about our Indian ways. If there's so much talk about a pipe, I just walk away and leave it alone," Joe says.

Josephine remarks how serious the subject of religious practice is. "These things are really touchy. It's best to watch your tongue if there is a lot of talk," says Josephine. The pipe demands respect, she adds.

When Joe prays in Blackfoot, he claims the words "come from my body, heart, and soul." He says emotional entreaties to the Great Spirit for guidance once preceded most activities and prayer was as natural as talking. "We used to always pray. Even before meetings in the early days, we had to get through our prayers first. I've been in parliament and prayed before I spoke, asking for guidance. Someone is always guiding us. But Prime Minister Trudeau asked us, 'Do you Indians have to pray all the time?'"

Both Joe and Josephine say they feel closer to people who go about their ordinary responsibilities with awareness and respect for the sacred, which is everywhere and in everything. Unmindful, disrespectful individuals who pray and sacrifice mightily upon occasion are fooling themselves, they say. Like most spiritual adepts, they are in constant communication with their Creator. Joe mentions that "all kinds of unexplainable things" come into his head, especially during sweatlodge ceremonies. He has slept by himself on the land to listen for the Creator's message and adds, "There is someone talking to every one of us today, but most of us are too busy to listen."

In his silence, under the sky and amidst God's creation, Joe realized a life force flowing through him that was limited only by his earthly worries. He began to tap into a new spiritual intelligence that made him feel strong and no longer at the mercy of the world. In this awareness, he has created a rich inner life and developed his soul to the point where his material life has become secondary.

"The birds take care of themselves. They don't worry what's going to take place tomorrow. The Great Spirit shall clothe you and feed you," Joe says. "Look at me. I don't have any money but my faith is strong. I can travel the world without a cent. I've been overseas. What money did I have in my pockets? I brought it all home to Josephine."

Living close to nature and respecting it helps develop the soul, Joe advises. "All the animals have a message for us. They too have a part in our religion. They have their songs just like those in a church book. The same thing, only there's few words in them."

Josephine adds, "A long time ago, nature had a meeting and different animals gave songs to bundles. They each contributed a song and said, 'This is the way I pray.' There're several animals given to us through the bundle to talk to, pray to, and help us. Not all animals do, just some."

A Blackfoot legend told in Walter McClintock's book *The Old North Trail* tells how Akaiyan, a Blackfoot ancestor, assembled the sacred Beaver Bundle and, with the help of certain animals, imbued it with power. After spending a winter in the beavers' underwater lodge, the beaver chief gave Akaiyan songs, prayers, and dances for the bundle. He told Akaiyan, "Whenever any of your people are sick, or dying, if you will give this ceremonial, they will be restored to health." After Akaiyan had returned to his people, he began assembling it and invited many birds and animals to offer their power to the beaver medicine and they obliged, giving him their skins and teaching him their songs. The elk, moose, and woodpecker each gave songs and dances, but the frog could neither sing nor dance, so he was not represented in the bundle. Turtle was in the same boat as frog, but he was smart enough to borrow a song from the lizard, who owned two. Akaiyan led the Beaver ceremonial as long as he lived and was known as a great medicine man. When he died, the ceremonial was passed on to his son and has been handed down ever since.[3]

When Joe opens his bundle, he must pay meticulous attention to performing numerous songs and dances of the ceremonial properly. To make a mistake might bring misfortune upon himself and others. This requires a remarkable memory and patience during the hours-long ceremony. If humans pray and sing messages to animals, showing they respect them and want to live beside them always, they will respond and perhaps offer, on a spiritual level, assistance. But if humans show no respect, animals can retaliate.

"I used to trap beaver for money, and I got bad luck one year. A mother beaver told me I didn't have any pity on her children, so she would take no pity on mine. Four days after I learned this, my boy got hurt. He almost lost his leg. So I gave my traps away. My dad did, too."

Josephine relates a story about a Blackfoot warrior, the only survivor of a raiding party, who owed his life to a bear. "Many years ago, this old man was telling us he went with a raiding party to another tribe and his people were all killed except him. He tried to go home, but he was wounded and he just laid on the ground. This bear came to him and the man wasn't scared because he knew he was dying anyway, but then the bear started licking his wounds. The bear stayed with him for a few days. He would bring him berries to eat, and he even took him down to the water for a drink. When this man was better, the bear took him on his back over the hills to his camp and back to his people."

Joe comments that animals don't have to do for him what the bear did for the warrior for him to appreciate them. They just have to be themselves.

"Have you ever seen an eagle flying up in the air, looking down on us? He whistles four times and says, 'I come down. My lodge is holy.' Seeing that makes an Indian happy.

"Just before the evening or early in the morning, I've watched the prairie chickens dance. There'd be maybe four of them and one in the middle. With his wings he'd make a sound, 'booomp boomp, booomp boomp.' Then they'd all call, 'kit a coco coco, kit a coco coco.' And I'd watch them dancing and calling. It really made me feel something."

Josephine says, "If you shoot one while they're dancing, they won't fly away. You could shoot them all while they're dancing." But Joe interjects that his uncle told him never to shoot dancing prairie chickens. "He said, 'It's not good to shoot them. They're not bothering us.' So I never shoot them anymore at all."

Perhaps the most mystical of nature's dances, as Josephine describes it, is that of the caterpillar. "Anybody, even a young child can go up to these caterpillar cocoons and clap their hands and sing to them in respect. What is the song, Joe?" she asks.

While her husband croons words that sound vaguely like "coombe why oh," Josephine explains how the caterpillar, at the sound of this song, emerges from its cocoon to undulate back and forth in a wavering dance. "And when you stop, it goes back in," Josephine claims. "My son sang to the caterpillars and made them dance one time for people at Head-Smashed-In visitor's centre. They couldn't believe it."

The Crowshoes marvel at the intelligence and power of animals and wonder how much humans don't realize about them. Swapping animal tales, I ask if they know that Crow Indians used to check inside a chickadee's mouth to determine what moon of the winter they were in. Apparently, in the fall, the tiny birds have two tongues, but during the following moons toward spring they grow a new tongue each month, so that by spring, when the birds sing their distinctive "summer's near" call, they have seven. By summertime, they are back to one tongue.[4]

Josephine smiles and nods her head in belief, then asks if I know about beaver time. "Some young men once took a beaver lodge apart, even though the old men told them to leave it alone. Inside they found twelve large sticks and 365 small sticks. Every day, the beaver family was putting a stick away to count the moons."

How else would the beaver know when to break open his lodge and come out into the world again, after seven months in his winter home?

1 Michael Ross, *Weasel Tail*, (NeWest Press, 2008) p.160.

2 Leslie Crossingham, "Joe Crowshoe Says Now Is the Time to Reveal Our Culture" (*Windspeaker*, 25 March 1988), p. 12.

3 Walter McClintock, *The Old North Trail: Life, Legends and Religion of the Blackfeet* (Lincoln and London: University of Nebraska Press), pp. 104–112.

4 Frank B. Linderman, *Pretty-shield, Medicine Woman of the Crows*, originally published under the title *Red Mother* 1932 (New York: Intext Press, 1972), p. 153.

Dianne Meili, the great-granddaughter of well-known Cree elder Victoria Callihoo, was born in Calgary in 1957. After studying journalism at the Southern Alberta Institute of Technology, she worked as a newspaper reporter and a public relations officer and was the editor of *Windspeaker* — Alberta's bi-weekly Native newspaper — for two years. It was during her time at *Windspeaker* that she became aware of the need for a book that would preserve the thoughts and experiences of Alberta's native elders. She spent the following eighteen months travelling throughout Alberta interviewing elders from many different tribes. She has returned to those communities, and visited new ones, to update and write additional biographies for this landmark edition of *Those Who Know*. Dianne currently lives in Stony Plain, Alberta.